1987

SO-BSB-814

3 0301 00080853 1

STRATEGIC MANAGEMENT

STRATEGIC MANAGEMENT

THOMAS L. WHEELEN
University of South Florida

J. DAVID HUNGER
Iowa State University

LIBRARY
College of St. Francis
JOLIET, ILL.

ADDISON-WESLEY PUBLISHING COMPANY
Reading, Massachusetts
Menlo Park, California
London • Amsterdam
Don Mills, Ontario • Sydney

Sponsoring Editor: *Janis Jackson Hill*
Developmental Editor: *Carol I. Beal*
Production Editor: *Marilee Sorotskin*

Text Designer: *Margaret Ong Tsao*
Illustrator: *Phil Carver & Friends, Inc.*
Cover Designer: *Richard Hannus*
Art Coordinator: *Susanah H. Michener*

Production Manager: *Sherry Berg*

The text of this book was composed in Zapf Book by
General Graphic Services, Inc. of York, Pennsylvania.

Library of Congress Cataloging in Publication Data

Wheelen, Thomas L.
    Strategic management.

    Includes index.
    1. Corporate planning.   I. Hunger, J. David, 1941-
II. Title.
HD30.28.W429 1984   658.4'012   84-418
ISBN 0-201-09036-8

Copyright © 1984 by Addison-Wesley Publishing Company, Inc.

All rights reserved. No part of this publication may be reproduced, stored in a retrieval system, or transmitted, in any form or by any means, electronic, mechanical, photocopying, recording, or otherwise, without the prior written permission of the publisher. Printed in the United States of America. Published simultaneously in Canada.

ISBN 0-201-09036-8
ABCDEFGHIJ-DO-8987654

658.4
W561

3-17-87 William Dodd *

123,745

To

Richard, Kathy, Tommy

Betty
Kari, Suzi, Lori, Merry

PREFACE

This book was written in order to provide the reader with a more comprehensive understanding of the business corporation. By taking a *strategic* view, it unites the various compartments, majors, and sub-disciplines usually taught within a school of business. Unlike many other areas of study, strategic management directly raises the issue of corporate existence and dares to ask WHY. Other areas deal in depth with procedures and activities designed to answer HOW. Business policy, partly because of its more holistic orientation and partly because strategic management is an emerging area of study, is often a difficult course to teach as well as to take. Consequently, this book is organized around the strategic management model that prefaces each chapter, providing a structure for both chapter content areas and complex case analyses by students.

This text was originally part of a hardcover book titled *Strategic Management and Business Policy* published in 1983 by Addison-Wesley. The hardcover book includes the eleven chapters of this text plus thirty-six comprehensive policy cases. Given the strong demand for the original book in its first year of publication, we decided to publish the text alone in a soft-cover version. This gives policy instructors the opportunity to continue using the textual material with cases or a simulation from another source. The same instructor's manual originally prepared for the hardcover book can be used with this text. The only change to the textual material is a supplementary *Appendix* at the end of the book summarizing Current Issues in Strategic Management.

OBJECTIVES

This book focuses on the following objectives, which are typically found in most business policy and strategic management courses:

☐ To develop *conceptual skills* so that a student is able to integrate previously learned aspects of corporations.

☐ To develop a *framework of analysis* to enable a student to identify central issues and problems in complex, comprehensive cases, to suggest alternative courses of action, and to present well-supported recommendations for future action.

☐ To develop an understanding of strategic management *concepts, research*, and *theories.*

☐ To develop an understanding of the *roles* and *responsibilities* of the Board of Directors, Chief Executive Officer, and other key managers in strategic management positions.

☐ To develop the ability to analyze and evaluate the *performance* of the people responsible for strategic management.

☐ To bridge the gap between theory and practice by developing an understanding of when and how to apply *concepts* and *techniques* learned earlier in courses focusing on marketing, accounting, finance, management, and production.

☐ To improve the *research capabilities* necessary to gather and interpret key environmental data.

☐ To develop a better understanding of the *present and future environments* within which corporations must function.

☐ To develop and refine *analytical and decision-making skills* to deal with complex conceptual problems.

This book achieves these objectives by presenting and explaining concepts and theories useful in understanding the strategic management process. It also provides studies in the field of strategy and policy in order to acquaint the student with the literature of this area and to help develop the student's research capabilities. It then describes the people who manage strategically and suggests a model of strategic management. It recommends a strategic audit as one approach to the systematic analysis of complex organization-wide issues. The book focuses on the business corporation because of its crucial position in the economic system of the free world.

STRUCTURE

Part I is an overview of the subject, surveying the basic skills and competencies needed to deal with strategic issues in modern corporations. Chapter 1 presents a descriptive model as well as key terms and concepts that will be used throughout the book. Chapter 2 focuses on the development of the skills necessary to understanding and applying strategic concepts to actual situations.

Part II discusses important concepts that arise from both the external and internal environments of a corporation. It also describes key people in the corporation who are responsible for strategic management. Chapter 3 discusses the role and importance of a corporation's board of directors and top management in the strategic management process. Chapter 4 discusses both the task and societal environments of a corporation and considers the impact of changing values on society's needs and desires. Chapter 5 examines the importance of a corporation's structure, culture, and resources to its strategic management.

Part III deals with strategy formulation. It emphasizes long-range planning and the development of alternative courses of action at both the corporate and business levels. Chapter 6 discusses the development of long-range plans. Chapter 7 examines the many possible corporate, business, and functional strategies.

Part IV considers the implementation of strategies and policies, as well as the process of evaluation and control, with continued emphasis on corporate-level strategic management. Chapter 8 explains strategic implementation in terms of programs, budgets and procedures. It tells who are in charge of implementation, what they need to do, and how they should do it. Chapter 9 focuses on evaluation and control. It considers the monitoring of corporate processes and the accomplishment of goals, as well as various methods and criteria used in evaluating performance.

Part V summarizes strategic concerns in areas of increasing importance. Chapter 10 deals with the strategic implications of operating within an international environment, and Chapter 11 describes the strategic management of not-for-profit organizations.

INSTRUCTOR'S MANUAL

A comprehensive Instructor's Manual has been constructed to accompany *Strategic Management and Business Policy,* the hardcover version of this text which includes cases. Except for the part dealing with cases, the Manual can be used in conjunction with the soft-cover text. It is composed of the following four parts.

Part I: *Introduction.* Suggested course outlines, case sequences, and teaching aids.

Part II: *Text Chapters.* A standardized format is provided for each chapter: (1) chapter abstract, (2) list of key concepts/terms, (3) suggested answers to discussion questions, and (4) multiple choice questions.

Part III. *Case Notes.* A standardized format is provided for each case: (1) case abstract, (2) case issues and subjects, (3) steps covered in strategic decision-making process (see Fig. 6.1, p. 121), (4) case objectives, (5) suggested classroom approaches to the case, (6) discussion questions, (7) student paper and/or case author's teaching note, and (8) student strategic audit.

Part IV: *Transparency Masters.* Selected figures and tables from the text chapters.

ACKNOWLEDGMENTS

We are grateful to the many people who reviewed drafts of this book for their constructive comments and suggestions. Their thought and effort has resulted in a book far superior to our original manuscript.

William Boulton, University of Georgia

William Crittenden, Florida State University

Keith Davis, Arizona State University

Roger Evered, Naval Postgraduate School

Kathryn Harrigan, Columbia University

John Logan, University of South Carolina

John Mahon, Boston University

James Miller, Georgia State University

Henry Odell, University of Virginia

Thomas Navin, University of Arizona

Neil Snyder, University of Virginia

Jeffrey Susbauer, Cleveland State University

James Thurman, George Washington University

William Warren, College of William & Mary

Carl Zeithaml, Texas A&M University

Our special thanks go to Janis Jackson Hill of the Addison-Wesley Publishing Company for her encouragement and concern as the book moved from being a series of interrelated ideas to a completed textbook. We are also grateful to Carol Beal, Marilee Sorotskin, and Barbara Gordon at Addison-Wesley for their comments and suggestions. (We never realized how complicated it is to publish a book!)

For prompt and accurate typing, we thank Barbara Brite, Sandra Ellis, Joyce Fowlkes, Kathy Johnson, Ann Joseph, and Cynthia Gaunt. We give special thanks to our families for helping us on many last minute chores and especially—for helping us to keep our sanity while we rewrote chapters for the fourth time!

In addition, we express our appreciation to William Shenkir, Dean of Virginia's McIntire School of Commerce, Charles B. Handy, Director of Iowa State's School of Business, and to Robert G. Cox, Dean of the College of Business of University of South Florida, for their help and encouragement as well as provision of resources. Both of us are grateful to the University of Virginia for granting us Sesquicentennial Associateships to work on this book.

Lastly, to the many policy instructors and students who have moaned to us about their problems with the policy course: We have tried to respond to your problems as best we could by providing a comprehensive yet usable text. To you, the people who work hard in the policy trenches, we acknowledge our debt. This book is yours.

Tampa, Florida   T. L. W.

Ames, Iowa   J. D. H.

March 1984

CONTENTS

STRATEGIC MANAGEMENT

INTRODUCTION TO STRATEGIC MANAGEMENT AND BUSINESS POLICY

PART I

STRATEGIC MANAGEMENT MODEL

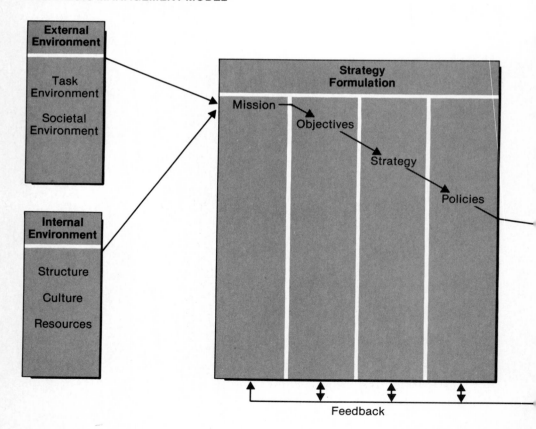

INTRODUCTION

CHAPTER 1

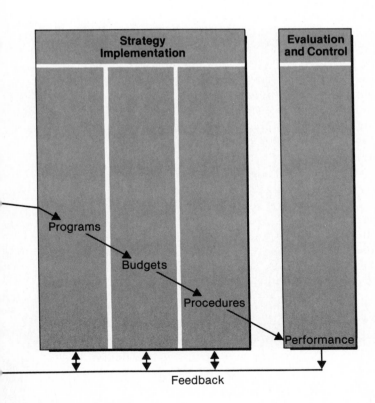

S trategic management and business policy is a fast-developing field of study. It looks at the corporation as a whole and attempts to explain why some firms develop and thrive while others stagnate and go bankrupt. Strategic management typically focuses on analyzing the problems and opportunities faced by people in top management. Unlike many decisions made at lower levels in a corporation, strategic decisions usually deal with the long-run future of the entire organization. The stakes can be very high. For instance, the strategic decision made after World War II by Sears, Roebuck and Company to expand from catalog sales into retail stores and insurance has given Sears many years of successful profits. A similar decision made independently during the 1960s by the top managements of General Motors, Ford, and Chrysler to emphasize the production of large, powerful automobiles over small, fuel-efficient ones resulted in their low profits and even the threat of bankruptcy in the early 1980s. Another key strategic decision was recently made by the President of the Fokker Aircraft Company of The Netherlands. In 1978, when Frans Swarttouw became head of Fokker Aircraft, the firm was beset by financial problems. It lacked not only new products to compete effectively in the world market for airplane sales, but the capital to develop and build these products. Swarttouw developed a strategic plan to make Fokker a competitive force among the world's airplane manufacturers. In May 1981, he announced a joint venture with McDonnell Douglas, the St. Louis firm, to build a Fokker-designed 150-seat, medium-range passenger jet. Both firms hoped that the new plane would capture a large share of the emerging replacement market for the McDonnell Douglas DC-9, and the Boeing 737 and 727. Although neither McDonnell Douglas nor Fokker alone had the more than $1 billion needed to develop such a plane, a joint venture would enable them to enter the $55 billion replacement market. Even though many people thought the new venture a gamble, Swarttouw calmly stated, "There are two ways to go broke. Do nothing, or do something."[1]

Frans Swarttouw's comment suggests why top management of large business corporations must manage firms strategically. They cannot make decisions based on long-standing rules, policies, or standard operating procedures. Instead, they must look to the future to plan organization-wide objectives, initiate strategy, and set policies. They must rise above their training and experience in such functional/operational areas as accounting, marketing, production, or finance to grasp the overall picture. They must be willing to ask these key strategic questions:

1. Where is the corporation now?
2. If no changes are made, where will the corporation be in one year, two years, five years, ten years? Are the answers acceptable?
3. If the answers are not acceptable, what specific actions should the corporation undertake? What are the risks and payoffs involved?

1.1 STUDY OF STRATEGIC MANAGEMENT AND BUSINESS POLICY

Most business schools offer a strategic management or business policy course. Although this course typically serves as a capstone or final integrative class in a business administration program, it—also typically—takes on some of the characteristics of a separate discipline.

In the 1950s the Ford Foundation and the Carnegie Corporation sponsored investigations into the business school curriculum.[2] The resulting Gordon and Howell report, sponsored by the Ford Foundation, recommended a broad business education and a course in business policy to "give students an opportunity to pull together what they have learned in the separate business fields and utilize this knowledge in the analysis of complex business problems."[3] The report also suggested the content which should be part of such a course:

> The business policy course can offer the student something he [or she] will find nowhere else in the curriculum: consideration of business problems which are not prejudged as being marketing problems, finance problems, etc.; emphasis on the development of skills in identifying, analyzing, and solving problems in a situation which is as close as the classroom can ever be to the real business world; opportunity to consider problems which draw on a wide range of substantive areas in business; opportunity to consider the external, nonmarket implications of problems at the same time that internal decisions must be made; situations which enable the student to exercise qualities of judgment and of mind which were not explicitly called for in any prior course. Questions of social responsibility and of personal attitudes can be brought in as a regular aspect of this kind of problem-solving practice. Without the responsibility of having to transmit some specific body of knowledge, the business policy course can concentrate on integrating what already has been acquired and on developing further the student's skill in using that knowledge.[4]

By the late 1960s most business schools included such a business policy course in their curriculum. But since that time the typical policy course has evolved to one that emphasizes the total organization and strategic management, with an increased interest in business social responsibilities and ethics as well as nonprofit organizations. This is in line with a recent survey of business school deans that reported a primary objective of undergraduate business education is to develop an understanding of the political, social, and economic environment of business.[5] This increasing concern with the effect of environmental issues on the management of the total organization has led leaders in the field to replace the term *business policy* with the more comprehensive *strategic management*.[6] *Strategic management* is that set of managerial decisions and actions that determine the long-run performance of a corporation. It includes strategy formulation, strategy implementation, and evaluation and control. The study of strategic management therefore emphasizes the monitoring and evaluating of environmental opportunities and constraints in light of a corporation's strengths and weaknesses. In contrast, the study of *business policy*, with its integrative orientation, tends to look inward by focusing on the efficient utilization of a corporation's assets and thus emphasizes the formulation of general guidelines that will better accomplish a firm's mission and objectives. We see, then, that strategic management incorporates the concerns of business policy with a heavier environmental and strategic emphasis.

1.2 RESEARCH IN STRATEGIC MANAGEMENT

Many researchers have conducted studies of corporations to learn if business firms that engage in long-range planning outperform firms that do not. Although both Rue and Fulmer, and Leontiades and Tezel failed to find any relationship between a firm's performance and strategic planning,[7] most researchers did. For example, Ansoff and Associates found that corporations involved in strategic planning outperformed nonplanners in all key sales and financial performance measures.[8] Similar results emerged in a study by Thune and House of medium-sized corporations in the drug, chemical, machinery, food, oil, and steel industries.[9] Other research supports the conclusion that organizations that manage strategically tend to outperform those that do not.[10]

Godiwalla, Meinhart, and Warde found that under different sets of environmental conditions firms need different mixes of organizational functions (general management, production, finance, marketing, research and development (R&D), personnel, external relations, and procurement) for effective performance. They concluded that managers must take care to blend the various functions in "correct proportions."[11] A landmark study by Schoeffler, Buzzel, and Heany found 37 basic factors that are related to corporate profitability. As a result of this research, Schoeffler, Buzzel, and Heany suggest that their PIMS model be used by managers in the development and assessment of strategic plans and choices.[12] Further work using the PIMS approach supports the value of this research to strategic management.[13]

Concern about external as well as internal factors seems to be increasing in today's large corporations. Recent research studies conducted by Henry indicate that the planning systems of 50 large companies are becoming increasingly sophisticated. For example, there is more effort to formulate, implement, and evaluate strategic plans. There is also a greater emphasis on strategic factors in the evaluation of a manager's performance.[14] Research further suggests that managers in corporations having volatile environments need to design and implement sophisticated strategic planning processes if their firms are to be successful.[15]

From these studies we may conclude that a knowledge of strategic management is very important for effective business performance. The use of long-range planning and the selection of alternative courses of action based upon external and internal factors are becoming key parts of a general manager's job.

1.3 HIERARCHY OF STRATEGY

The typical large multidivisional business firm has three levels of strategy: (1) corporate, (2) business, and (3) functional.

Corporate strategy explores the ways a firm can develop a favorable "portfolio strategy" for its many activities.[16] It includes such factors as decisions about the type of businesses a firm should be in, the flow of financial and other resources to and from its divisions, and the way a corporation can increase its return on investment (ROI).

Business strategy, in contrast, usually occurs at the divisional level, with emphasis on improving the competitive position of a corporation's products or services in a specific industry or market segment the division serves. A division may be organized as a *strategic business unit* (SBU) around a group of similar products, such as housewares or electric turbines. Top management usually treats an SBU as an autonomous unit with, generally, the authority to develop its own strategy within corporate objectives and strategy. A division's business strategy would probably stress increasing its profit margin in the production and sales of its products and services. Business strategies also should integrate various functional activities to achieve divisional objectives.

The principal focus of *functional strategy* is on maximizing resource productivity.[17] Given the constraints of corporate and business strategies around them, functional departments develop strategies to pull together their various activities and competencies to improve performance. For example a typical strategy of a marketing department might center on developing the means to increase the current year's sales over those of the previous year.

The three levels of strategy—corporate, business, and functional—form a *hierarchy of strategy* within a large corporation. They interact closely with each other and must be well integrated if the total corporation is to be successful. As depicted in Fig. 1.1, each level of strategy forms the strategic environment of the next level in the corporation. (The interaction among the three levels is depicted later in the chapter in Fig. 1.5.)

1.4 DESCRIPTIVE MODEL OF STRATEGIC MANAGEMENT

The process of strategic management involves three basic elements: (1) strategy formulation, (2) strategy implementation, and (3) evaluation and control. Figure 1.2 shows how these three elements interact. We will discuss these interactions later in this section.

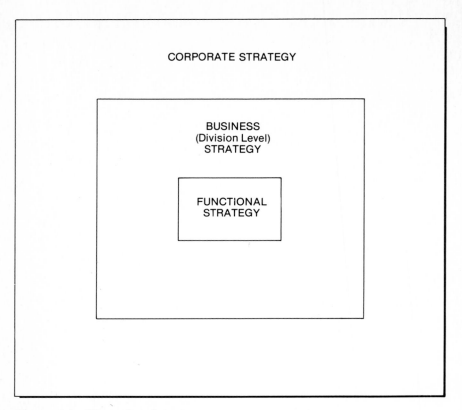

Figure 1.1   *Hierarchy of strategy.*

At the corporate level, the strategic management process includes activities that range from the initial statement of corporate mission to the evaluation of performance. Top management scans both the external environment for opportunities and threats, and the internal environment for strengths and weaknesses. Then it evaluates the strategic factors to determine corporate mission, which is the first step in strategy formulation. A statement of mission leads to a determination of corporate objectives, strategies, and policies. These strategies and policies are implemented through programs, budgets, and procedures. Finally perfor-

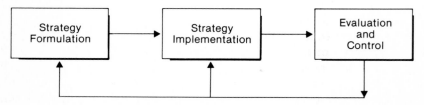

Figure 1.2   *Basic elements of the strategic management process.*

mance is evaluated, and information is fed back into the system to ensure adequate control of organizational activities. Figure 1.3 depicts this process as a continuous one. It is an expansion of the basic model presented in Fig. 1.2.

The model in Fig. 1.3, with minor changes, also reflects the strategic management process at both divisional and functional levels of the corporation. A division's external environment, for example, includes not only task and societal variables, but also the mission, objectives, strategy, and policies of corporate headquarters. Similarly, both corporate and divisional constraints form the external environment of a functional department. Excepting mission, which may exist only at the corporate level, the model depicted in Fig. 1.3 is appropriate for any strategic level of a corporation.

External Environment

The *external environment* consists of variables that exist outside the organization and are not typically within the short-run control of top management. These variables form the context within which the corporation exists. The external environment has two parts: task environment and societal environment. The *task environment* includes those elements or groups that directly affect and are affected by an organization's major operations. Some of these are stockholders, governments, suppliers, local communities, competitors, customers, creditors, labor unions, and trade associations. The *societal environment* includes more general forces—ones that do not directly touch upon the activities of the organization but that can, and often do, influence its decisions. Such economic, socio-cultural, technological, and political-legal forces are depicted in Fig. 1.4 in relation to a firm's total environment. (These external variables are discussed in more detail in Chapter 4.)

Internal Environment

The *internal environment* of a corporation consists of those variables within the organization itself that are also not usually within the short-run control of top management. These variables form the context in which work is done. They include the corporation's structure, culture, and resources. The *corporate structure* is the way a corporation is organized in terms of communication, authority, and workflow. It is often referred to as the "chain of command" and is graphically described in an organization chart. The *corporation's culture* is that pattern of beliefs, expectations, and values shared by the corporation's members. In a typical firm norms emerge that define the acceptable behavior of people from top management down to the operative employees. *Corporate resources* are those assets that form the raw material for the production of an organization's products or services. These include people and man-

8

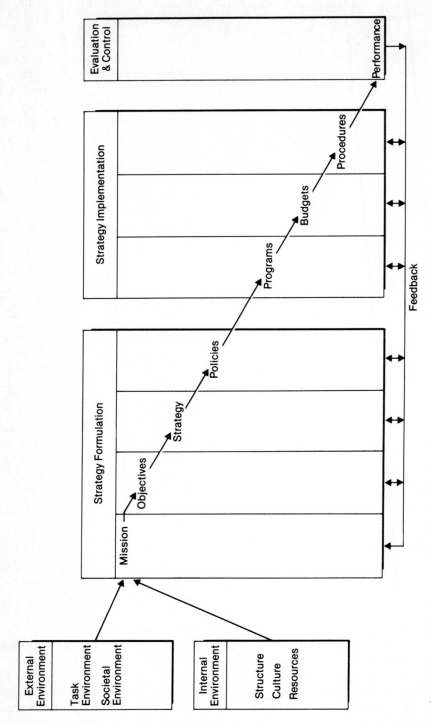

Figure 1.3 *Strategic management model.*

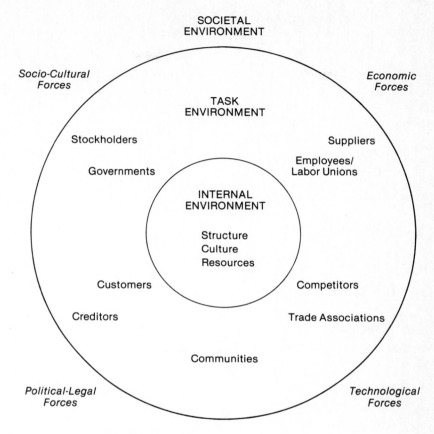

Figure 1.4 *Environmental variables.*

agerial talent as well as financial assets, plant facilities, and functional area skills and abilities. (These internal variables in a firm's environment are discussed in more detail in Chapter 5.)

Strategy Formulation

Strategy formulation is the process of developing long-range plans to deal effectively with environmental opportunities and challenges in light of corporate strengths and weaknesses. It includes defining the corporate mission, specifying achievable objectives, developing strategies, and setting policy guidelines.

Mission. The corporate mission is the purpose or reason for the corporation's existence. For example, the mission of a savings and loan association might be to provide mortgage money to people of the community. By fulfilling this mission, the S&L would hope to provide a reasonable rate of return to its depositors. A mission may be *narrow*, like that of the S&L, or it may be *broad*. A broad statement of mission for another S&L might be to offer financial services to anyone who can pay the interest.

Objectives. The corporate mission, as depicted in Fig. 1.3, determines the parameters of the specific objectives top management chooses to achieve. These objectives are listed as an end result of planned activity. They state *who* is responsible for accomplishing *what* by *when* and at what *cost*. (The terms *goals* and *objectives* are often used interchangeably.) The achievement of corporate objectives should result in a corporation's fulfilling its mission. An S&L, for example, might set objectives for the year of loaning $1 million in mortgage money and earning a fifteen percent rate of return on its investment portfolio.

Strategy. The strategy of a corporation is a comprehensive master plan stating *how* a corporation will achieve its mission and objectives. The strategy of an S&L might be to increase both demand for mortgage loans and the amount of money deposited in its savings accounts. Another strategy might be to expand its financial services so that it is not so dependent on mortgages for income.

Policies. As broad guidelines for making decisions, policies flow from the strategy. They provide guidance for decision making throughout the organization. In attempting to increase the amount of mortgage loans as well as the amount of deposits available for mortgages, an S&L might set policies of always offering the highest legal interest rate on savings deposits or to offer mortgage borrowers the best deal possible in the area. (Strategy formulation is discussed in more detail in Chapters 6 and 7.)

Strategy Implementation

Strategy implementation is the process of putting strategies and policies into action through the development of programs, budgets, and procedures. It is typically conducted by middle and lower level managers but reviewed by top management. Sometimes referred to as operational planning, it is concerned with day-to-day resource allocation problems.

Division and/or functional managers work to fully develop the programs, budgets, and procedures that will be used to achieve the objectives of the corporate strategy. At the same time, these managers are involved in strategy formulation at the divisional or functional level. If, for example, a corporate program for a steel company is to close down all inefficient plants within two years, a divisional objective might be to close down two specific production facilities. A divisional (business) strategy would then be developed to detail the specifics of the closing.

Programs. A program is a statement of activities or steps needed to accomplish a single-use plan. It makes the strategy action-oriented. For instance, to implement its strategy and policies, a savings and loan association might initiate an advertising program in the local area, develop close ties with the local realtors' association, and offer free silverware with every $1,000 savings deposit.

Budgets. A budget is a statement of a corporation's programs in dollar terms. It lists the detailed cost of each program for planning and control purposes. The S&L might thus draw up separate budgets for each of its three programs: the advertising budget, the public relations budget, and the premium budget.

Procedures. Sometimes referred to as standard operating procedures (SOP), procedures are a system of sequential steps or techniques that describe how to perform a particular task or job. They typically detail the various activities that must be carried out to complete a corporation's program. The S&L, for example, might develop procedures for placing ads in newspapers and on radio. They might list persons to contact, techniques for writing acceptable copy (with samples), and details about payment. They might establish detailed procedures concerning eligibility requirements for silverware premiums. (Strategy implementation is discussed in more detail in Chapter 8.)

Evaluation and Control

Evaluation and control is the process of monitoring corporate activities and performance results so that actual performance can be compared with desired performance. Managers at all levels use the resulting information to take corrective action and resolve problems. Although evaluation and control is the final major element of strategic management, it may also serve to stimulate the beginning of the entire process by pinpointing weaknesses in previously implemented strategic plans.

For effective evaluation and control, managers must obtain clear, prompt, and unbiased feedback from the people below them in the corporation's hierarchy. The model in Fig. 1.3 indicates how feedback in the form of performance data and activity reports runs through the entire management process. Managers use this information to compare what is actually happening with what was originally planned in the formulation stage.

Top management of large corporations typically monitors and evaluates results by using periodic reports dealing with key performance indicators, such as return on investment, net profits, earnings per share, and net sales. Corporations are sometimes structured in ways to pinpoint performance problem areas with profit centers, investment centers, expense centers, and revenue centers. (These are discussed in detail in Chapter 9.)

Activities are much harder to monitor and evaluate than are performance results. Because of the many difficulties in deciding which activities to monitor and because of the bias inherent in evaluating job performance, some firms now manage by objectives. Management by objectives (MBO) has been criticized, however, for ignoring many of the intermediate activities that can lead to the desired results. To counter this criticism, consulting firms have developed management "audits," which assess key organizational activities and provide in-depth feedback to consultants and managers. Management audits complement standard measures of performance and provide a more complete picture of the corporation's activities. (We discuss an example of a comprehensive audit in Chapter 2.)

1.5 ILLUSTRATION OF THE MODEL

We illustrate the strategic management model for a large, multi-divisional corporation. A fictitious automobile manufacturer called Murphy Motors begins the process by scanning its external environment for any relevant information. It also scans its internal environment to assess the strengths and weaknesses in its divisions and functional areas. Officers of divisions and functional areas are normally requested to provide input for top management's use. This information provides the data necessary for the formulation and implementation stages of strategic management. As depicted in Illustrative Example 1.1, the firm begins with redefining its mission and ends with developing a feedback system to aid in evaluation and control.

A corporation the size of a modern automobile company would tend to be structured on a divisional and a functional basis. Each car line, for example, might form its own division. Each division would have its own production facilities as well as marketing, finance, and human resource departments. As depicted in Fig. 1.5, the corporate level goes through all three stages of the strategic management process. Top management with input from the divisions formulates strategy and makes plans for implementation. These implementation plans initiate the strategy formulation process at the division level. Each division formulates objectives, strategies, and policies in order to accomplish the corporate programs. The evaluation and control information from each division feeds upward to the corporate level for its use in evaluation and control.

Just as the implementation stage of corporate strategic planning initiates the formulation stage of the same process at the divisional level, implementation planning at the divisional level causes each functional department to begin formulating its own strategic plans. For example, a corporate-level program of Murphy Motors might have as its goal the conversion of 80% of the auto fleet to front-wheel drive by 1985. To implement this program, each division must formulate an objective specifying which cars will be converted by what time and at what cost.

Illustrative Example 1.1 ———————————————————
STRATEGIC MANAGEMENT AT MURPHY MOTORS

STRATEGY FORMULATION

Mission

Broad. Provide transportation.

Narrow. Build and sell cars and trucks.

Corporate Objectives

1. Achieve an ROI of 10% for 1985–86 fiscal year on cars and trucks.
2. Achieve an Environmental Protection Agency (EPA) rating of 30 miles per gallon (mpg) on entire auto fleet.

Strategy

1. Update and automate plant facilities to reduce costs.
2. Develop fuel-efficient cars and trucks to meet EPA requirements and to challenge competition.

Policies

1. Emphasize research and development to reduce costs and to improve auto efficiency and safety.
2. Emphasize efficiency at all levels. Reward high performers and retire or fire unproductive workers and managers. Increase plant efficiency at all locations.
3. Emphasize the building of safe, fuel-efficient cars and trucks at a quality level equal to the No. 1 competitor.

STRATEGY IMPLEMENTATION

Programs

1. Close down most inefficient plants by end-1985.
2. Install robots at 40% of work stations by end-1985.
3. Increase use of light-weight metals and plastics by 40% from 1983 to 1986.
4. Convert 80% of auto fleet to front-wheel drive by 1985.

Budgets

Prepare budgets showing cost-benefit analysis of each planned program.

Procedures

Develop procedures to dispose of plant equipment.

1. Develop criteria (depreciation value, replacement cost, age, condition, etc.) to determine disposition status (scrap, auction, storage, transfer) by Manufacturing Engineer of each piece of equipment.
2. Tag and record the disposition status of each piece of equipment by Manufacturing Engineer.
3. Estimate costs and revenues for each piece of equipment: (a) scrap value, (b) transfer cost, (c) storage costs, and (d) auction value by Manufacturing Engineer.
4. Transfer selected equipment to designated plant on company trucks.
5. Sell scrap items to TLW Scrap Corporation.
6. Hire Doyle Auction Company to auction selected equipment.

   ☐ Hold auction on January 15th.
   ☐ Equipment not sold—determine new status (scrap, storage, transfer).

EVALUATION AND CONTROL

Require monthly status reports on the following:

1. Actual versus standard costs.
2. Actual versus planned sales.
3. Progress toward closing inefficient plants.
4. Progress toward installing robots.
5. Progress toward utilizing light-weight materials.
6. Progress toward front-wheel drive conversion.

Require annual reports on the following:

1. ROI for each division.
2. EPA rating on fleet in terms of miles per gallon.
3. Strategic audit of entire corporation and each division.

As each division develops its own programs for implementation, separate functional departments within each division begin to formulate their own strategies. For example, Division A's manufacturing department sets an objective of retooling its assembly line for front-wheel drive cars by 1984. The purchasing department of Division A sets objectives and

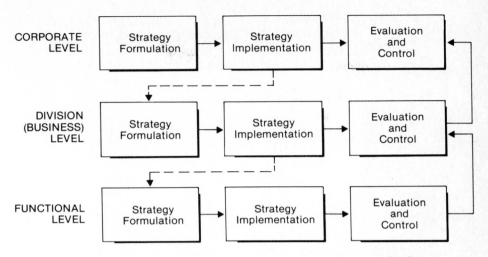

Figure 1.5 *Strategic management process at three corporate levels.*

plans strategies to begin ordering new parts from suppliers. Division A's marketing department initiates plans to change its advertising and promotional activities in order to ready the consumer for front-wheel drive vehicles. Each level develops its own objectives, strategies, and policies to complement the level above.

The strategic management process operates in this manner at all three levels of a large multidivisional corporation.

1.6 SUMMARY AND CONCLUSION

This chapter sets the stage for the study of strategic management and business policy. It explains the rationale for including the subject in a business school curriculum. In addition to serving as a capstone to integrate the various functional areas, the course provides a framework for analyzing top management's decision process and the effects of environmental issues on the corporation. Research generally supports the conclusion that corporations that manage strategically perform at higher levels than do those firms that do not. Strategic management is thus an important area of study for anyone interested in organizational productivity.

Our model of strategic management includes formulation and implementation, plus evaluation and control. The mission of a corporation derives from the interaction of internal and external environmental factors, modified by the needs and values of top management. A precise statement of mission guides the setting of objectives and the formulation of strategy and policies. Strategy is implemented through specific programs, budgets, and procedures. Management continually monitors and evaluates performance and activities on the basis of measurable results and audits of key areas. These data feed back into the corporation at all phases of the strategic management process. If results and activities fail to measure up to the plans, managers may then take the appropriate actions.

Although top management and the board of directors have primary responsibility for the strategic management process, many levels of the corporation conduct strategy formulation, implementation, evaluation, and control. Large multidivisional corporations utilize divisional and functional levels that integrate the entire corporation by focusing activities on the accomplishment of the mission.

DISCUSSION QUESTIONS

1. What is strategic management?
2. Why does a course like business policy/strategic management need to be part of a business school curriculum?
3. What is meant by the hierarchy of strategy?
4. Does every business firm have business strategies? Explain.
5. What information is needed to properly formulate strategy? Why?

NOTES

1. "Dutch Treat: Fokker's Challenge to Boeing," *Time Magazine* (May 18, 1981), p. 68.

2. R. A. Gordon and J. E. Howell, *Higher Education for Business* (New York: Columbia University Press, 1959).

   F. C. Pierson, et. al., *The Education of American Businessmen* (New York: McGraw-Hill, 1959).

3. Gordon and Howell, p. 206.

4. Gordon and Howell, pp. 206–207.

5. J. D. Hunger and T. L. Wheelen, *An Assessment of Undergraduate Business Education in the United States* (Charlottesville, Va.: McIntire School of Commerce Foundation, 1980). Also summarized in "A Performance Appraisal of Undergraduate Business Education," *Human Resource Management* (Spring 1980), pp. 24–31.

6. M. Leontiades, "The Confusing Words of Business Policy," *Academy of Management Review* (January 1982), p. 46.

7. M. Leontiades and A. Tezel, "Planning Perceptions and Planning Results," *Strategic Management Journal* (January–March 1980), pp. 65–75.

   W. Rue and R. M. Fulmer, "Is Long-Range Planning Profitable?" *Proceedings, Academy of Mangement* (August 1973), pp. 66–73.

8. H. I. Ansoff, et al. "Does Planning Pay?" *Long Range Planning* (December 1970), pp. 2–7.

9. S. Thune and R. J. House, "Where Long-Range Planning Pays Off," *Business Horizons* (August 1970), pp. 81–87.

10. D. M. Herold, "Long-Range Planning and Organizational Performance: A Cross-Validation Study," *Academy of Management Journal* (March 1972), pp. 91–104.

    D. Burt, "Planning and Performance in Australian Retailing," *Long Range Planning* (June 1978), pp. 62–66.

    J. O. Eastlack and P. R. McDonald, "CEO's Role in Corporate Growth," *Harvard Business Review* (May–June 1970), pp. 150–163.

    D. R. Wood and R. L. LaForge, "The Impact of Comprehensive Planning on Financial Performance," *Academy of Management Journal* (September 1979), pp. 516–526.

    Stanford Research Institute, "Why Companies Grow," *Nation's Business* (November 1957), pp. 80–86.

    D. W. Karger and Z. A. Malik, "Long Range Planning and Organizational Performance," *Long Range Planning* (December 1975), pp. 60–64; and Z. A. Malik and D. W. Karger, "Does Long-Range Planning Improve Company Performance?" *Management Review* (September 1975), pp. 27–31.

11. Y. M. Godiwalla, W. A. Meinhart, and W. D. Warde, "The Strategic Configurations and Influence—Mixes of Organizational Functions for Overall Corporate Strategy," *Proceedings, Academy of Management* (August 1978), pp. 111–115.

12. S. Schoeffler, R. D. Buzzell, and D. F. Heany, "Impact of Strategic Planning on Profit Performance," *Harvard Business Review* (March–April 1974), pp. 137–145.

13. C. P. Zeithaml, C. R. Anderson, and F. T. Paine, "An Empirical Reexamination of Selected PIMS Findings," *Proceedings, Academy of Management* (August 1981), pp. 12–16.

14. H. W. Henry, "Evolution of Strategic Planning in Major Corporations," *Proceedings, American Institute of Decision Sciences* (November 1980), pp. 454–456.

    H. W. Henry, "Then and Now: A Look at Strategic Planning Systems," *Journal of Business Strategy* (Winter 1981), pp. 64–69.

15. N. H. Snyder, "Environmental Volatility and Planning Effectiveness," a *Working Paper* (Charlottesville, Va.: McIntire School of Commerce, University of Virginia, 1981).

16. P. Lorange, *Corporate Planning: An Executive Viewpoint* (Englewood Cliffs, N.J.: Prentice-Hall, 1980), p. 18.

17. C. W. Hofer and D. Schendel, *Strategy Formulation: Analytical Concepts* (St. Paul, Minn.: West Publishing Co., 1978), p. 29.

STRATEGIC MANAGEMENT MODEL

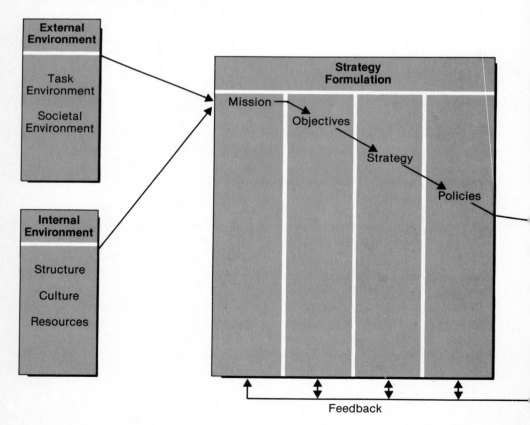

DEVELOPING CONCEPTUAL SKILLS: THE CASE METHOD AND THE STRATEGIC AUDIT

CHAPTER 2

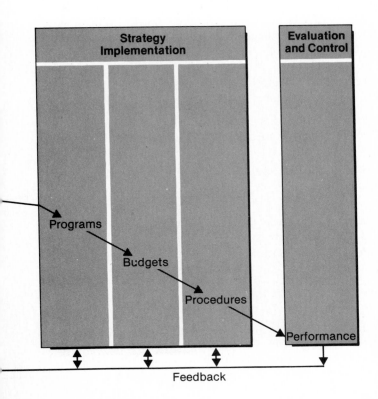

A n analysis of a corporation's strategic management calls for a top-down view of the organization. In our analysis we view the corporation as an entity composed of interrelated units and systems, such as accounting, marketing, and finance. We examine the interrelationships of these areas in light of the opportunities and threats in the corporation's environment. We carry out our analysis through the use of complex cases or management simulations. These techniques will give you the opportunity to move from a narrow, specialized view to a broader, less precise analysis of the overall corporate picture. Consequently, the emphasis in case analysis is on developing and refining conceptual skills, which are different from the skills you developed in your technical and function-oriented courses. As you will see, conceptual skills are vital to performing successfully in the business world.

2.1 IMPORTANCE OF CONCEPTUAL SKILLS IN BUSINESS

Many have attempted to specify the characteristics necessary for a person to successfully advance from an entry-level position to one in top management. Few of these studies have been successful.[1] But Robert L. Katz has suggested one interesting approach. He focused on the skills successful managers exhibit in performing their jobs, an approach that negates the need to identify specific personality traits.[2] These skills imply abilities that can be developed and are manifested in performance.

Katz suggests that effective administration rests on three basic skills: technical, human, and conceptual. He defines them as follows:[3]

☐ *Technical skills* pertain to *what* is done and to working with *things*. They comprise one's ability to use technology to perform an organizational task.

☐ *Human skills* pertain to *how* something is done and to working with *people*. They comprise one's ability to work with people to achieve goals.

☐ *Conceptual skills* pertain to *why* something is done and to seeing the corporation as a *whole*. They comprise one's ability to understand the complexities of the corporation as it affects and is affected by its environment.

Katz further suggests that the optimal mix of these three skills varies at the different corporate levels:

> At lower levels, the major need is for technical and human skills. At higher levels, the administrator's effectiveness depends largely on human and conceptual skills. At the top, conceptual skill becomes the most important of all for successful administration.[4]

Results of a survey of 300 presidents of *Fortune's* list of the top fifty banking, industrial, insurance, public utility, retailing, and transportation firms support Katz's conclusion regarding the different skill mixes needed at the different organizational levels.[5] As shown in Fig. 2.1, the need for technical skills decreases and the need for conceptual skills increases as a person moves from entry level to top management.

In addition, when executives were asked, "Are there certain skills necessary to move from one organizational level to another?" fifty-five percent reported conceptual skills to be the most crucial in moving from middle to top management.[6] Similar results have been reported concerning accountants in CPA firms.[7]

The strategic management and business policy course attempts to develop conceptual skills through the use of comprehensive cases or complex simulations. Of course, you also need technical skills in order to analyze various aspects of each case. And you will use human skills in team presentations, study groups, or team projects. But in this course you will primarily develop and refine your conceptual skills by focusing on strategic issues. Concentrating on strategic management processes forces you to develop a better understanding of the political, social, and economic environment of business and to appreciate the interactions of the functional specialties required for corporate success.

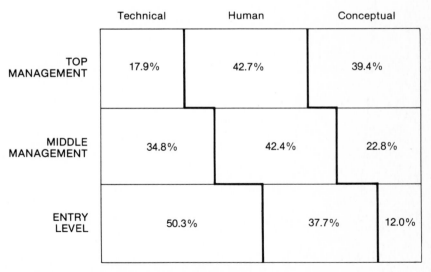

	Technical	Human	Conceptual
TOP MANAGEMENT	17.9%	42.7%	39.4%
MIDDLE MANAGEMENT	34.8%	42.4%	22.8%
ENTRY LEVEL	50.3%	37.7%	12.0%

SOURCE: T. L. Wheelen, G. K. Rakes, and J. D. Hunger, "Skills of an Executive," a paper presented to the Academy of Management, Kansas City, Mo., August 1976.

Figure 2.1 *Optimal skill mix of a manager by hierarchical level.*

2.2 AUDITS

Consulting firms, boards of directors, and managers are increasingly suggesting the use of audits of corporate activities. Audits may evaluate such activities as marketing and such divisions as international as well as an entire corporation (in, for example, a corporate strategic audit).[8] An audit provides a checklist of questions by area or issue to enable a systematic analysis of various corporate activities. It is extremely useful as a diagnostic tool to pinpoint problem areas and to highlight strengths and weaknesses.

Management Audit

The National Association of Regulatory Utility Commissioners analyzed thirty-one management audits that had been completed or were in progress. The report concluded that the regulatory agencies using management audits were pleased with the results and intended to continue using them. In general, these audits recommended changes in the operating practices of management and suggested areas where substantial reductions in operating costs could be made. The audits gave the boards of directors and management the opportunity to establish new priorities in their objectives and planning, and provided specific recommendations that had impact on the "bottom line."[9]

Most business analysts predict that the use of audits will increase in the 1980s. As corporate boards of directors become more aware of their expanding duties and responsibilities, they will call for more corporate-wide audits to be conducted. Typically, however, the term *management audit* refers to an internal analysis of a corporation. Rarely does it include a consideration of environmental issues. Therefore, since management audits fail to provide a complete assessment of a corporation's situation in the full strategic sense, strategic audits better serve a corporation's needs.

Strategic Audit

As contrasted with the typical management audit, the strategic audit considers external as well as internal factors and includes alternative selection, implementation, and evaluation and control. It therefore covers the key aspects of the strategic management process and places them within a decision-making framework. This framework is composed of the following eight interrelated steps:

1. Evaluation of a corporation's current performance results in terms of (a) return on investment, profitability, etc., and (b) the current mission, objectives, strategies, and policies.
2. Examination and evaluation of a corporation's strategic managers— its board of directors and top management.

3. A scanning of the external environment to locate strategic factors that pose opportunities and threats.

4. A scanning of the internal corporate environment to determine strategic strengths and weaknesses.

5. Analysis of the strategic factors (a) to pinpoint problem areas and (b) to review and revise the corporate mission and objectives as necessary.

6. Generation, evaluation, and selection of the best alternative strategy in light of the analysis conducted in step 5.

7. Implementation of selected strategies via programs, budgets, and procedures.

8. Evaluation of the implemented strategies via feedback systems, and the control of activities to ensure minimum deviation from plans.

This strategic decision-making process, which is depicted in Fig. 2.2, is made operational by the strategic audit. The audit presents an integrated view of strategic management in action. It not only shows how objectives, strategies, and policies are formulated as long-range decisions, but also how they are implemented, evaluated, and controlled by programs, budgets, and procedures. The strategic audit, therefore, enables a person to better understand the *ways* in which various functional areas are interrelated and interdependent, as well as the *manner* in which they contribute to the achievement of the corporate mission. Consequently, the strategic audit is very useful to those people, such as boards of directors, whose job is to evaluate the overall performance of a corporation and its management.

Appendix 2.A at the end of this chapter is an example of a strategic audit proposed for use in analyzing complex business policy cases and for strategic decision making. It is a series of questions organized by the steps in the strategic decision-making process. It is not an all-inclusive list, but it presents many of the critical questions needed to strategically analyze any business corporation. You should consider the audit as a guide for analysis. Some questions or even some areas may be inappropriate for a particular case; in other areas, the questions may be insufficient for a complete analysis. However, each question in a particular area of the strategic audit can be broken down into an additional series of subquestions. It is up to you to develop these subquestions when they are needed.

A strategic audit fulfills three major *functions* in a case-oriented strategy and policy course:

1. It serves to highlight and review important concepts from previously studied subject areas.

2. It provides a systematic framework for the analysis of complex cases. (It is especially useful if you are unfamiliar with the case method.)

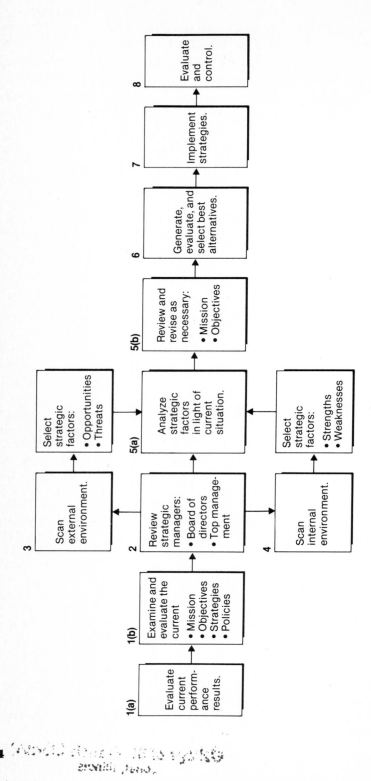

NOTE: Steps 1 through 6 are *strategy formulation.*
Step 7 is *strategy implementation.*
Step 8 is *evaluation and control.*

Figure 2.2 *Strategic decision making process.*

3. It generally improves the quality of case analysis and reduces the amount of time you might spend in learning how to analyze a case.

Students also find the audit helpful in organizing a case for written or oral presentation and in seeing that all areas have been considered. The strategic audit thus enables both students and teachers to maximize the amount of time spent both in analyzing why a certain area is creating problems for a corporation and in considering solutions to the problems.

2.3 CASE METHOD

The analysis/discussion of case problems has been the most popular method of teaching strategy and policy for many years. Cases present actual business situations and enable you to examine both successful and unsuccessful corporations. For example, you may be asked to critically analyze a situation where a manager had to make a decision of long-run corporate importance. This approach gives you a feel for what it is like to work in a large corporation and to be faced with making a business decision.

Case Analysis and Presentation

There is no one best way to analyze or present a case report. Each instructor has personal preferences in terms of format and approach. Nevertheless, we present one suggested approach for both written and oral reports in Appendix 2.B at the end of the chapter. This approach utilizes the strategic audit and provides a systematic method for successfully attacking a case.

The focus in case discussion is on critical analysis and logical development of thought. A solution is satisfactory if it resolves important problems and is likely to be successfully implemented. What the corporation may actually have done to deal with the case problems has no real bearing on the analysis, because its management may have analyzed its problems incorrectly and implemented a series of flawed solutions.

Researching the Case

You should undertake outside research to provide the environmental setting of the case. Check each case to find out when the case situation occurred and then screen the business periodicals for that time period. This background will give you an appreciation for the situation as it was experienced by the people in the case. A company's annual report from that year can be very helpful. An understanding of the economy during that period will help you avoid making a serious error in your analysis— for example, suggesting a sale of stock when the stock market is at an all-time low. Information on the industry will provide insights on its

123,745

College of St. Francis Library
Joliet, Illinois

competitive activities. Some resources available for research into the economy and a corporation's industry are suggested in Appendix 2.C at the end of the chapter.

Financial Analysis: A Place to Begin

A review of key financial ratios may help you assess the company's overall situation and pinpoint some problem areas. Table 2.1 lists some of the most important financial ratios. Included are (1) *liquidity ratios*, which measure the corporation's ability to meet its financial obligations, (2) *profitability ratios*, which measure the degree of corporate success in achieving desired profit levels, (3) *activity ratios*, which measure the effectiveness of the corporation's use of resources, and (4) *leverage ratios*, which measure the contributions of owners' financing compared with creditors' financing.

In your analysis do *not* simply make an exhibit including all the ratios, but select and discuss only those ratios that have an impact on the company's problems. For instance, external resources, accounts receivable, and inventory may provide a source of funds. If receivables and inventories are double the industry average, reducing them may provide needed cash. In this situation, the case report should include not only sources of funds, but also the number of dollars freed for use.

A typical financial analysis of a firm would include a study of the operating statements for five or ten years, including a trend analysis of sales, earnings, profits per share, debt/equity ratio, return on net worth, etc., plus a ratio study comparing the firm under study with industry standards. To begin, scrutinize historical income statements and balance sheets. These two basic statements provide most of the data needed for analysis. Compare the statements over time if a series of statements is available. Calculate changes that occur in individual categories from year to year, as well as the total change over the years. Determine the percentage change along with the absolute amount and the amount *adjusted for inflation*. Examination of this information may reveal developing trends. Compare trends in one category with trends in related categories. For example, an increase in sales of 15% over three years may appear to be satisfactory until you note an increase of 20% in the cost of goods sold during the same period. The outcome of this comparison may suggest that further investigation into the manufacturing process is necessary.

Another approach to analyzing financial statements is to convert them into *common-size* statements. Convert every category from dollar terms to percentages. In the case of the balance sheet, give the total assets or liabilities a value of 100%, and calculate all other categories as percentages of the total assets or liabilities. For the income statement, net sales represent 100%: calculate the percentage of each category so that the categories sum to the net sales percentage (100%). When you convert statements to this form, it is relatively easy to note the percentage each category represents of the total. Comparisons over the years may point out areas for additional analysis. To get a proper picture, however, make comparisons with industry data, if available, to see if fluctuations are merely reflecting industry-wide trends. If a firm's trends are generally in line with those of the rest of the industry, there is less likelihood of problems than if the firm's trends are worse than industry averages.

Adjusting for Inflation

Many of the cases in business policy/strategy textbooks take place during a period of rapid inflation. When analyzing these cases, you should calculate sales and profits in constant dollars in order to perceive the "true" performance of the corporation in comparison with that of the industry, or of the economy in general. Remember that chief executive officers wish to keep their jobs and that some will tend to bias the figures in their favor. Sales stated in current dollars may look like substantial growth, but when they're converted to constant dollars, they may show a steady decline. In 1980, Peter Drucker, a renowned author and consultant, stated, ". . . corporate profits of the last ten years would be all wiped out if they were adjusted for inflation."[10]

As of 1980, the Financial Accounting Standards Board required corporations to report the last five years' sales, dividends, and market price in constant dollar terms.[11] Table 2.2 shows a page from the 1980 annual report of Holiday Inns, Inc., which provided constant dollar figures so that investors could make comparisons quickly. Note that, as originally stated, Holiday Inn revenues increased 208% from 1976 to 1980. When recalculated in 1980 dollars, however, revenues only increased 144%.

As an additional method of dealing with the distortions caused by inflation, firms such as DuPont and General Electric use inflation-adjusted figures throughout their operations. To adjust for inflation, most firms use the Consumer Price Index (CPI). Table 2.3 presents the index for all items.

2.4 SUMMARY AND CONCLUSION

The strategic management/business policy course is concerned with developing the conceptual skills that successful top management needs. The emphasis is therefore on improving your analytical and problem-solving abilities. The case method develops those skills and gives you an appreciation of environmental issues and the interdependencies among the functional units of a large corporation. The strategic audit is one recommended technique for systematizing the analysis of fairly long and

Table 2.1 FINANCIAL RATIOS

RATIO	FORMULA	HOW EXPRESSED
1. *Liquidity Ratios*		
Current ratio	$\dfrac{\text{Current assets}}{\text{Current liabilities}}$	Decimal
Quick (acid test) ratio	$\dfrac{\text{Current assets} - \text{Inventory}}{\text{Current liabilities}}$	Decimal
2. *Profitability Ratios*		
Net profit margin	$\dfrac{\text{Net profit before taxes}}{\text{Net sales}}$	Percentage
Gross margin	$\dfrac{\text{Sales} - \text{Cost of sales}}{\text{Net sales}}$	Percentage
Return on investment (ROI)	$\dfrac{\text{Net profit before taxes}}{\text{Total assets}}$	Percentage
Return on equity (ROE)	$\dfrac{\text{Net profit after taxes}}{\text{Average equity}}$	Percentage
Earnings Per Share (EPS)	$\dfrac{\text{Net profit after taxes} - \text{Preferred burdens}}{\text{Average number of common shares}}$	Dollar per share
Productivity of Assets	$\dfrac{\text{Gross income} - \text{Taxes}}{\text{Equity}}$	Percentage
3. *Activity Ratios*		
Inventory turnover	$\dfrac{\text{Net sales}}{\text{Inventory}}$	Decimal

Ratio	Formula	Unit
Net working capital turnover	$\dfrac{\text{Net sales}}{\text{Net working capital}}$	Decimal
Asset turnover	$\dfrac{\text{Sales}}{\text{Total assets}}$	Decimal
Average collection period	$\dfrac{\text{Accounts receivable}}{\text{Sales for year} \div 365}$	Days
Accounts payable period	$\dfrac{\text{Accounts Payable}}{\text{Purchases for year} \div 365}$	Days
Cash turnover	$\dfrac{\text{Cash}}{\text{Net sales for year} \div 365}$	Days
Days of inventory	$\dfrac{\text{Inventory}}{\text{Cost of goods sold} \div 365}$	Days
Price earning ratio	$\dfrac{\text{Market price per share}}{\text{Earnings per share}}$	Ratio

4. Leverage Ratios

Ratio	Formula	Unit
Debt ratio	$\dfrac{\text{Total debt}}{\text{Total assets}}$	Percentage
Times interest earned	$\dfrac{\text{Profit before taxes} + \text{Interest charges}}{\text{Interest charges}}$	Decimal
Coverage of fixed charges	$\dfrac{\text{Profit before taxes} + \text{Interest charges} + \text{Lease charges}}{\text{Interest charges} + \text{Lease obligations}}$	Decimal
Current liabilities to equity	$\dfrac{\text{Current liabilities}}{\text{Equity}}$	Percentage

Note: In using ratios for analysis, calculate ratios for the corporation and compare them to the average ratios for the particular industry. Refer to Standard and Poor's and Robert Morris Associates for average industry data. For an in-depth discussion of ratios and their use, refer to J. F. Weston and E. F. Brigham, *Managerial Finance*, 7th ed. (Hinsdale, Ill.: Dryden Press, 1981), pp. 134–160.

29

Table 2.2   HOLIDAY INN'S ANNUAL REPORT ADJUSTED FOR INFLATION: AN EXCERPT

	1980	1979	1978	1977	1976
	(In thousands, except per share)				
Revenues					
As reported	1,533,758	1,112,645	935,823	791,430	736,366
In 1980 dollars	1,533,758	1,263,113	1,181,991	1,076,170	1,065,895
Income from continuing operations					
As reported	108,275	71,296	52,504	42,623	32,710
In 1980 dollars	76,173	54,583	42,005	33,612	23,851
At current cost in 1980 dollars	65,277	43,252			
Income per common and common equivalent share-continuing					
As reported	2.92	2.25	1.71	1.39	1.07
In 1980 dollars	2.10	1.72	1.36	1.09	.78
At current cost in 1980 dollars	1.82	1.36			
Net assets at year end					
As reported	707,961	624,491	550,080	502,496	465,751
In 1980 dollars	1,155,120	1,083,452	1,029,539	1,001,355	982,926
At current cost in 1980 dollars	1,350,981	1,249,617			
Gain from decline in purchasing power of net amounts owed in 1980 dollars	50,292	29,238	26,071	22,226	18,088
Cash dividends declared per common share					
As reported	.70	.66	.56	.465	.40
In 1980 dollars	.70	.75	.71	.63	.58
Market price per common share at year end					
As reported	26.75	18.25	16.375	15.75	13.125
In 1980 dollars	25.55	19.63	19.92	20.89	18.58
Average consumer price index	246.8	217.4	195.4	181.5	170.5

SOURCE: Holiday Inns, Inc., *1980 Annual Report*, p. 46

complex policy cases. It also provides a basic checklist for investigating any large corporation. Nevertheless, the strategic audit is only one of many techniques with which you can analyze and diagnose case problems. We expect that during the 1980s consultants, managers, and boards of directors will increasingly employ the audit as an analytical technique.

Table 2.3   CONSUMER PRICE
             INDEX FOR ALL
             ITEMS

Year	CPI	Year	CPI
1967	100.0	1974	147.7
1968	104.2	1975	161.2
1969	109.8	1976	170.5
1970	116.3	1977	181.5
1971	121.3	1978	195.4
1972	125.3	1979	217.4
1973	133.1	1980	246.8

SOURCE: U.S. Department of Commerce, "1980 Statistical Abstract of the United States," Chart no. 806, p. 486.

DISCUSSION QUESTIONS

1. Should people be selected for top management positions primarily on the basis of their having a particular combination of skills? Explain.

2. What are the strengths and weaknesses of the strategic audit as a technique for assessing corporate performance?

3. What value does the case method hold for the study of strategic management/business policy?

4. Why should one begin a case analysis with a financial analysis? When are other approaches appropriate?

5. Reconcile the strategic decision making process depicted in Fig. 2.2 with the strategic management model depicted in Fig. 1.3.

NOTES

1. B. M. Bass, *Stogdill's Handbook of Leadership* (New York: Free Press, 1981), p. 73.

2. R. L. Katz, "Skills of an Effective Administrator," *Harvard Business Review* (January–February 1955), p. 33.

3. Katz, pp. 33–42. These definitions were adapted from the material in this article.

4. Katz, p. 42.

5. T. L. Wheelen, G. K. Rakes, and J. D. Hunger, "Skills of an Executive" (Paper presented at the Thirty-Sixth Annual Meeting of the Academy of Management, Kansas City, Mo., August 1976).

6. Wheelen, Rakes, and Hunger, p. 7.

7. W. G. Shenkir, T. L. Wheelen, and R. H. Strawser, "The Making of an Accountant," *CPA Journal* (March 1973), p. 219.

8. R. B. Buchele, "How to Evaluate a Firm," *California Management Review* (Fall 1962), pp. 5–16.

    W. T. Greenwood, *Business Policy: A Management Audit Approach* (New York: Macmillan, 1967), pp. 41–142.

    A. Elkins, *Management: Structures, Functions, and Practices* (Reading, Mass.: Addison-Wesley, 1980), pp. 441–454.

    A. B. Carroll and G. W. Beiler, "Landmarks in the Evolution of the Social Audit," *Academy of Management Journal* (September 1975), pp. 589–599.

    B. H. Marcus and E. M. Tauber, *Marketing Analysis and Decision Making* (Boston: Little, Brown & Co., 1979), p. 25.

    J. A. F. Stoner, *Management*, 2nd ed. (Englewood Cliffs, N.J.: Prentice-Hall, 1982), p. 526.

    J. Martindell, *The Appraisal of Management* (New York: Harper & Row, 1962).

    R. Bauer, L. T. Cauthorn, and R. P. Warner, "Management Audit Process Guide," (Boston: Intercollegiate Case Clearing House, no. 9-375-336, 1975).

9. T. Barry, "What a Management Audit Can Do for You," *Management Review* (June 1977), p. 43.

10. D. Pauly, "Tomorrow's Rules for World Business," *Newsweek*, April 28, 1980, p. 71.

11. "Financial Statements Restated for General Price-Level Changes," *Financial Accounting Standards*, APB Statement no. 3 (Stamford, Conn.: Financial Accounting Standards Board, July 1, 1979).

Appendix 2.A
STRATEGIC AUDIT OF A CORPORATION

I. Current Situation

   A. How is the corporation performing in terms of return on investment, overall market share, profitability trends, earnings per share, etc.?

   B. What are the corporation's current mission, objectives, strategies, and policies?

      1. Are they clearly stated or are they merely implied from performance?

      2. *Mission*: What business(es) is the corporation in? Why?

      3. *Objectives*: What are the corporate, business, and functional objectives? Are they consistent with each other, with the mission, and with the internal and external environments?

      4. *Strategies*: What strategy or mix of strategies is the corporation following? Are they consistent with each other, with the mission and objectives, and with the internal and external environments?

      5. *Policies*: What are they? Are they consistent with each other, with the mission, objectives, and strategies, and with the internal and external environments?

II. Strategic Managers

   A. Board of Directors

      1. Who are they? Are they internal or external?

      2. Do they own significant shares of stock?

      3. Is the stock privately held or publicly traded?

      4. What do they contribute to the corporation in terms of knowledge, skills, background, and connections?

      5. How long have they served on the board?

      6. What is their level of involvement in strategic management? Do they merely rubber stamp top management's proposals or do they actively participate and suggest future directions?

   B. Top Management

      1. What person or group constitutes top management?

      2. What are top management's chief characteristics in terms of knowledge, skills, background, and style?

      3. Has top management been responsible for the corporation's performance over the past few years?

      4. Has it established a systematic approach to the formulation, implementation, and evaluation and control of strategic management?

      5. What is its level of involvement in the strategic management process?

      6. How well does top management interact with lower-level management?

SOURCE: T. L. Wheelen and J. D. Hunger, "Strategic Audit of a Corporation." Copyright © 1982 by Wheelen and Hunger Associates. Reprinted by permission.

7. How well does top management interact with the board of directors?

8. Is top management sufficiently skilled to cope with likely future challenges?

III. External Environment: Opportunities and Threats

    A. Societal Environment

        1. What general environmental factors (that is, socio-cultural, economic, political-legal, and technological factors) are affecting the corporation?

        2. Which of these are the most important at the present time? In the next few years?

    B. Task Environment

        1. What key factors in the immediate environment are affecting the corporation (customers, competitors, suppliers, creditors, labor unions, governments, trade associations, local community, and stockholders)?

        2. Which of these are most important at the present time? In the next few years?

IV. Internal Environment: Strengths and Weaknesses

    A. Corporate Structure

        1. How is the corporation presently structured?

            a) Is decision-making authority centralized around one group or decentralized to many groups or units?

            b) Is it organized on the basis of functions, projects, geography, or some combination of these?

        2. Is the structure clearly understood by everyone in the corporation?

        3. Is the present structure consistent with current corporate objectives, strategies, policies, and programs?

        4. In what ways does this structure compare with those of similar corporations?

    B. Corporate Culture

        1. Is there a well-defined or emerging culture composed of shared beliefs, expectations, and values?

        2. Is the culture consistent with the current objectives, strategies, policies, and programs?

        3. What is the culture's position on important issues facing the corporation (that is, on productivity, quality of performance, adaptability to changing conditions)?

    C. Corporate Resources

        1. Marketing

            a) What are the corporation's current marketing objectives, strategies, policies, and programs?

                i) Are they clearly stated or merely implied from performance and/or budgets?

                ii) Are they consistent with the corporation's mission, objectives, strategies, policies, and with internal and external environments?

b) How well is the corporation performing in terms of analysis of market position and marketing mix (that is, of product, price, place, and promotion)?

i) What trends emerge from this analysis?

ii) What impact have these trends had on past performance and will probably have on future performance?

iii) Does this analysis support the corporation's past and pending strategic decisions?

c) How well does this corporation's marketing performance compare with those of similar corporations?

d) Are marketing managers using accepted marketing concepts and techniques to evaluate and improve product performance? (Consider product life cycle, market segmentation, market research, and product portfolios.)

e) What is the role of the marketing manager in the strategic management process?

2. Finance

a) What are the corporation's current financial objectives, strategies, policies, and programs?

i) Are they clearly stated or merely implied from performance and/or budgets?

ii) Are they consistent with the corporation's mission, objectives, strategies, policies, and with internal and external environments?

b) How well is the corporation performing in terms of financial analysis? (Consider liquidity ratios, profitability ratios, activity ratios, leverage ratios, capitalization structure, and constant dollars.)

i) What trends emerge from this analysis?

ii) What impact have these trends had on past performance and will have on future performance?

iii) Does this analysis support the corporation's past and pending strategic decisions?

c) How well does this corporation's financial performance compare with that of similar corporations?

d) Are financial managers using accepted financial concepts and techniques to evaluate and improve current corporate and divisional performance? (Consider financial leverage, capital budgeting, and ratio analysis.)

e) What is the role of the financial manager in the strategic management process?

3. Research and Development (R&D)

a) What are the corporation's current R&D objectives, strategies, policies, and programs?

i) Are they clearly stated or implied from performance and/or budgets?

      ii) Are they consistent with the corporation's mission, objectives, strategies, policies, and with internal and external environments?

      iii) What is the role of technology in corporate performance?

      iv) Is the mix of basic, applied and engineering research appropriate given the corporate mission and strategies?

  b) What return is the corporation receiving from its investment in R&D?

  c) Is the corporation technologically competent?

  d) How well does the corporation's investment in R&D compare with the investments of similar corporations?

  e) What is the role of the R&D manager in the strategic management process?

4. Manufacturing

  a) What are the corporation's current manufacturing objectives, strategies, policies, and programs?

      i) Are they clearly stated or merely implied from performance and/or budgets?

      ii) Are they consistent with the corporation's mission, objectives, strategies, policies, and with internal or external environments?

  b) What is the type and extent of manufacturing capabilities of the corporation? Consider plant facilities, type of production system (continuous mass production or intermittent job shop), age and type of equipment, degree and role of automation and/or robots, plant capacities and utilization, productivity ratings, availability and type of transportation.

  c) What is the vulnerability of each of these plants to natural disasters, local or national strikes, reduction or limitation of resources from suppliers, substantial cost increases of materials, and nationalization of foreign holdings?

  d) Is operating leverage being used successfully?

  e) How well is the corporation performing in terms of competitive manufacturing analysis? Consider costs—unit, labor, material, and overhead; downtime; inventory control management; production ratings; plant utilization; and percentage of orders shipped on time.

      i) What trends emerge from this analysis?

      ii) What impact have these trends had on past performance and will probably have on future performance?

      iii) Does this analysis support the corporation's past and pending strategic decisions?

  f) Are manufacturing managers using manufacturing concepts and techniques to evaluate and improve current corporate performance? Consider cost systems, quality control and reliability systems, inventory control management, learning curves, safety programs, and manufacturing engineering programs.

     g) What is the role of the manufacturing manager in the strategic management process?

  5. Human Resources Management (HRM)

     a) What are the corporation's current HRM objectives, strategies, policies, and programs?

        i) Are they clearly stated or merely implied from performance?

        ii) Are they consistent with the corporation's mission, objectives, strategies, policies, and with internal and external environments?

     b) How well is the corporation's HRM performing in terms of improving the fit between the individual employee and the job? Consider turnover, grievances, strikes, layoffs, quality of work life.

        i) What trends emerge from this analysis?

        ii) What impact have these trends had on past performance and will probably have on future performance?

        iii) Does this analysis support the corporation's strategic decisions of the past and pending decisions?

     c) How does this corporation's HRM performance compare with that of similar corporations?

     d) Are HRM managers using appropriate concepts and techniques to evaluate and improve corporate performance? Consider job analysis program, performance appraisal system, up-to-date job descriptions, training and development programs, attitude surveys, job design programs, quality of relationship with unions.

     e) What is the role of the HRM manager in the strategic management process?

V. Analysis of Strategic Factors

  A. What are the key internal and external factors that strongly affect the corporation's present and future performance?

    1. What are the short-term problems facing this corporation?

    2. What are the long-term problems facing this corporation?

  B. Are the current mission and objectives appropriate in light of the key strategic factors and problems?

    1. Should the mission and objectives be changed?

    2. If changed, what will the effect be on the firm?

VI. Strategic Alternatives

  A. Can the current or revised objectives be met by simply implementing more carefully those strategies presently in use (for example, fine tuning the strategies)?

  B. What are the feasible alternative strategies available to this corporation?

    1. Do you recommend stability, growth, retrenchment, or a combination?

    2. What are the pros and cons of each?

  C. What is the *best* alternative (that is, *your* recommended strategy)?

    1. Does it adequately resolve the long- and short-term problems?

      2. Does it take into consideration the key strategic factors?

      3. What policies should be developed to guide effective implementation?

VII. Implementation

    A. What kinds of programs (for example, restructuring the corporation) should be developed to implement the recommended strategy?

      1. Who should develop these programs?

      2. Who should be in charge of these programs?

    B. Are the programs financially feasible? Can *pro forma* budgets be developed and agreed upon?

    C. Will new standard operating procedures need to be developed?

VIII. Evaluation and Control

    A. Is the current information system capable of providing sufficient feedback on implementation activities and performance?

      1. Can performance results be pinpointed by area, unit, project, or function?

      2. Is the information timely?

    B. Are adequate control measures in place to ensure conformance with the recommended strategic plan?

      1. Are appropriate standards and measures being used?

      2. Are reward systems capable of recognizing and rewarding good performance?

Appendix 2.B
SUGGESTED TECHNIQUES FOR CASE
ANALYSIS AND PRESENTATION

A. Case Analysis

    1. Read the case rapidly to get an overview of the nature of the corporation and its environment. Note the date the case was written so that you can put it into proper context.

    2. Read the case a second time, giving it a detailed analysis according to the strategic audit (see Appendix 2. A) when appropriate. The audit will provide a conceptual framework to examine the corporation's objectives, mission, policies, strategies, problems, symptoms or problems, and issues. You should end up with a list of the salient issues and problems in the case. Perform a financial analysis.

    3. Undertake outside research, when appropriate, to uncover economic and industrial information. Appendix 2.C suggests possible sources for outside research. These data should provide the environmental setting for the corporation.

    4. Marshal facts and evidence to support selected issues and problems. De-

velop a framework or outline to organize the analysis. Your method of organization could be one of the following:

   a) The case as organized around the strategic audit.

   b) The case as organized around the key individual(s) in the case.

   c) The case as organized around the corporation's functional areas: production, management, finance, marketing, and R&D.

   d) The case as organized around the decision making process.

5. Clearly identify and state the central problem(s) as supported by the information in the case.

6. Develop a logical series of alternatives that evolve from the analysis to resolve the problem(s) or issue(s) in the case.

7. Evaluate each of the alternatives in light of the company's environment (both external and internal), mission, objectives, strategies, and policies. For each alternative, consider both the possible obstacles to its implementation and its financial implications.

8. Make recommendations on the basis of the fact that action must be taken. (Don't say, "I don't have enough information." The individuals in the case had the same or even less information than is in the case.)

   a) Base your recommendations on a total analysis of the case.

   b) Provide the evidence gathered in step A4 to justify suggested changes.

   c) List the recommendations in order of priority—those to be done immediately and those to be done in the future.

   d) Show how your recommendation(s) will solve each of the problems mentioned in step A5.

   e) Explain how each recommendation will be implemented. How will the plan(s) deal with anticipated resistance?

   f) Suggest feedback and control systems to ensure that the recommendations are carried out as planned and to give advance warning of needed adjustments.

B. Written Presentation

1. Use the audit or outline to write the first draft of the case analysis.

   a) Don't rehash the case material; rather supply the salient evidence and data to support your recommendations.

   b) Develop exhibits on financial ratios and other data for inclusion in your report. The exhibits should provide meaningful information. Mention key elements of an exhibit in the text of the written analysis. If you include a ratio analysis as an exhibit, explain the meaning of the ratios in the text and cite only the critical ones in your analysis.

2. Review your case analysis after it is written for content and grammar. Remember to compare the audit or outline (step A4) with the final product. Make sure you've presented sufficient data or evidence to support your problem analysis and recommendations. If the final product requires rewriting, do so. Keep in mind that the written report is going to be judged not only on *what* is said but also on the *manner* in which it is said.

C. Oral Presentation by Teams

   1. Each team member should develop his or her own outline or strategic audit.

   2. The team should consolidate member outlines into one comprehensive team audit or outline.

   3. Divide the work of the case analysis among the team members for further modification and for presentation.

   4. Modify the team outline or audit, if necessary, and have one or two rehearsals of the presentation. If there is a time constraint, apply it to the practice presentation. If exhibits are used, make sure to allow sufficient time to explain them. Critique one another's presentations and make the necessary modifications to the analysis.

   5. During the class presentation, if a presenter misses a key fact, either slip a note to him or her, or deal with it in the summary speech.

   6. Answer the specific questions raised by the instructor or classmates. If one person acts as a moderator for the questions and refers the questions to the appropriate team member, the presentation runs smoother than it will if everyone (or no one!) tries to deal with each question.

Appendix 2.C
RESOURCES FOR CASE RESEARCH

A. Company Information

   1. Annual Reports

   2. *Moody's Manuals on Investment* (a listing of companies within certain industries that contains a brief history of each company and a five-year financial statement)

   3. Securities and Exchange Commission Annual Report Form 10-K

   4. *Standard and Poor's Register of Corporations, Directors, and Executives*

B. Economic Information

   1. Regional statistics and local forecasts from large banks

   2. *Business Cycle Development* (Department of Commerce)

   3. Chase Econometric Associates' publications

   4. Census Bureau publications on population, transportation, and housing

   5. *Current Business Reports* (Department of Commerce)

   6. *Economic Indicators* (Joint Economic Committee)

   7. *Economic Report of the President to Congress*

   8. *Long-Term Economic Growth* (Department of Commerce)

   9. *Monthly Labor Review* (Department of Labor)

   10. *Monthly Bulletin of Statistics* (United Nations)

   11. "Survey of Buying Power," *Sales Management*

   12. Standard and Poor's Statistical Service

13. *Statistical Abstract of the United States* (Department of Commerce)

14. *Statistical Yearbook* (United Nations)

15. *Survey of Current Business* (Department of Commerce)

16. *U.S. Industrial Outlook* (Department of Defense)

17. *World Trade Annual* (United Nations)

C. Industry Information

1. Analysis of companies and industries by investment brokerage firms

2. *Annual Report of American Industry* (a compilation of statistics by industry and company published by *Fortune*)

3. *Business Week* (provides weekly economic and business information and quarterly profit and sales rankings of corporations)

4. *Fortune Magazine* (publishes listings of financial information on corporations within certain industries)

5. *Industry Survey* (published quarterly by Standard and Poor's Corporation)

D. Directory and Index Information

1. *Business Information: How to Find and Use It*

2. *Business Periodical Index*

3. *Directory of National Trade Association*

4. *Encyclopedia of Associations*

5. *Funk and Scott Index of Corporations and Industries*

6. *Thomas's Register of American Manufacturers*

7. *Wall Street Journal Index*

E. Ratio Analysis Information

1. *Almanac of Business and Industrial Ratios* (Prentice-Hall)

2. *Annual Statement Studies* (Robert Morris Associates)

3. *Dun's Review* (Dun and Bradstreet: published annually in September–December issues)

F. General Sources

1. *Commodity Yearbook*

2. *U.S. Census of Business*

3. *U.S. Census of Manufactures*

4. *World Almanac and Book of Facts*

G. Periodicals

1. *Business Horizons*

2. *Business Week*

3. *California Management Review*

4. *Forbes*

5. *Fortune*

6. *Harvard Business Review*

7. *Long-Range Planning*

8. *Wall Street Journal*

SCANNING THE ENVIRONMENT

PART II

STRATEGIC MANAGEMENT MODEL

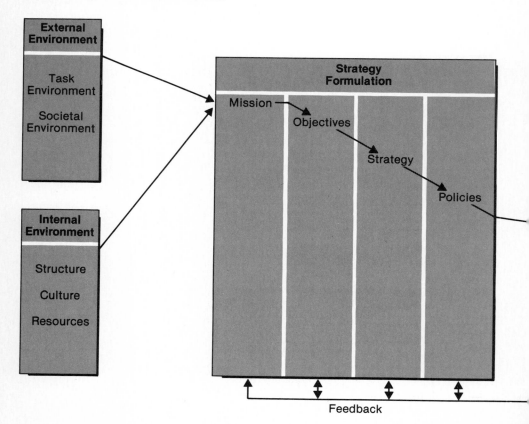

STRATEGIC MANAGERS

CHAPTER 3

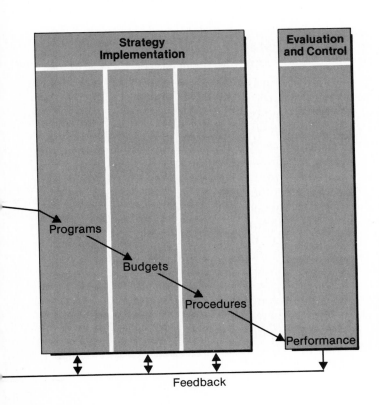

S trategic managers are the people in a corporation who are involved in the strategic management process. They are the people who scan the internal and external environments, formulate and implement objectives, strategies and policies, and evaluate and control the results. The people with direct responsibility for this process are the board of directors and top management. The chief executive officer (CEO), the chief operations officer (COO) or president, the executive vice-president, and the vice-presidents in charge of operating divisions and functional areas typically form the top management group. Traditionally, boards of directors have engaged in strategic management only to the extent that they passively approved proposals from top management and hired and fired their CEOs. Their role, however, is changing dramatically. The strategic management process, therefore, is also changing.

3.1 CORPORATE BOARD OF DIRECTORS

Directors conduct a far different meeting from those in the past. Pressures—from regulatory agencies, shareholders, lenders, and the public—have practically forced greater awareness of directors' responsibilities. The board as a rubber stamp or a bastion of the "old-boy" selection system has largely been replaced by more active, more professional boards.[1]

Even in the recent past, boards of directors have functioned rather passively. Members were selected because of their prestige in the community, regardless of their knowledge of the specific functioning of the corporation they were to oversee. Traditionally, members of the board were requested to simply approve proposals by top management or the firm's legal counsel, and the more important board activities were generally conducted by an executive committee composed of insiders.[2] Even now, the boards in some family-owned corporations are more figureheads than overseers; they exist on paper because the laws of incorporation require their presence, but they rarely, if ever, meet.

Over the past decade stockholders and various interest groups have seriously questioned the role of the board of directors. As a result, the general public has become more aware and more critical of many boards' apparent lack of responsibility for corporate activities. Who is responsible for radioactive leaks in nuclear power plants? For the manufacture and sale of unsafe toys? For insect poison sold by mistake as cattle feed? For bribery attempts by corporate officers? Can boards, especially those of multinational corporations, realistically monitor the decisions and actions of corporate employees? What are the legal liabilities of a board for the actions of its corporation?

Responsibilities of the Board

At this time, there are no national standards defining the accountability or responsibility of a board of directors. The law offers little guidance on this question. Specific requirements of directors vary, depending on the state in which the corporate charter is issued. According to Conference Board reports authored by Bacon and Brown, "State corporation laws give boards of directors rather sweeping powers couched in general language that does not specify to whom they are accountable nor clarify what it is they are accountable for."[3] There is, nevertheless, a developing consensus concerning the major responsibilities of a board. The board of directors of a corporation is appointed or elected by the stockholders for the following purposes: To oversee the management of the corporation's assets; to establish or approve the corporation's mission, objectives, strategy, and policies; to review management's actions and financial performance of the corporation; and to hire and fire the principal operating officers of the corporation. In a legal sense, the board is required to direct the affairs of the corporation but not to manage them. It is charged by law to act with "due care." As Bacon and Brown put it, "Directors must act with that degree of diligence, care and skill which ordinarily prudent men would exercise under similar circumstances in like positions."[4] If a director or the board as a whole fails to act with due care and, as a result, the corporation is in some way harmed, the careless director or directors may be held personally liable for the harm done. The increasing popularity of personal liability insurance for board members suggests that a number of people on boards of directors are becoming very concerned that they might be held personally responsible not only for their own actions but also for the actions of the corporation as a whole. This is reinforced by the requirement of the Securities and Exchange Commission (SEC) that a majority of directors must sign the Annual Report Form 10-K. A recent survey found that of 606 major U.S. corporations, 51% go beyond the SEC requirement by requiring that *all* directors sign the 10-K.[5]

In addition to these duties, directors must make certain that the corporation is managed in accordance with the laws of the state in which it is incorporated. They must also ensure management's adherence to laws and regulations, such as those dealing with the issuance of securities, insider trading, and other conflict-of-interest situations. They must also be aware of the needs and demands of constituent groups so that they can achieve a judicious balance among the interests of these diverse groups while ensuring the continued functioning of the corporation.

Role of the Board in
Strategic Management

In terms of strategic management, a board of directors has three basic tasks:[6]

☐ *To initiate and determine.* A board can delineate a corporation's mission and specify strategic options to its management.

☐ *To evaluate and influence.* A board can examine management proposals, decisions, and actions; agree or disagree with them; give advice and offer suggestions; develop alternatives.

☐ *To monitor.* By acting through its committees, a board can keep abreast of developments both inside and outside the corporation. It can thus bring to management's attention developments it may have overlooked.

Even though any board will be composed of people with varying degrees of commitment to the corporation, we can make some generalizations about a board of directors as a whole in its attempt to fulfill these three basic tasks. We can characterize a board as being at a specific point on a continuum on the basis of its degree of involvement in corporate strategic affairs. As types, boards may range from phantom boards with no real involvement to catalyst boards with a very high degree of involvement. Highly involved boards tend to be very active. They take their tasks of initiating, evaluating and influencing, and monitoring very seriously by providing advice when necessary and keeping management alert. As depicted in Fig. 3.1, they may be deeply involved in the strategic management process. At Texas Instruments, for example, the board attends a four-day strategic planning conference each year to discuss business opportunities of the next decade. Several members of the board also attend, during the following two days, management meetings attended by 500 managers from throughout the company. Kenneth Andrews, an authority on the role of the board of directors in strategic management, indicates the result:

> By the time the board comes to approve the company's plans, via ten days' annual work of the corporate objectives committee, it is presumably informed enough to play an important role in the company's planning processes.[7]

As a board becomes less involved in the affairs of the corporation, it is found further to the left on the continuum. These are passive boards that typically *never* initiate or determine strategy unless a crisis occurs. Most publicly owned large corporations probably have boards that operate at some point between nominal and active participation. Few have catalyst boards, except for those with major problems (that is, pending bankruptcies, mergers, or acquisitions).

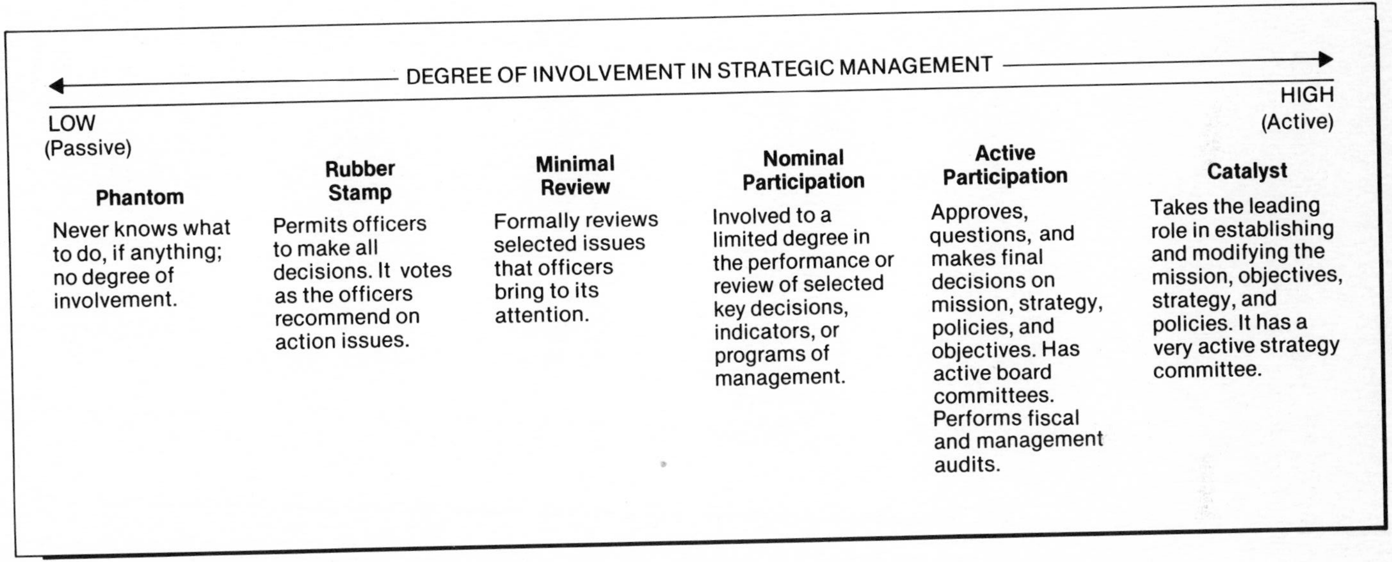

————— DEGREE OF INVOLVEMENT IN STRATEGIC MANAGEMENT —————

LOW
(Passive)

HIGH
(Active)

Phantom	Rubber Stamp	Minimal Review	Nominal Participation	Active Participation	Catalyst
Never knows what to do, if anything; no degree of involvement.	Permits officers to make all decisions. It votes as the officers recommend on action issues.	Formally reviews selected issues that officers bring to its attention.	Involved to a limited degree in the performance or review of selected key decisions, indicators, or programs of management.	Approves, questions, and makes final decisions on mission, strategy, policies, and objectives. Has active board committees. Performs fiscal and management audits.	Takes the leading role in establishing and modifying the mission, objectives, strategy, and policies. It has a very active strategy committee.

Figure 3.1 *Board of directors continuum.*

Many CEOs and board members do not want the board to be involved in strategy matters at more than a superficial level. Andrews suggests why:

> Many chief executive officers, rejecting the practicality of conscious strategy, preside over unstated, incremental, or intuitive strategies that have never been articulated or analyzed—and therefore could not be deliberated by the board. Others do not believe their outside directors know enough or have time enough to do more than assent to strategic recommendations. Still others may keep discussions of strategy within management to prevent board transgression onto management turf and consequent reduction of executives' power to shape by themselves the future of their companies.[8]

Board Membership: Inside versus Outside Directors

The boards of most publicly owned corporations are comprised of both inside and outside directors. Inside directors are typically officers or executives employed by the corporation. The outside director may be an executive of another firm but is not an employee of the board's corporation. A survey sponsored by the Financial Executives Institute found that an average of 72% of the board members of nearly 800 responding *publicly* held corporations were nonmangement (outside) directors. In comparison, only 55% of the board members of approximately 200 *privately* held corporations were outside directors.[9] Although outside directors are typically compensated for their work on the board at a rate ranging in 1981 from $14,441 to $19,248 per person, few inside directors are paid for assuming this extra duty.[10]

In 1977, R. P. Neuschel, then of McKinsey & Company, Inc., a management consulting firm, suggested that in the future board composition will be 80% outsiders and 20% insiders, such as the president or CEO.[11] Today the SEC requires corporations whose stock is listed on the New York Exchange to have at least two outside directors. The SEC apparently takes the view that outside directors are less biased and more likely to evaluate objectively management's performance than are inside directors.

Surveys of manufacturing companies disclose that a majority (51%) of the outside directors are presidents, managing partners, or chairmen of the boards of other corporations. Outside directors come from a variety of organizations, some even from the ministry, but a majority of them come from the manufacturing, banking, law, and investment industries. A majority (58%) of the inside directors include the president, chairman of the board, and vice-presidents; the rest are key officers or former employees. Lower-level operating employees, including managers, form only one percent of the total employee board membership of the companies surveyed.[12]

Codetermination. The dearth of nonmanagement employee directors on the boards of U.S. corporations may be changing. Codetermination, the inclusion of a corporation's employees on its board, began only recently in the United States. The addition of Douglas Frazer, President of the United Auto Workers, to the board of Chrysler Corporation in 1980 was a controversial move designed to placate the union while Chrysler was attempting to avoid bankruptcy. Critics of this plan raise the issue of conflict of interest. Can a member of the board who is privy to confidential managerial information function as a union leader whose primary duty is to fight for the best benefits for his members?[13]

While the movement to place employees on the boards of directors of American companies is only just beginning, the European experience reveals an increasing acceptance of worker participation on corporate boards. The Federal Republic of Germany pioneered the practice with its Co-Determination Act of 1951 and Works Constitution Act (originally adopted in 1952 and revised in 1972). Worker representatives in the coal, iron, and steel industries were given equal status with management on policy-making boards. Management in other industries, however, retained a two-thirds majority on policy-making boards. Other countries such as Sweden, Norway, and the Netherlands have passed or are considering similar legislation.[14]

Interlocking Directorates. Boards that are primarily composed of outside directors will not necessarily be more objective than those primarily composed of insiders. CEOs may nominate for board membership chief executives from other firms for the purpose of exchanging important information and guaranteeing the stability of key marketplace relationships. One or more individuals serving on the boards of directors of two or more corporations create an *interlocking directorate*. Although the Clayton Act and the Banking Act of 1933 prohibit interlocking directorates in many circumstances,[15] interlocking continues to occur in almost all corporations, especially large ones. Research has shown that the larger the firm, the greater the number of different corporations represented on its board of directors. Corporations also have members of their management teams on the boards of other corporations. General Motors, for example, has 284 connections (11 through ownership, 67 through direct interlocking, and 206 through indirect interlocking).[16] Interlocking occurs because large firms have a large impact on other corporations; and these other corporations, in turn, have some control over the firm's inputs and marketplace. Interlocking directorates are also a useful method to gain both inside information about an uncertain environment and objective expertise about a firm's strategy. As a result, capital-intensive firms tend to be involved in extensive interlocking.[17] Family-owned corporations, however, are less likely to have interlocking directorates than are corporations with highly dispersed stock ownership, probably because family-owned corporations do not like to dilute their corporate control by adding outsiders to boardroom discussions.[18]

Nomination and Election of Board Members

Traditionally, the CEO of the corporation decided whom to invite to board membership and merely asked the stockholders for approval. This practice continues to occur in approximately 40% of all corporations.[19] The chief criteria used by most CEOs in nominating board members are that the persons be compatible with the CEO and that they bring some prestige to the board.[20]

There are some dangers, however, in allowing the CEO free reign in nominating directors. The CEO may select board members who, in the CEO's opinion, will not disturb the company's policies and functioning. More importantly, directors selected by the CEO often feel that they should go along with any proposals made by the CEO. Thus, board members find themselves accountable to the very management they are charged to oversee. Because of the likelihood of these occurrences, there is an increasing tendency for a special board committee to nominate new outside board members. A recent survey reveals that the percentage of corporations using nominating committees to select new directors has risen from 19% in 1977 to 58% in 1981.[21]

Term of Office. A survey of 855 executives reported that 81% of the companies responding elected all directors annually for one year terms. Seventeen percent elected them for three-year terms, with the remainder elected for two or five years. Virtually every corporation whose directors serve terms of more than one year divided its board into classes and staggered elections so that only a portion of the board stood for election each year. Arguments in favor of this practice are that it provides continuity by reducing the chance of an abrupt turnover in its membership and that it reduces the likelihood of people unfriendly to management being elected through cumulative voting.[22]

Cumulative Voting. The practice of cumulative voting allows a stockholder to concentrate his or her votes in an election of directors. Cumulative voting is required by law in 18 states and is mandatory on request or permitted as a corporate option in 32 other states or territories. Under cumulative voting, the number of votes allowed are determined from multiplying the number of voting shares held by the number of directors to be elected. Thus, a person owning 1,000 shares in an election of 12 directors would have 12,000 votes. These votes may then be distributed in any manner—for instance, divided evenly (or unevenly) between two directors or concentrated on one. This is contrasted with straight voting in which the stockholder votes shares individually for each director to be elected.[23]

Only a minority of companies surveyed provide for cumulative voting in their by-laws or certificate of incorporation.[24] Although few stockholders use this privilege, it is a powerful way for them to influence a board of directors. For example, a minority of stockholders could concentrate their voting power and elect one or more directors of their choice. In contrast, straight voting allows the holders of the majority of outstanding shares to prevent the election of any director not to their liking.

Those in favor of cumulative voting argue that it is the only system under which a candidate not on the management slate can hope to be elected to the board. Otherwise, under straight voting, an entrenched management could insulate itself from criticism and use the board as a rubber stamp. Critics of cumulative voting argue that it allows the board to deteriorate into interest groups more concerned with protecting their own special concerns than in working for the good of the corporation. This could become a serious problem if the corporation is in danger of being bought or controlled by another firm. For instance, by purchasing some shares, another firm (such as a potential acquirer) could, through cumulative voting, elect enough board members to directly influence or even incapacitate the board. Nevertheless, the practice of cumulative voting has been recommended as a way to achieve minority representation on the boards of directors of major corporations.

Organization of the Board

The size of the board is determined by the corporation's charter and its bylaws in compliance with state laws. Although some states require a minimum number of board members, most corporations have quite a bit of discretion in determining board size. Surveys of U.S. business corporations reveal that the average *privately* held company has eight board members who meet four times a year as compared to the average *publicly* held company with thirteen directors who meet seven times a year. In addition, there appears to be a direct relationship between company size as measured by sales volume and the number of people on the board.[25]

Chairman. A fairly common practice in U.S. corporations is to have the chairman of the board also serve as the chief executive officer (CEO). The CEO concentrates on strategy, planning, external relations, and responsibility to the board. The chairman's responsibility is to ensure that the board and its committees perform their functions as stated in their charter. Further, the chairman schedules board meetings and presides over the annual stockholders' meeting. In most U.S. corporations the chairman comes from inside the company.[26]

Committees. The most effective boards of large corporations accomplish much of their work through committees.[27] Although the committees do not have legal duties, unless detailed in the bylaws, most committees are granted full power to act with the authority of the board between board meetings. Typical standing committees are the executive committee, audit committee, compensation committee, finance committee, and stock option committee. The executive committee is formed from local directors who can meet between board meetings to attend to matters that must be settled quickly. This committee acts as an extension of the board and, consequently, may have almost unrestricted authority in certain areas.[28] Other less common committees are the nominating, strategy, corporate responsibility, investments (pension funds), and conflict-of-interest committees.[29]

Trends for the Future

A study by Northwestern University and McKinsey & Company, Inc. sees several following trends for future responsibilities and organizations of boards.[30] Although the study concludes that it is not likely there will be significant changes in the typical board structure, it does predict a reduction in board size and a greater use of committees. The board of the future will tend to direct its own affairs with less reliance on the CEO. It will have fewer inside members and will be under less CEO influence in the selection of its members. There will be greater emphasis on systematically monitoring and appraising top management's performance, with more involvement by the board in the management succession process. Boards will also have more influence in determining executive compensation, and there will probably be more open communication between the board and management as the boards become more active. Boards will most likely form audit committees for the purpose of ensuring a formalized evaluation of overall corporate performance. Their membership will become more representative of minorities and women. In addition, there will be a continuing pressure on board members in terms of their liabilities, plus greater expectations by the public for higher standards of public responsibility.

3.2 TOP MANAGEMENT

The top management function is usually conducted by the CEO of the corporation in coordination with the COO or president, executive vice-president, and vice-presidents of divisions and functional areas. As we mentioned earlier in this chapter, some corporations combine the office of CEO with that of chairman of the board of directors. Although this plan has the advantage of freeing the president or COO of the firm from many strategic responsibilities so that he or she may focus primarily on operational matters, it has been criticized because it gives the combined CEO/chairman too much power and serves to undercut the independence of the board.[31]

Responsibilities of Top Management

Top management, and especially the CEO, is responsible to the board of directors for the overall management of the corporation. It is tasked with getting things accomplished through and with others in order to meet corporate objectives. Top management's job is thus multidimensional and oriented toward the welfare of the total organization. Specific top management tasks vary from firm to firm and are developed from an analysis of the mission, objectives, strategies, and key activities of the corporation. But all top managers are people who see the business as a whole, who can balance the present needs of the business against the needs of the future, and who can make final and effective decisions.[32]

Fulfill Key Roles. From five weeks of in-depth observation of five chief executives, Henry Mintzberg concluded that the job of a top manager contains ten interrelated *roles*. The importance of each role and the amount of time demanded by each probably varies from one job to another. These roles are as follows:

Figurehead	Acts as legal and symbolic head; performs obligatory social, ceremonial, or legal duties (hosts retirement dinners, luncheons for employees, and plant dedications; attends civic affairs; signs contracts on behalf of firm).
Leader	Motivates, develops, and guides subordinates; oversees staffing, training, and associated activites (introduces management by objectives (MBO), develops a challenging work climate, provides a sense of direction, acts as a role model).
Liason	Maintains a network of contacts and information sources outside top management in order to obtain information and assistance (meets with key people from the task environment, meets formally and informally with corporate division managers and with CEOs of other firms).
Monitor	Seeks and obtains information in order to understand the corporation and its environments; acts as nerve center for the corporation (reviews status reports from vice-presidents, reviews key indicators of corporate performance, scans *Wall Street Journal* and key trade journals, joins select clubs and societies).

Disseminator	Transmits information to the rest of the top management team and other key people in the corporation (chairs staff meetings, transmits policy letters, communicates five-year plans).
Spokesman	Transmits information to key groups and people in the task environment (prepares annual report to stockholders, talks to the Chamber of Commerce, states corporate policy to the media, participates in advertising campaigns, speaks before Congressional committees).
Entrepreneur	Searches the corporation and its environment for projects to improve products, processes, procedures, and structures; then supervises the design and implementation of these projects (introduces cost reduction programs, makes plant trips to divisions, changes forecasting system, brings in subcontract work to level the work load, reorganizes the corporation).
Disturbance Handler	Takes corrective action in times of disturbance or crisis (personally talks with key creditors, interest groups, Congressional committees, union leaders; establishes investigative committees; revises objectives, strategies, and policies).
Resource Allocator	Allocates corporate resources by making and/or approving decisions (reviews budgets, revises program scheduling, initiates strategic planning, plans personnel load, sets objectives).
Negotiator	Represents the corporation in negotiating important agreements; may speak directly with key representatives of groups in the task environment or work through a negotiator; negotiates disagreements within the corporation by working with conflicting division heads (works with labor negotiator; resolves jurisdictional disputes between divisions; negotiates with key creditors, suppliers, and customers).[33]

Provide Corporate Leadership. People who work in corporations look to top management for leadership. Their doing so, says Drucker, reflects a need for standard setting and example setting.[34] According to Mintzberg, this is a key role of any manager.

Corporate leadership is important because it sets the tone for the entire corporation. Since most middle managers look to their boss for guidance and direction, they will tend to emulate the characteristics and style of successful top managers. People in an organization want to have a vision of what they are working toward—a sense of mission. Only top management is in the position to specify and communicate this sense of mission to the general work force. Top management's enthusiasm (or lack of it) about the corporation tends to be contagious. For instance, a positive attitude characterizing many well-known industrial leaders—such as Alfred Sloan at General Motors, Ed Watson at IBM, Dr. Land at Polariod, and Lee Iacocca at Chrysler—have energized their respective corporations.

Chief executive officers with a clear sense of mission are often perceived as dynamic and charismatic leaders. They are able to command respect and to influence strategy formulation and implementation because they tend to have three key characteristics:[35]

1. The CEO *presents a role* for others to identify with and to follow. The leader sets an example in terms of behavior and dress. The CEO's attitudes and values concerning the corporation's purpose and activities are clear-cut and constantly communicated in words and deeds.

2. The CEO *articulates a transcendent goal* for the corporation. The CEO's vision of the corporation goes beyond the petty complaints and grievances of the average work day. This vision puts activities and conflicts in a new perspective, giving renewed meaning to everyone's work activities and enabling them to see beyond the details of their own jobs to the functioning of the total corporation.

3. The CEO communicates *high performance standards* but also shows *confidence* in the followers' abilities to meet these standards. No leader ever improved performance by setting easily attainable goals that provide no challenge. The CEO must be willing to follow through by coaching people.

Manage Strategic Planning. Top management must initiate and manage the strategic planning process. It must take a very long-range view in order to specify the corporate mission, delineate corporate objectives, and formulate appropriate strategies and policies. As depicted in Fig. 3.2, the ideal time horizon varies according to one's level in the corporate hierarchy. The president of a corporation, for example, should allocate the largest proportion of planning time to looking two to four *years* ahead. A department manager, however, should put the heaviest proportion of planning time on looking only three to six *months* ahead.

To accomplish its tasks, top management must use information provided by three key corporate groups: a long-range planning staff, division or SBU managers, and managers of functional departments.

A *long-range planning staff* typically consists of six people, headed by a senior vice-president or director of corporate planning.[36] It continu-

	Today	1 Week Ahead	1 Month Ahead	3-6 Months Ahead	1 Year Ahead	2 Years Ahead	3-4 Years Ahead	5-10 Years Ahead
President	1%	2%	5%	10%	15%	27%	30%	10%
Executive Vice-President	2%	4%	10%	29%	20%	18%	13%	4%
Vice-President of Functional Area	4%	8%	15%	35%	20%	10%	5%	3%
General Manager of a Major Division	2%	5%	15%	30%	20%	12%	12%	4%
Department Manager	10%	10%	24%	39%	10%	5%	1%	1%
Section Supervisor	15%	20%	25%	37%	3%			
Group Supervisor	38%	40%	15%	5%	2%			

SOURCE: Reprinted with permission of Macmillan Publishing Co., Inc. from *Top Management Planning* (p. 26) by G. A. Steiner. Copyright © by the Trustees of Columbia University of the City of New York.

Figure 3.2   *"Ideal" allocations of time for planning in the "average" company.*

ously monitors both internal and external environments in order to generate data for strategic decisions by top management. It also suggests to top management possible changes in the corporate mission, objectives, strategies, and policies.

Divisional or *SBU managers* typically perform the strategic planning function for the business segments in the division or SBU. They therefore respond both to requests from top management for suggested divisional plans and to finalized corporate plans the divisions must implement. In addition, divisional managers request input from managers of functional units for their use in developing divisional objectives, strategies, and policies.

Managers of functional departments (marketing, engineering, R&D managers, etc.) report directly either to divisional managers in a multidivision corporation or to top management if the corporation has no divisions. Although they may develop specific functional strategies, they generally do so within the framework of divisional or corporate strategies. They also respond to initiatives from above that ask them for input or require them to develop strategies to implement divisional plans.

Characteristics of Top Management Tasks

Top management tasks have two characteristics that differentiate them from other managerial tasks.[37] First, *very few of them are continuous*. Rarely does a manager work on these tasks all day. The responsibilities, however, are always present, even though the tasks themselves are sporadic. And when the tasks do arise, they are of crucial significance, such as the selection of a person to head a new division.

Mintzberg reports that the activities of most executives are characterized by brevity, variety, and fragmentation: "Half of the observed activities were completed in less than nine minutes and only one-tenth took more than an hour. In effect, the managers were seldom able or willing to spend much time on any one issue in any one session."[38]

It is likely that serious objective-setting and strategy formulation will not occur in corporations if most top managers are as activity-oriented as those in the Mintzberg study. John De Lorean suggests as much in his comments about "The Fourteenth Floor" (the executive offices) of General Motors.

> I was trying to bring a set of new eyes to the job of group executive, as one only can do in the first few months in a new position. But I had no time to perform the real function of my position. Instead, I was being tied down and totally consumed by this constant parade of paperwork and meetings.[39]

The second characteristic of top management tasks is that *they require a wide range of capabilities and temperaments*. Some tasks require the capacity to analyze and carefully weigh alternative courses of action. Some require an awareness of and an interest in people; whereas others call for the ability to pursue abstract ideas, concepts, and calculations: "The top-management tasks require at least four different kinds of human being: the 'thought man,' the 'action man,' the 'people man,' and the 'front man.' Yet those four temperaments are almost never found in one person."[40]

One result of these two task characteristics is that top managers are often drawn back into the functional work of the corporation. Since the activities of top management are not continuous, people in top management often have unplanned free time. They tend therefore to get caught up in the day-to-day work in manufacturing, marketing, accounting, engineering, or in other operations of the corporation. They may find themselves constantly solving crises that could probably have been better handled by lower-level managers. These managers are also usually fond of protesting "How can I be expected to drain the swamp when I'm up to my eyeballs in alligators!?"

A second result of the task characteristics is that top managers tend to perceive only those aspects and responsibilities of the top management function that are compatible with their abilities, experience, and temperaments. And, if the board of directors fails to state explicitly what it considers to be the key responsibilities and activities of top management, the top managers are free to define the job themselves. As a result, important tasks may be overlooked until a crisis occurs.

Top Management Team

Many executives believe that top management work is a job for a team rather than for one person. The large amount and variety of the work may be too great for one person to handle capably. Furthermore, when one person is in charge, he or she becomes extremely involved in the organization and tends to take personally any criticism of corporate activities. Consequently, that person is less willing to change personal management practices as situations change. According to Drucker, "... one-man top management is a major reason why businesses fail to grow."[41]

Analysts argue, therefore, that a large complex corporation needs a clearly structured top management team. This team may be organized as an office of the president in which a number of people serve as equals, each with an assigned area of primary responsibility. Corporations such as DuPont, Standard Oil of New Jersey, Royal Dutch Shell, and Unilever have taken this approach.[42] Or the team may include one person who carries the title of CEO and several colleagues, each of whom has clearly assigned authority and responsibility for a segment of the top management task. Another common structure is a three- or four-person team, each person having clearly assigned top management responsibilities even though one person is officially in charge. General Motors uses this structure. GM's team includes a chairman, a vice-chairman, a chairman of the executive committee, and a president. General Electric has taken a similar approach, although it refers to its four-man top management group as the Corporate Executive Office.

An advantage of the team approach to top management is the sharing of roles, responsibilities, and tasks, a sharing that depends on the strengths and weaknesses of the people involved. It makes more sense for large corporations to put together a top management team to achieve synergy, rather than try to find the perfect person to be CEO. Certainly succession problems are minimized by the team approach; decisions can be made even though the CEO has resigned, is incapacitated or otherwise absent.

3.3 STRATEGIC MANAGEMENT STYLES

Just as boards of directors vary widely on a continuum of involvement in the strategic management process, so do top management teams. For example, a top management team with low involvement in strategic management will tend to be functionally oriented and will focus its energies on day-to-day operational problems; this type of team is likely either to be disorganized or to have a dominant CEO who continues to identify with his or her old division. In contrast, a top management team with high involvement will be active in long-range planning. It will try to get division managers involved in planning so that it will have more time to scan the environment for challenges and opportunities.

Both the board of directors and top management can be placed on a matrix to reflect four basic styles of corporate strategic management. These styles are depicted in Fig. 3.3.

Chaos Management

When both the board of directors and top management have little involvement in the strategic management process, their style is referred to as chaos management. The board waits for top management to bring it proposals. Top management is operationally oriented and continues to carry out strategies, policies, and programs specified by the founding entrepreneur who died years ago. The basic strategic philosophy seems to be, "If it was good enough for old J. B., it's good enough for us." There is no strategic management being done here.

Entrepreneurship Management

A corporation with an uninvolved board of directors but with a highly involved top management has entrepreneurship management. The board is willing to be used as a rubber stamp for top management. The CEO, operating alone or with a team, dominates the corporation and its strategic decisions. An example is the Calhoun First National Bank of Cal-

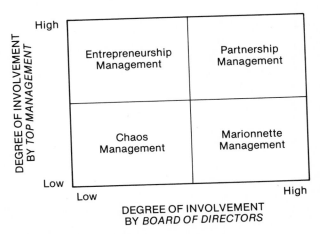

Figure 3.3 *Strategic management styles.*

houn, Georgia, whose CEO is Bert Lance. Returning to the bank after serving in the cabinet of President Jimmy Carter, Lance tried to regain control of the corporation as its president. He wanted, among other things, the bank to initiate new loan policies and to hire his 26-year-old son as an officer. After the board turned him down, Lance began a proxy fight for control of the bank. The resulting new board not only approved all the changes desired by Lance, it fired both the previous chairman of the board and the president without severance pay. Lance, of course, returned to his job as president of the bank and gained total control of all strategic management.[43]

Marionnette Management

Probably the rarest form of strategic management styles, marionnette management occurs when the board of directors is deeply involved in strategic decision making, whereas top management is primarily concerned with operations. Such a style evolves when a board is composed of key stockholders who refuse to delegate strategic decision making to the president. The president is forced into a COO role and can do only what the board allows him to do. This style also occurs when a board fires a CEO but is slow to find a replacement. The COO or executive vice-president stays on as "acting" president or CEO until the selection process is complete. In the meantime, strategic management is firmly in the hands of the board of directors. In one specific bank (which will remain unnamed), the board of directors is so involved in managing that it requires the president to ask its permission before offices are painted. The board actually votes on the color!

Partnership Management

Probably the most effective style of strategic management, partnership management is epitomized by a highly involved board and top management. The board and the top management team work closely to establish mission, objectives, strategies, and policies. Board members are active in committee work and utilize strategic audits to provide feedback to top management on its actions in implementing agreed-upon strategies and policies. This appears to be the style emerging in a number of successful corporations such as Texas Instruments and General Electric Company.[44]

3.4 SUMMARY AND CONCLUSION

The strategy makers of a modern corporation are the board of directors and top management. Both must be actively involved in the strategic management process if the corporation is to have long-term success in accomplishing its mission.

An effective board is the keystone of the modern corporation. Without it, management would tend to focus on short-run problems and solutions or go off on tangents at odds with the basic mission. The personal needs and goals of executives would tend to overrule the interests of the corporation. Even the strongest critics of boards of directors are more interested in improving and upgrading boards than in eliminating them.[45] An active board is critical in determining an organization's mission, objectives, strategy, and policies.

Top management, in contrast, is responsible for the overall functioning of the corporation. People in top management must view the corporation as a whole rather than as a series of functional departments or decentralized divisions. They must constantly visualize and plan for the future, setting objectives, strategies, and policies that will allow the corporation to successfully meet that future. They must set standards and provide a vision not only of what the corporation is but also of what it is trying to become. They must develop working relationships with the board of directors, key staff personnel, and managers from divisions and functional areas.

The interaction between the board of directors and the top management of a corporation usually results in an overall strategic management style. The long-run success of a corporation is best ensured through a partnership style in which both the board and top management are genuinely involved in strategic issues.

DISCUSSION QUESTIONS

1. What are the responsibilities of a corporation's board of directors?
2. What aspects of a corporation's environment should be represented on a board of directors?
3. Should cumulative voting for the election of board members be *required* by law in all political jurisdictions?
4. Do you agree that a chief executive officer (CEO) should fulfill Mintzberg's ten roles in order to be effective?
5. Is partnership management always the best style of strategic management?

NOTES

1. W. L. Shanklin and J. K. Ryans, Jr., "Should the Board Consider This Agenda Item?" *MSU Business Topics* (Winter 1981), p. 35.
2. W. R. Boulton, "The Evolving Board: A Look at the Board's Changing Roles and Information Needs," *Academy of Management Review* (October 1978), p. 828.
3. J. Bacon and J. K. Brown, *Corporate Directorship Practices: Role, Selection and Legal Status of the Board* (New York: The Conference Board, Report no. 646, 1975), p. 7.

4. Bacon and Brown, p. 75.

5. L. B. Korn and R. M. Ferry, *Board of Directors Ninth Annual Study* (New York: Korn/Ferry International, February 1982), p. 8.

6. Bacon and Brown, p. 15.

7. K. R. Andrews, "Corporate Strategy as a Vital Function of the Board," *Harvard Business Review* (November–December 1981), p. 175.

8. K. R. Andrews, "Directors' Responsibility for Corporate Strategy," *Harvard Business Review* (November–December 1980), p. 30.

9. E. Mruk and J. Giardina, *Organization and Compensation of Boards of Directors* (New York: Financial Executives Institute, Arthur Young & Co., 1981), pp. 11 and 39.

10. L. Barker, "Pricing the Director Market," *Directors and Boards: The Journal of Corporate Actions* (Winter 1982), pp. 36–37.

11. R. P. Neuschel, Conference Summary (p. 60), "The Changing Role of the Corporate Board," proceedings of a conference held in Chicago on April 13, 1977 and sponsored jointly by Northwestern University's Graduate School of Management and McKinsey & Company, Inc. Privately published by the sponsors.

12. J. Bacon, *Corporate Directorship Practices: Membership and Committees of the Board* (New York: The Conference Board, Report no. 588, 1973), pp. 28–29.

13. K. Sawyer, "Chrysler-UAW Deal: More Than Just a Peek at the Books," *Washington Post* (January 19, 1980), p. A5.

14. Bacon and Brown, p. 50.

15. E. F. Donaldson and J. K. Pfahl, *Corporate Finance*, 3rd ed. (New York: Ronald Press, 1969), p. 742.

    F. D. Schoorman, M. H. Bazerman, and R. S. Atkin, "Interlocking Directorates: A Strategy For Reducing Environmental Uncertainty," *Academy of Management Review* (April 1981), p. 244.

16. R. S. Burt, "Cooptive Corporate Actor Networks: A Reconsideration of Interlocking Directorates Involving American Manufacturing," *Administrative Science Quarterly* (December 1980), p. 566.

17. Burt, p. 559.

18. For a more in-depth discussion of this topic, refer to J. M. Pennings, *Interlocking Directorates* (San Francisco: Jossey-Bass, 1980).

19. J. W. Goodrich, Structural and Behavioral Means of Improving Board Effectiveness (p. 6), "The Changing Role of the Corporate Board," proceedings of a conference held in Chicago on April 13, 1977 and sponsored jointly by Northwestern University's Graduate School of Management and McKinsey & Company, Inc. Privately published by the sponsors.

20. R. F. Lewis, "Choosing and Using Outside Directors," *Harvard Business Review* (July–August 1974), p. 71.

21. Korn and Ferry, p. 5.

22. Bacon, p. 6.

23. Bacon, pp. 7–8.

24. Bacon, p. 6.

25. Korn and Ferry, p. 3; and Mruk and Giardina, p. 39.

26. L. Barker, p. 40.

27. W. Wommack, "The Board's Most Important Function," *Harvard Business Review* (September–October 1979), p. 48.

28. Bacon and Brown, pp. 106–108.

29. For further information on board committees, refer to Bacon and Brown, pp. 99–140. For detailed information on the audit committee, see L. Braiotta, *The Audit Director's Guide* (New York: John Wiley & Sons, 1981).

30. Neuschel, pp. 60–61.

31. Bacon and Brown, p. 25; and Andrews, 1980, p. 36.

32. P. F. Drucker, *Management: Tasks, Responsibilities, Practices* (New York: Harper & Row, 1974), p. 613.

33. Adapted from H. Mintzberg, *The Nature of Managerial Work* (New York: Harper & Row, 1973), pp. 54–94.

34. Drucker, pp. 611–612.

35. Adapted from R. J. House, "A 1976 Theory of Charismatic Leadership," *Leadership: The Cutting Edge*, eds. J. G. Hunt and L. L. Larson (Carbondale, Ill.: SIU Press, 1977), pp. 189–207.

36. S. Matlins and G. Knisely, "Update: Profile of the Corporate Planners," *Journal of Business Strategy* (Spring 1981), pp. 75 and 77.

37. Drucker, pp. 615–617.

38. Mintzberg, p. 33.

39. J. P. Wright, *On A Clear Day You Can See General Motors* (Grosse Pointe, Mich.: Wright Enterprises, 1979), p. 28.

40. Drucker, p. 616.

41. Drucker, p. 618.

42. Drucker, p. 619.

43. D. Russakoff, "Bert Lance on the Rebound," *Washington Post* (May 17, 1981), pp. A6–A7.

44. K. Andrews, "Corporate Strategy as a Vital Function of the Board," *Harvard Business Review* (November–December 1981), p. 175.

45. R. P. Neuschel, Introductory Remarks (p. 11), "The Changing Role of the Corporate Board," proceedings of a conference held in Chicago on April 13, 1977 and sponsored jointly by Northwestern University's Graduate School of Management and McKinsey & Company, Inc. Privately published by the sponsors.

STRATEGIC MANAGEMENT MODEL

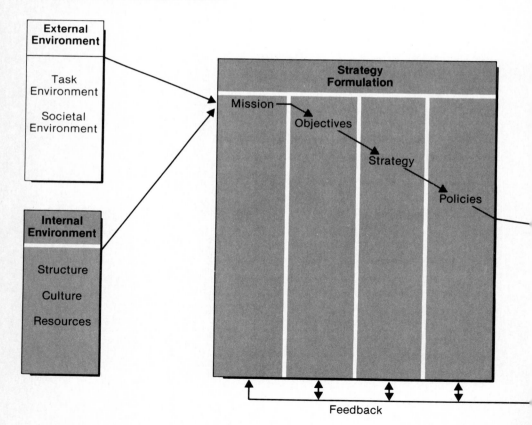

THE EXTERNAL ENVIRONMENT

CHAPTER 4

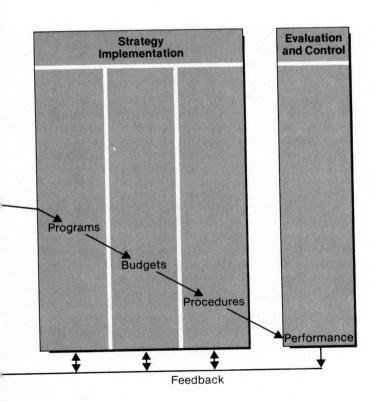

Strategy
Implementation

Evaluation
and Control

Programs

Budgets

Procedures

Performance

Feedback

B usiness corporations do not exist in a vacuum. They arise out of society's need for a particular product or service and can continue to exist in freedom only so long as they acknowledge their role in the larger society. As a result, corporations must constantly be aware of the key variables in their environment. These variables may be within a firm's task environment or in its larger societal environment (see Fig. 4.1). The *task environment* includes those elements or groups that directly affect the corporation and, in turn, are affected by it. These are governments, local communities, suppliers, competitors, customers, creditors, employees/labor unions, and trade associations. The *societal environment* includes the more general forces that do not directly touch on the activities of the organization but that can, and often do, influence its decisions. These, also shown in Fig. 4.1, are as follows:

☐ *Economic forces* that regulate exchange of materials, money, energy, and information.

☐ *Socio-cultural forces* that regulate values, mores, and customs.

☐ *Technological forces* that generate problem solving inventions.

☐ *Political-legal forces* that allocate power and provide constraining and protecting laws and regulations.

All of these variables and forces constantly interact with each other. In the short run, societal forces affect the decisions and actions of a corporation through the groups in its task environment. In the long run, however, the corporation also affects these groups through its activities. For example, the possible collapse of Chrysler Corporation in 1980 had wide-ranging and serious effects upon almost every group and force in its task and societal environment.

4.1 BUSINESS AND SOCIETY:
A DELICATE RELATIONSHIP

For centuries, business corporations have lived an uneasy truce with society. Exchange and commercial activities, along with laws governing them, are as old as recorded history. The Code of Hammurabi, established about 2000 B.C., provided guidelines for merchants and peddlers.[1] The Old Testament is filled with examples of commercial activity and the laws and regulations governing them. Greek philosophers, in general, regarded commercial activities as necessary but distasteful. The Romans, like the Greeks, were necessarily tolerant of commercial activity, but gave those who engaged in it a low status.[2] During the early years of the Middle Ages, the Christian Church held business and commercial activity in disdain and governed it through strict rules and limitations. Usury, the lending of money at interest, was for instance, decreed a mortal sin for Christians, who were forbidden the practice, although Jews were per-

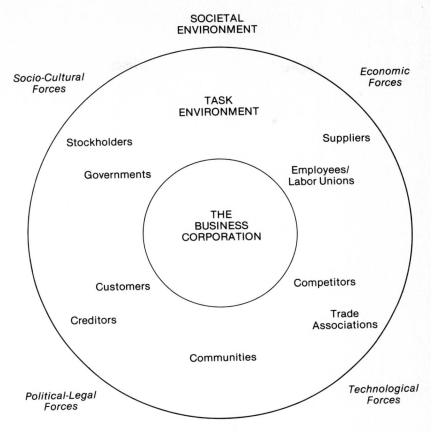

Figure 4.1 *Key environmental variables.*

mitted to engage in it. Trade itself was of dubious purity, and the gathering of wealth was considered an action directly opposed to the charitable teachings of Jesus Christ. This view of trade and commerce and the associated accumulation of capital as necessary evils was commonly accepted in the Western World until the Protestant Reformation.

Development of the Capitalistic Ethic

With the end of the Middle Ages, values began to change in the West, and business activities were viewed more positively. Max Weber, noted economist and sociologist, postulated that changes in the religious ethic resulting from the Reformation and the Protestant movement provided an economic climate highly favorable for the development of capitalism.[3] A new spirit of individualism developed out of the Renaissance and was encouraged by humanism and Protestantism. Society placed a high value on frugality, thrift, and hard work—key elements of what is commonly referred to as the *Protestant ethic.*

Free trade was not, however, commonly accepted until much later. After the Reformation, kings and queens replaced the Church as earthly rulers. They established their right to regulate business activity through the concept of mercantilism. According to this concept, the individual was subordinate to the state, and all economic and business activity was dedicated to support the power of the state. Under mercantilism, Europeans set up organizations, such as the East India Company, to trade with the natives of distant lands and to return with goods valuable to crown and country.

In 1776, however, economist Adam Smith advanced a theory justifying and underlying capitalism in his book *An Inquiry Into the Nature and Causes of the Wealth of Nations.* Smith argued that economic freedom would enable individuals through self-interest to fulfill themselves and thereby benefit the total society. He used the term *laissez faire* to suggest that government should leave business alone. The "invisible hand" of the marketplace would, through pure competition, ensure maximum benefit to society.

The doctrine of *laissez faire*, as postulated by Smith and refined by others, called for society to give business corporations increasing autonomy so that they could accomplish their work—the production and sale of goods and services. In the rapidly changing world of the eighteenth and nineteenth centuries such work was considered worthwhile and valuable to society. For example, James Watt's development of a usable steam engine permitted muscle power to be replaced by an external power source and resulted in enormous increases in the production and distribution of scarce goods. Because of these benefits, governments relaxed many of their restrictions on commerce and trade, and allowed capital to accumulate and business to flourish.

Society Supports Free Enterprise

With changes in socio-cultural values fed by the benefits of new technology and *laissez faire* economics, governments began to support independent businesses. During much of the early part of the nineteenth century in the United States, government favored the development of commerce and industry. The Supreme Court, for example, ruled that the private corporation was a legal entity, and Congress passed tariff laws protecting business interests. In addition, the government provided vast sums of money and land for the rapidly expanding railroads.[4] As pointed out by McGuire,

> . . .the Federal government attempted to encourage business activities with a minimum of regulation and intervention. . . . Government's task in these years, it was thought by many politicians and businessmen, was to aid business enterprise in accord with the best principles of mercantilism and still

leave business free to grow and develop without restraint, as set forth in the doctrine of *laissez faire*. The tradition thus grew that businessmen in the United States could do what so few people were able to do—have their cake and eat it too.[5]

Beginnings of Regulation

In the late 1800s and early 1900s, the public began to find some business practices antisocial, and increasingly this dissatisfaction was expressed. Karl Marx, who wrote *The Communist Manifesto* with Frederick Engels in 1848 and *Das Kapital* in 1867, put into words much of this dissatisfaction. He, as well as many others, rejected the capitalistic ethic because of its many unsavory side effects, such as child labor, unsafe working conditions, and subsistence wages. The development of monopolistic corporations and cartels caused various groups within the United States to demand some form of regulation. Although most U.S. citizens rejected the Marxist view, they challenged the *laissez faire* concept by suggesting that Adam Smith's economic system was based on a pure, competitive model that was ineffective in a system of entrenched monopolies and oligopolies. As a result, the federal government reclaimed some of the freedom and autonomy it had granted business by enacting such legislation as the Interstate Commerce Act (1887), the Sherman Antitrust Act (1890), the Pure Food and Drug Act (1906), the Clayton Act (1914), and the Federal Trade Commission Act (1914).

A Question of Autonomy

The Great Depression of the 1930s, Keynesian economics, and the increasing popularity of socialism as a political force resulted in business losing even more of its autonomy to government. Governments all over the world assumed responsibility for their economies. In 1946, the U.S. Congress passed the Fair Employment Act, which states that the federal government has prime responsibility for the maintenance of full employment and full utilization of economic resources.[6] Through the decades of the 50s, 60s, and 70s, *laissez faire*, if not dead, was certainly forgotten as people put their faith in a democratically elected central government rather than the self-interest of capitalists. Businesses were threatened by government with more regulations and, therefore, less autonomy unless they became more "socially responsible."

4.2 SOCIAL RESPONSIBILITY

The concept that business must be socially responsible sounds appealing until one asks, "Responsible to whom?" As was shown in Fig. 4.1, the task environment includes a large number of groups with interest in a corporation's activities. Should a corporation be responsible only to some of these groups, or does business have a responsibility to society at large?

The corporation must pay close attention to its task environment because its groups are very responsive to the general trends in the societal environment and will typically translate these trends into direct pressure to affect corporate activities. Even if top management assumes the traditional *laissez faire* stance that the major concern of its corporation is to make profits, it will find (often to its chagrin) that it must also be concerned with the effect of its profit making on key groups within its task environment. Each task group uses its own criteria to determine how well a corporation is performing, and each is constantly judging top management's actions by their effect on the group. Therefore top management must be aware not only of the key task groups in its corporation's task environment but also of the criteria each group uses to judge the corporation's performance. The following is a list of some of these task groups and their probable criteria.

Stockholders	Price appreciation of securities. Dividends (How much and how often?).
Unions	Comparable wages. Stability of employment. Opportunity for advancement.
Governments	Support of government programs. Adherence to laws and regulations.
Suppliers	Rapidity of payment. Consistency of purchases.
Creditors	Adherence to contract terms. Dependability.
Customers/Distributors	Value given for the price paid. Availability of product or service.
Trade associations	Participation in association programs (*time*). Participation in association programs (*money*).
Competitors	Rate of growth (encroachment on their markets). Product or service innovation (source of new ideas to use).
Communities	Contribution to community development through taxes, participation in charitable activities, etc. Employment of local people.

Priority of Concerns

In any one decision regarding corporate strategy, the interests of one task group can conflict with another. For example, a business firm's decision to build a plant in an inner-city location may have a positive effect on community relations but a negative effect on stockholder dividends. Which group's interests have priority? In a survey of *Harvard Business Review* readers, executives were asked to rank various groups in their businesses' task environment.[7] As shown in Table 4.1, executives felt the greatest responsibility for customers. Stockholders and employees ranked second and third. The interests of society at large and its elected governments received much less consideration.

Pressures on the Business Corporation

Given the wide range of interests and concerns present in any corporation's task environment, one or more groups, at any one time, will probably be dissatisfied with a corporation's activities. For example, consider General Motors' decision to build a new plant in a run-down area of Detroit (sometimes referred to as "Poletown"). In 1980, when corporate profits were turning to losses, General Motors advised the city of Detroit that in 1983 it would close its Cadillac and Fisher Body plants, both located within city boundaries. Realizing its responsibility to Detroit, GM suggested that if the city could find a rectangular area of 450 to 500 acres with access to highways and long-haul railroad lines, it would build a new plant within the city. The city government in cooperation with the

Table 4.1 EXECUTIVES' PERCEIVED RESPONSIBILITY TO VARIOUS GROUPS

GROUP	RANK
Customers	1.83
Stockholders	2.52
Employees	2.86
Local community where company operates	4.44
Society in general	4.97
Suppliers	5.10
Government	5.72

Note: The ranking is calculated on a scale of 1 (most responsibility) to 7 (least responsibility).

SOURCE: Steven N. Brenner and Carl A. Molander, "Is the Ethics of Business Changing?" *Harvard Business Review*, January–February 1977, p. 69. Copyright © 1977 by the President and Fellows of Harvard College. All rights reserved.

town of Hamtramck decided on the vacant Dodge "main plant" (abandoned previously by Chrysler Corporation), along with the adjacent area. As Detroit and Hamtramck began to appropriate the homes, factories, and churches in the area, protests developed. Lawsuits were filed. General Motors was in a situation of being damned if it left Detroit and damned if it stayed![8]

Other examples of task group protests reveal the dark side of corporate decision making. Top management has sometimes made decisions that have emphasized short-term profitability to the detriment of long-run relations with governments, local communities, suppliers, and even customers and employees. For example, here are some questionable practices that have been exposed in recent years:

☐ Possible negligent construction and management practices at nuclear power plants (for example, at Three Mile Island and Diablo Canyon).[9]

☐ Improper disposal of toxic wastes (for instance, at Love Canal).[10]

☐ Production and sale of unsafe products (for instance, Firestone "500" tires).[11]

☐ Insufficient safeguarding of employees from exposure to dangerous chemicals and materials in the workplace (for instance, the asbestos problem at Johns-Manville).[12]

☐ Bribery, fraud, and price-fixing scandals at 117 of the United States' largest corporations between 1970 and 1980.[13]

Ethics: A Question of Values

Such questionable practices by business corporations run counter to the values of society as a whole and are justly criticized and prosecuted. Why are actions taken that so obviously harm important groups in the corporation's task environment? Are business corporations and the people who run them amoral, or are they simply ignorant of the many consequences of their actions?

Cultural Differences. One reason for such behavior is that there is no world-wide standard of conduct for businesspeople. Cultural norms and values vary between countries and even between different geographic regions and ethnic groups within a country. One example is the use of payoffs and bribes to influence a potential customer to buy from a particular supplier. Although this practice is considered illegal in the United States, it is deeply entrenched in many countries. In Mexico, for instance, the payoff, referred to as *la mordida* (the bite), is considered a fringe benefit or *prorpina* (a tip).[14]

Differences in Personal Values. Another possible reason for a corporation's questionable practices lies in differences in values between top management and key groups in the task environment. Some businesspeople may believe profit maximization is the key goal of their firm, whereas concerned interest groups may have other goals, such as the hiring of minorities and women or the safety of their neighborhoods.

Economist Milton Friedman, in urging a return to a *laissez-faire* style world-wide economy, argues against the concept of social responsibility. If a businessperson acts "responsibly" by cutting the price of the firm's product to prevent inflation, or by making expenditures to reduce pollution, or by hiring the hard-core unemployed, that person, according to Friedman, is spending the stockholder's money for a general social interest. Even if the businessperson has stockholder permission or encouragement to do so, he or she is still acting from motives other than economic and may, in the long run, cause harm to the very society the firm is trying to help. By taking on the burden of these social costs, the business becomes less efficient; and either prices go up to pay for the increased costs, or investment in new activities and research is postponed. These results negatively affect—perhaps fatally—the long-term efficiency of a business. Friedman thus referred to the social responsibility of business as a "fundamentally subversive doctrine" and stated that "there is one and only one social responsibility of business—to use its resources and engage in activities designed to increase its profits so long as it stays within the rules of the game, which is to say, engages in open and free competition without deception or fraud."[15]

Friedman's stand on free enterprise has been both criticized and praised. Businesspeople tend to agree with Friedman because his views are compatible not only with their own self-interests but also with their hierarchy of values. Research by Guth and Tagiuri points out that high-level U.S. executives hold most highly a combination of economic, theoretical, and political values. Religious, aesthetic, and social values have less importance in their lives. The following comparison of the value systems of business executives and ministers shows large differences (the values are arranged in order from most important to least important).[16]

EXECUTIVES	MINISTERS
Economic	Religious
Theoretical	Social
Political	Aesthetic
Religious	Political
Aesthetic	Theoretical
Social	Economic

Imagine the controversy that would result if a group composed of ministers and executives had to decide the following strategy issues: Should business firms close on Sunday? Should the corporation hire handicapped workers and accept the increased training costs associated with their employment? In discussing these issues, the executive would probably be very concerned with the effects on the "bottom line" (profits), whereas the minister would probably be concerned with the effects on society and salvation (a very different bottom line).

This conclusion is supported by the results of a study conducted by the *Harvard Business Review* of 1200 of its U.S. readers. The readers were asked to express the degree of responsibility they felt in the nine areas depicted in Table 4.2. The results suggest that businesspeople wish to limit their responsibilities to those areas where they can clearly see benefits to the corporation in terms of reduced costs and governmental regulation.[17]

This very narrow view of businesses' responsibilities to society will typically cause conflicts between the business corporation and certain members of its task environment. Carroll, in his research on social responsibility, suggests that in addition to the obvious economic and legal responsibilities, businesses have ethical and discretionary ones.[18] The *economic* responsibilities of a business corporation are to produce goods

Table 4.2   BUSINESSPEOPLE'S PERCEIVED DEGREE OF RESPONSIBILITY IN NINE KEY AREAS

AREA	DEGREE OF RESPONSIBILITY
Being an efficient user of energy and natural resources.	4.00
Assessing the potential environmental effects flowing from the company's technological advances.	3.96
Maximizing long-run profits.	3.78
Using every means possible to maximize job content and satisfaction for the hourly worker.	3.35
Having your company's subsidiary in another country use the same occupational safety standards as your company does in the United States.	3.05
Acquiescing to State Department requests that the company not establish operations in a certain country.	3.01
Making implementation of corporate Affirmative Action plans a significant determinant of line officer promotion and salary improvement.	2.91
Instituting a program for hiring the hard-core unemployed.	2.23
Contributing to the local United Fund.	2.17

Note: The ranking is calculated on a scale of 1 (absolutely voluntary) to 5 (absolutely obligatory).
SOURCE: Steven N. Brenner and Carl A. Molander, "Is the Ethics of Business Changing?" *Harvard Business Review,* January–February 1977, p. 70. Copyright © 1977 by the President and Fellows of Harvard College. All rights reserved.

and services of value to society. Its *legal* responsibilities are defined by governments in the laws that corporations are expected to obey. Its *ethical* responsibilities are to follow the generally held beliefs about how one should act in a society. *Discretionary* responsibilities, in contrast, are the purely voluntary obligations a corporation assumes. Examples are philanthropic contributions, training the hard-core unemployed, and providing day-care centers. Carroll suggests that to the extent that business corporations fail to acknowledge discretionary or ethical responsibilities, society, through government, will act, making them legal responsibilities. This may be done by governments, moreover, without regard to a corporation's economic responsibilities. As a result, the corporation may have greater difficulty in earning a profit than it would have had in assuming voluntarily some ethical and discretionary responsibilities. For example, it has been suggested by some people in the American automobile industry that the large number of safety and pollution regulations passed in the 1960s and 1970s are partially responsible for the poor health of the industry in the 1980s.

The issue seems clear. If corporations are unable or unwilling to police themselves by considering their responsibilities to all members of their task environment, then society—usually in the form of government—will police their doing so, and once again governments will reduce corporate autonomy via increased rules and regulations.

Although at present U.S. voters appear less willing than in the past to absorb the costs of a vast government police effort directed at business, the situation may change. Under President Reagan and his supply-side economics, deregulation has increased and Congress has passed reform laws suggesting a more *laissez-faire* based attitude. But history suggests that the current trend toward deregulation by the U.S. government may only be a short-run phenomenon, its life-span depending on the willingness of business corporations to perform their functions in an ethically and socially responsible manner. If they do not do so, it seems likely that the pendulum of public opinion will swing back toward increasing rather than decreasing regulation.

4.3 ENVIRONMENTAL SCANNING

Because they are a part of a larger society that constantly affects them in many ways, corporations must be aware of changes and potential changes within the key variables in their task and societal environments. In 1973, for example, the Arab oil embargo caught many firms completely by surprise, with the result that goods dependent on oil as a raw material or energy source could not be produced. The resulting shortages and price adjustments caused chaos in the American economy. Since then, the increasing scarcity and escalating cost of fossil-fuel energy have created long-term changes, such as a push for nuclear energy and a decline in demand for large "gas guzzling" automobiles.

Before strategy makers can begin formulating strategy, they must scan the external environment to identify possible opportunities and threats. Environmental scanning is the monitoring, evaluating, and disseminating of information from the external environment to key people within the corporation.[19] It is a tool used by a corporation to avoid strategic surprise and to ensure its long-run health.[20] Both the societal and task environments must be monitored to detect strategic factors that are likely to have a strong impact on corporate success or failure.

Monitoring Strategic Factors

Usually environmental scanning begins with the identification of strategic factors in the societal and task environments. *Strategic factors* are those variables that top management believes have great potential for affecting its corporation's activities. They are the patterns of events that will influence the corporation in the future. These factors are typically ones that have strongly affected a corporation in the past or are presently doing so. But, unfortunately, few firms attempt to anticipate them.[21] Furthermore, the values of the top managers are likely to bias both their perceptions of what is or is not important to monitor in the external environment and their interpretations of what they perceive.

Societal Environment. The number of possible strategic factors in the societal environment are enormous. Some of the factors likely to be of strategic importance to most corporations are listed in Table 4.3. For example, the recent decrease in the number of teenagers in the United States population when coupled with the increasing cost of energy plus a recessionary economic climate has put pressure on corporations in the amusement-park industry to review their strategies for earning profits. Of course, each corporation will develop its own list of key factors to monitor, a task typically performed by its long-range planning staff.

A 1980 survey of the chief corporate planners in major U.S. firms identified the six external environment issues most important to them. These were issues that a majority of planners felt would strongly affect their companies through 1985. Interestingly, most of them are societal issues.

- ☐ Government intervention/regulation
- ☐ Inflation
- ☐ Energy
- ☐ Economic climate in the United States
- ☐ Foreign competition
- ☐ International political/economic instability

Table 4.3   SOME IMPORTANT FACTORS IN THE SOCIETAL ENVIRONMENT

SOCIO-CULTURAL	ECONOMIC	TECHNOLOGICAL	POLITICAL-LEGAL
Life-style changes.	GNP Trends.	Total federal spending for R&D.	Antitrust regulations.
Career expectations.	Interest rates.	Total industry spending for R&D.	Environmental protection laws.
Consumer activism.	Money supply.	Focus of technological efforts.	Tax laws.
Rate of family formation.	Inflation rates.		Special incentives.
Growth rate of population.	Unemployment levels.	Patent protection.	Foreign trade regulations.
Age distribution of population.	Wage/Price controls.	New products.	Attitudes towards foreign companies.
Regional shifts in population.	Devaluation/ revaluation.	New developments in technology transfer from lab to marketplace.	Laws on hiring and promotion.
Life expectancies.	Energy availability and cost.	Productivity improvements through automation.	Stability of government.
Birth rates.			

Other issues of some importance to the planners were increased domestic competition, low productivity, changing consumer preferences, rapid technological changes, cost and availability of raw materials, labor supply problems, and changing demographics.[22]

Task Environment. As was noted earlier, changes in the societal environment tend to be reflected in pressures on the corporation from task environment groups. As shown in Fig. 4.2, a corporation's scanning of the environment will include analyses of all the relevant elements in the task environment—interest groups, its industry, resources, the marketplace, competitors, suppliers, and governments. Most corporations tend to be most interested in analyses of customers, suppliers, competitors, economic conditions, and government.[23]

Porter, an authority on competitive strategy, contends that a corporation is most concerned with the intensity of competition within its industry. The level of this intensity is determined by five basic competitive forces, which are depicted in Fig. 4.3. "The collective strength of these forces," he contends, "determines the ultimate profit potential in the industry, where profit potential is measured in terms of long-run return on invested capital."[24]

A corporation must carefully scan the task environment to assess the importance to its success of each of the following five forces.[25]

1. *Threat of New Entrants*: New entrants to an industry typically bring to it new capacity, a desire to gain market share, and substantial resources and are, therefore, threats to an established corporation.

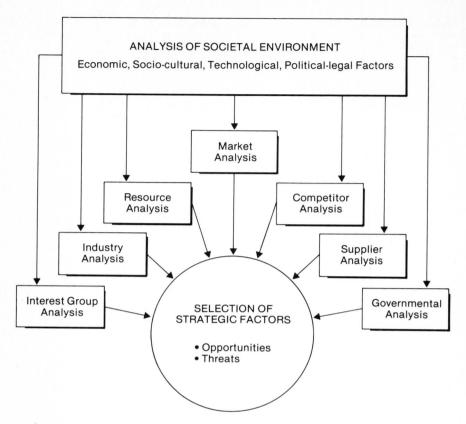

Figure 4.2   *Scanning the external environment.*

The threat of entry depends on the presence of entrance barriers and the reaction that can be expected from existing competitors.

2. *Rivalry Among Existing Firms*: In most industries, corporations are mutually dependent. A competitive move by one firm can be expected to have a noticeable effect on its competitors and thus may cause retaliation or efforts to counter the move.

3. *Threat of Substitute Products or Services*: In effect, all corporations in an industry are competing with industries that produce substitute products. According to Porter, "Substitutes limit the potential returns of an industry by placing a ceiling on the prices firms in the industry can profitable charge."[26] In the 1970s, for example, the high price of cane sugar caused soft drink manufacturers to turn to high fructose corn syrup as a sugar substitute. Sometimes a difficult task, the identification of possible substitute products or services means searching for products or services that can perform the same *function*, even though they may not appear to be easily substitutable.

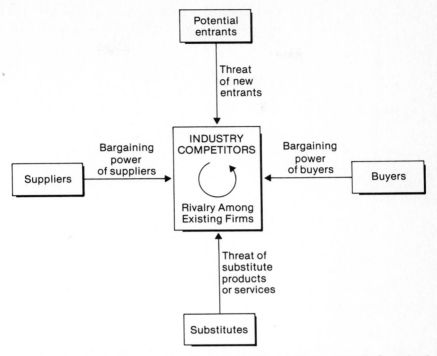

SOURCE: M. E. Porter, *Competitive Strategy* (New York: Free Press, 1980), p. 4. Copyright © 1980 by The Free Press, a division of Macmillan Publishing Co., Inc. Reprinted by permission.

Figure 4.3 *Forces driving industry competition.*

4. *Bargaining Power of Buyers*: Buyers affect an industry through their ability to force down prices, bargain for higher quality or more services, and play competitors against each other. A buyer or a group of buyers is powerful if some of the following hold true:

   □ It purchases a large proportion of the seller's product or service.

   □ It has the potential to integrate backward by producing the product itself.

   □ Alternative suppliers are plentiful.

   □ Changing suppliers costs very little.

5. *Bargaining Power of Suppliers*: Suppliers can affect an industry through their ability to raise prices or reduce the quality of purchased goods and services. A supplier group is powerful if some of the following apply:

   □ The supplier industry is dominated by a few companies, but sells to many.

   □ Substitutes are not readily available.

☐ Suppliers are able to integrate forward and compete directly with its present customers. An example is the construction of oil refineries by Saudi Arabia.

☐ A purchasing industry buys only a small portion of the supplier group's goods and services.

Sources of Information

Studies have shown that environmental scanning is, typically, done on an informal and individual basis. Information is obtained from a variety of sources such as customers, suppliers, bankers, consultants, publications, personal observations, subordinates, superiors, and peers.[27] For example, scientists and engineers working in a firm's R&D lab may learn about new products and competitors' ideas at professional meetings; or speaking with supplier representatives personnel in the purchasing department may uncover valuable bits of information about a competitor. Some of the main sources of information about an industry's environment are shown in Fig. 4.4. Because people throughout a corporation may obtain an extraordinary amount of data in any given month, top management must develop a system to get these data from those who obtained it to the people who can integrate it with other information to form a comprehensive environmental assessment.

As one would suspect, research suggests that corporations develop and implement more appropriate scanning procedures for following, anticipating, and responding to changes in the activites of *competitors* than for other groups in the environment. This may be explained by the likelihood that information about competitors is more readily available than information about the other groups.[28] This is not to suggest, however, that other groups and forces are ignored. It merely means that, *at present*, business corporations are more adept at monitoring competitive activity than any other environmental activity.

There is danger in focusing one's scanning efforts too closely on one's own industry, though. According to research by Snyder, "History teaches that most new developments which threaten existing business practices and technologies do not come from traditional industries."[29] For instance, *technology transfer*, the process of taking new technology from the laboratory to the marketplace, has become an important issue in recent decades. Consider just one example. With the development of the integrated circuit, electronics firms, such as Texas Instruments, were able to introduce high-volume, low-cost electronic digital watches. These firms' entry into the watch-making industry took well-established mechanical watchmakers by surprise. Timex, Seiko, and especially the Swiss firms found that their market had changed overnight. Their production facilities, however, had not; and they spent a lot of money buying the new technology.

Most corporations rely on outside organizations to provide them with environmental data. Firms such as A. C. Nielsen Co. provide subscribers

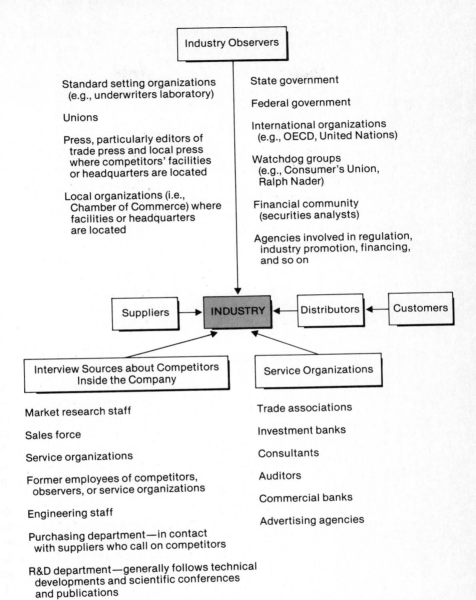

Industry Observers

Standard setting organizations
(e.g., underwriters laboratory)

Unions

Press, particularly editors of
trade press and local press
where competitors' facilities
or headquarters are located

Local organizations (i.e.,
Chamber of Commerce) where
facilities or headquarters
are located

State government

Federal government

International organizations
(e.g., OECD, United Nations)

Watchdog groups
(e.g., Consumer's Union,
Ralph Nader)

Financial community
(securities analysts)

Agencies involved in regulation,
industry promotion, financing,
and so on

Suppliers → INDUSTRY ← Distributors ← Customers

Interview Sources about Competitors
Inside the Company

Service Organizations

Market research staff

Sales force

Service organizations

Former employees of competitors,
observers, or service organizations

Engineering staff

Purchasing department—in contact
with suppliers who call on competitors

R&D department—generally follows technical
developments and scientific conferences
and publications

Trade associations

Investment banks

Consultants

Auditors

Commercial banks

Advertising agencies

SOURCE: M. E. Porter, *Competitive Strategy* (New York: Free Press, 1980), p. 378. Copyright © 1980 by The Free Press, a division of Macmillan Publishing Co., Inc. Reprinted by permission.

Figure 4.4 *Sources of data for industry analysis.*

with bimonthly data on brand share, retail prices, percentages of stores stocking an item, and percentages of stock-out stores. These data can be used to spot regional and national trends as well as to assess market share. Information on market conditions, government regulations, competitors, and new products can be bought from "information brokers."

Such firms as FIND/SVP, a New York company, get their data from periodicals, reference books, computer data banks, directors, and experts in the area.[30]

4.4 FORECASTING

Once a business corporation has collected data about its current environmental situation, it must analyze present trends to learn if they will continue into the future. The strategic planning horizon for many large corporations is from five to ten years in the future. A long-term planning horizon is especially necessary for large, capital-intensive corporations, such as automobile or heavy-machinery manufacturers. These corporations require many years to move from an accepted proposal to a finished product. As a result, most corporations must make future plans on the basis of a forecast, a set of assumptions about what that future will look like. These assumptions may be derived from an entrepreneur's vision, from a head-in-the-sand hope that the future will be similar to the present, or from the opinions of experts. Figure 4.5 depicts the role of forecasting in the strategy formulation process.

The Danger of Assumptions

A forecast is nothing more than a leap of faith into the future. Environmental scanning provides reasonably hard data on the present situation, but intuition and luck are needed to predict the future. Nevertheless, many firms formulate and implement strategic plans with little or no realization that their success is based on a series of assumptions. Many long-range plans are simply based on projections of the current situation. One example of what can happen when corporate strategy rests on the very questionable assumption that the future will simply be an extension of the present is that of Texaco, Incorporated.

During the 1950s, Texaco set in place a long-range strategy based on the key assumption that crude oil supplies would remain cheap and plentiful forever. From that assumption developed the strategy of minimizing exploration while emphasizing marketing. In 1973, the year of

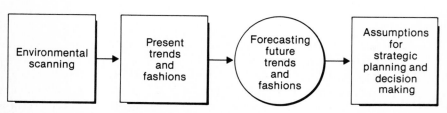

Figure 4.5   *The role of forecasting.*

the Arab oil boycott, Texaco had the largest and least efficient refining and marketing system in the industry, as well as a very weak exploration program. With almost no diversification to cushion the shock, Texaco fell from being, in the late 1960s, the most profitable of the major oil companies ("the Seven Sisters") to that of least profitable by 1978. Because its management was centralized and introverted, the corporation was the least responsive and most inflexible of its peers.

As a result of being an oil company without oil, Texaco has been forced to develop an entirely new strategy based upon radically different assumptions. They now envision far narrower markets and an intensive, expensive search for new supplies. The new strategy anticipates a gradual, but steady shifting of capital investments away from sources of conventional oil into such unconventional sources as coal gasification, shale oil, and tar sands.[31]

Techniques

Various techniques are used to forecast future situations.[32] Each has its proponents and critics. Generally speaking, forecasting techniques can be placed in three broad categories: (1) extrapolation, (2) simulations, and (3) expert opinion. No one method is considered appropriate for use in all situations.

Extrapolation. Simply stated, *extrapolation* is the extension of present trends into the future. It rests upon the assumption that the world is reasonably consistent and changes slowly in the short-run. There are two mathematical approaches: single variable extrapolation and theoretical limit envelopes. Both approaches attempt to predict what will happen to a single variable, such as the demand for cigarettes, on the basis of changes in a wide range of present and past variables, like disposable personal income and demographic data. Examples are life-cycle curves, exponential smoothing, and least-means-square smoothing.[33] As a rule of thumb, the further back into the past one can find relevant data, the more confidence one can have in the prediction.

Simulations. The availability of computers, with their ability to handle simultaneously the interrelationships of many variables, has increased the use of simulations. *Simulations* are simply a complicated way of asking "What if?" Given a large amount of historical data on certain interrelated factors, one attempts to conceptualize alternative futures. Various possibilities, such as the world-wide acceptance of birth-control methods, can be entered into the computer to see the probable demographic effect on cigarette smoking in the twenty-first century, for example. To date, however, the use of simulation for forecasting has been only an exploratory effort due to measurement problems and a lack of understanding of underlying relationships.[34]

Expert Opinion. Probably the most popular of forecasting techniques, the *expert opinion* approach merely involves asking some authorities in the area to make an "informed guess" about future events. One well-known approach is the *Delphi technique* developed by the RAND Corporation. In this approach an anonymous panel of experts is asked to estimate the probability of certain events occurring in the future. Each member of the panel is given several opportunities to revise the estimate after seeing the responses from the other experts. Other approaches are *brain-storming* and *scenario construction*. Figure 4.6 shows an example of scenario construction as used by General Electric. Scenarios attempt to combine environmental scanning with historical data, Delphi panels, and trend extrapolations to predict likely future scenarios. As with all other techniques of forecasting, the closer the future to be forecast is to the present, the higher is the likelihood of accuracy.

4.5 SUMMARY AND CONCLUSION

Anyone concerned with how strategic decisions are made in large corporations should be aware of the impact of the external environment on top management and the board of directors. Long-run developments in the economic, technological, political-legal, and socio-cultural aspects of the societal environment strongly affect the corporation's activities through the more immediate pressures in its task environment.

Business and commerce have lived an uneasy truce with society for centuries. Vacillating between heavy regulation and *laissez faire* economics, business corporations are learning that they must be socially responsible if they are to operate with some autonomy. Top management and the board of directors must constantly balance the needs of one group in the corporation's task environment against the needs of another. They must work to ensure that their priorities do not get too far away from those valued by society.

Before strategy can be formulated, strategy makers must scan the external environment for possible opportunities and threats. They must identify which strategic factors to monitor, as well as assess which are likely to affect the corporation in the future. Then they must analyze the resulting information and disseminate it to the people involved in strategic planning and decision making.

Just as environmental scanning provides an understanding of present trends in the environment, forecasting provides assumptions about the future that are crucial for strategic management. Modern corporations use the techniques of extrapolation, computer simulations, and expert opinion to predict their future environment. Even if the predictions prove to be wrong, the very act of scanning and forecasting the environment help managers take a broader perspective. These techniques also help prevent the development of reactive managers who dare

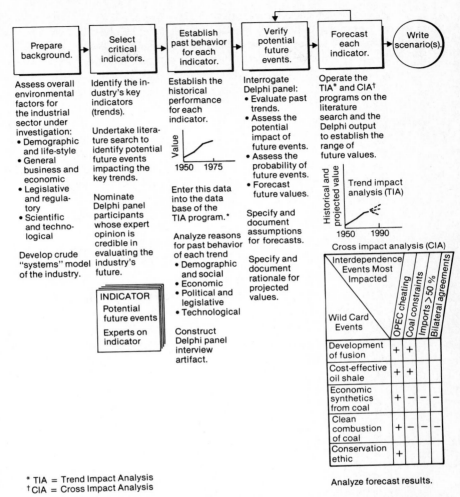

Prepare background. → Select critical indicators. → Establish past behavior for each indicator. → Verify potential future events. → Forecast each indicator. → Write scenario(s).

Assess overall environmental factors for the industrial sector under investigation:
• Demographic and life-style
• General business and economic
• Legislative and regulatory
• Scientific and technological

Develop crude "systems" model of the industry.

Identify the industry's key indicators (trends).

Undertake literature search to identify potential future events impacting the key trends.

Nominate Delphi panel participants whose expert opinion is credible in evaluating the industry's future.

INDICATOR
Potential future events
Experts on indicator

Establish the historical performance for each indicator.

Value
1950 1975

Enter this data into the data base of the TIA program.*

Analyze reasons for past behavior of each trend
• Demographic and social
• Economic
• Political and legislative
• Technological

Construct Delphi panel interview artifact.

Interrogate Delphi panel:
• Evaluate past trends.
• Assess the potential impact of future events.
• Assess the probability of future events.
• Forecast future values.

Specify and document assumptions for forecasts.

Specify and document rationale for projected values.

Operate the TIA* and CIA† programs on the literature search and the Delphi output to establish the range of future values.

Historical and projected value
Trend impact analysis (TIA)
1950 1990

Cross impact analysis (CIA)

Interdependence Events Most Impacted / Wild Card Events	OPEC cheating	Coal constraints	Imports >50 %	Bilateral agreements
Development of fusion	+	+		
Cost-effective oil shale	+	+		
Economic synthetics from coal	+	−	−	−
Clean combustion of coal	+	−	−	−
Conservation ethic	+			

Analyze forecast results.

* TIA = Trend Impact Analysis
†CIA = Cross Impact Analysis

SOURCE: W. F. Glueck, *Business Policy and Strategic Management* (New York: McGraw-Hill, 1980), p. 116. Copyright © 1980 by McGraw-Hill, Inc. Reprinted by permission.

Figure 4.6 *Scenario construction at General Electric.*

not take the time to plan for the future because they are caught up in the crises and problems of the present.

DISCUSSION QUESTIONS

1. How appropriate is the theory of *laissez faire* in today's world?
2. Why should a business corporation be socially responsible?
3. What can a corporation do to ensure that information about strategic environmental factors get to the attention of strategy makers?

4. To what extent do you agree with Porter's conclusion that the ultimate profit potential of an industry depends on the collective strength of five key forces: the threat of new entrants, the rivalry among existing firms, the threat of substitutable products or services, the bargaining power of buyers, and the bargaining power of suppliers? Defend your view.

5. If most long-term forecasts are usually incorrect, why bother doing them?

NOTES

1. E. C. Bursk, D. T. Clark, and R. W. Hidy, "The Oldest Business Code: Nearly 4000 Years Ago," *The World of Business*, vol. 1 (New York: Simon and Schuster, 1962), pp. 9–10.

2. F. E. Kast and J. E. Rosenzweig, *Organization and Management*, 2nd ed. (New York: McGraw-Hill, 1974), p. 28.

3. M. Weber, *The Protestant Ethic and the Spirit of Capitalism*, trans. Talcott Parson (New York: Charles Scribner's Sons, 1958).

4. Kast and Rosenzweig, p. 35.

5. J. W. McGuire, *Business and Society* (New York: McGraw-Hill, 1963), p. 78.

6. Kast and Rosenzweig, pp. 37–39.

7. S. N. Brenner and E. A. Molander, "Is the Ethics of Business Changing?" *Harvard Business Review* (January–February 1977), p. 69.

8. "Pushing the Boundaries of Eminent Domain," *Business Week* (May 4, 1981), p. 174.

9. "Three Mile Island's Lingering Ills," *Business Week* (October 22, 1979), p. 75. T. Redburn, "Stalled Nuclear Power Plant: PG&E Feels Powerless," *Los Angeles Times* (February 24, 1980), part 4, p. 1.

10. "Who Will Be Liable for Toxic Dumping?" *Business Week* (August 28, 1978), p. 32.

11. S. A. Frildstein, "How to React to a Safety Controversy," *Business Week* (November 6, 1978), p. 65.

12. S. Soloman, "The Asbestos Fallout at Johns-Manville," *Fortune* (May 7, 1979), pp. 197–206.

13. I. Ross, "How Lawless Are Big Companies?" *Fortune* (December 1, 1980), pp. 58–61.

14. W. M. Pride and O. C. Ferrell, *Marketing*, 2nd ed. (Boston: Houghton Mifflin, 1980), p. 720.

15. M. Friedman, "The Social Responsibility of Business Is To Increase Its Profits," *New York Times Magazine* (September 13, 1970), pp. 30, 126–127; and *Capitalism and Freedom* (Chicago: University of Chicago Press, 1963), p. 133.

16. W. D. Guth and R. Tagiuri, "Personal Values and Corporate Strategy," *Harvard Business Review* (September–October 1965), pp. 126–127.

17. Brenner and Molander, p. 70.

18. A. B. Carroll, "A Three-Dimensional Conceptual Model of Corporate Performance," *Academy of Management Review* (October 1979), pp. 497–505.

19. N. H. Snyder, "Environmental Volatility, Scanning Intensity and Organization Performance," *Journal of Contemporary Business* (September 1981), p. 7.

20. H. I. Ansoff, "Managing Strategic Surprise by Response to Weak Signals," *California Management Review* (Winter 1975), pp. 21–33.

21. F. J. Aguilar, *Scanning the Business Environment* (New York: Macmillan, 1967).

22. S. Matlins and G. Knisely, "Update: Profile of the Corporate Planner," *Journal of Business Strategy* (Spring 1981), p. 81.

23. Snyder, p. 6.

24. M. E. Porter, *Competitive Strategy* (New York: Free Press, 1980), p. 3.

25. This summary of the five forces driving competitive strategy is taken from M. E. Porter, *Competitive Strategy* (New York: Free Press, 1980), pp. 7–29.

26. Porter, p. 23.

27. Aguilar, op. cit.

    W. J. Keegan, "Multinational Scanning: A Study of Information Sources Utilized by Headquarters Executives in Multinational Companies," *Administrative Science Quarterly* (September 1974), pp. 411–421.

    H. Mintzberg, *The Nature of Managerial Work* (New York: Harper & Row, 1973).

28. Snyder, p. 13.

29. Snyder, p. 16.

30. A. Nag, "Information Brokers Thrive by Helping Firms Get Facts," *Wall Street Journal* (July 7, 1981), p. 31.

31. "Texaco Restoring Luster to the Star," *Business Week* (December 22, 1980), pp. 54–61.

32. D. Lebell and O. J. Krasner, "Selecting Environmental Forecasting Techniques from Business Planning Requirements," *Academy of Management Review* (July 1977), pp. 376–378.

    J. M. Utterback, "Environmental Analysis and Forecasting," *Strategic Management: A New View of Business Policy and Planning*, eds. D. E. Schendel and C. W. Hofer (Boston: Little, Brown & Co., 1979), pp. 134–144.

33. Lebell and Krasner, pp. 376–378.

34. Utterback, p. 137.

STRATEGIC MANAGEMENT MODEL

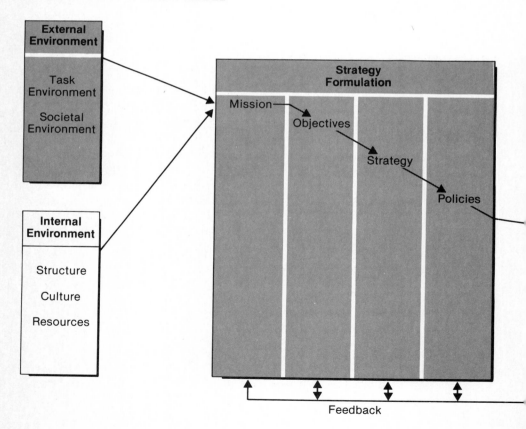

THE INTERNAL ENVIRONMENT

CHAPTER 5

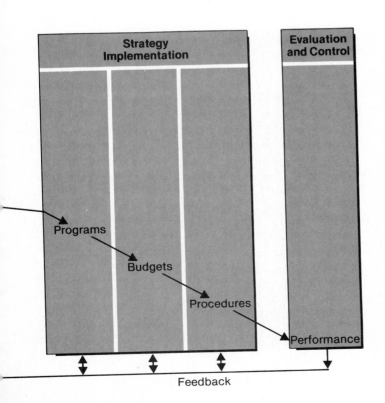

S trategic planning and decision making cannot be successful at the corporate level without an in-depth understanding of the strategic factors within the corporation. These factors are the internal *strengths* and *weaknesses* that act to either constrain or support a strategy. Part of a firm's internal environment, these factors are not within the short-run control of strategic managers. Instead they form the context within which work is accomplished. Strategic factors in a corporation's internal environment are *structure*, *culture*, and *resources*.

5.1 STRUCTURE

The structure of a corporation is often defined in terms of communication, authority, and work flow. It is the corporation's pattern of relationships, its "anatomy." It is a formal arrangement of roles and relationships of people so that the work is directed toward meeting the goals and accomplishing the mission of the corporation.[1] Sometimes it is referred to as the chain of command and is often graphically described in an organization chart.

Although there are an almost infinite variety of structural forms, certain types are predominant in modern complex organizations. These are simple, functional, divisional, matrix, and conglomerate structures.[2] Figure 5.1 illustrates some of these structures.

Simple Structure

Firms with a simple structure are usually small in size and undifferentiated laterally—that is, there are no functional or product categories. A firm with a simple structure is likely to be managed by an owner-manager who either does all the work or oversees a group of unspecialized people who do whatever needs to be done to provide a single product or service. The simple structure is appropriate if the owner-manager can grasp all the intricacies of the business and if the demand for the product or service is reasonably stable.

Functional Structure

In a functional structure, work is divided into subunits on the basis of such functions as manufacturing, finance, and sales. Functional structure enables a firm to take advantage of specialists and to deal with complex production or service-delivery problems more efficiently than it could if everyone performed an undifferentiated task. The functional structure is appropriate as long as top management is willing to invest a lot of energy in coordinating the many activities. The typical long vertical channels of communication and authority tend to make the firm rather in-

I. SIMPLE STRUCTURE

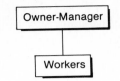

II. FUNCTIONAL STRUCTURE

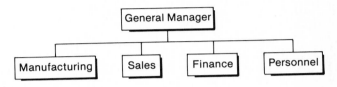

III. DIVISIONAL STRUCTURE*

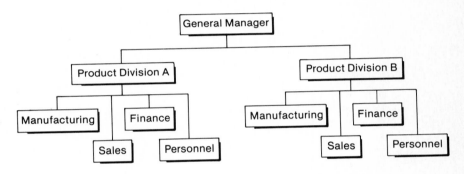

*Conglomerate structure is a variant of the division structure.

IV. MATRIX STRUCTURE

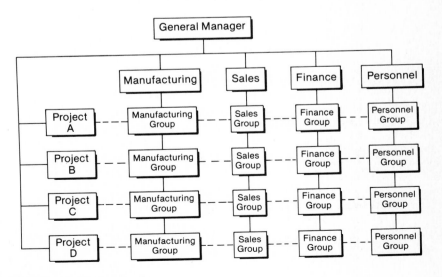

Figure 5.1 *Basic structures.*

flexible to the requirements of a changing environment, but very successful when adaptability is not required and predictability is important.

Divisional Structure

When a corporation is organized on the basis of divisions, an extra management layer—division chiefs—is added between top management and functional managers. The standard functions are then designed around products, clients, or territories.[3] A recent innovation in this area is the use of *strategic business units* (SBUs). Organizational groups composed of discrete, independent *product-market* segments are identified and given primary responsibility and authority to manage their functional areas. For example, instead of food preparation appliances being housed in three different divisions—such as large appliances, small appliances, and cookware—they can be merged into a single SBU serving the housewares market. (For more information on SBUs, refer to Chapter 8.) The divisional structure is appropriate for a firm with many products serving many different markets. It gives the corporation the flexibility it needs to deal with a complex and changeable environment. It can be potentially inefficient, however, if there is much duplication of equipment and support staff. Furthermore, one division can be operating at overcapacity while in another division much of its facilities and staff are idle.

Matrix Structure

In matrix structures, functional and divisional areas are combined *simultaneously* at the same level of the corporation. Employees have two superiors, a project manager and a functional manager. The "home" department—that is, engineering, manufacturing, or sales—is usually functional and is reasonably permanent. People from these functional units are assigned on a temporary basis to one or more project units. The project units act like divisions in that they are differentiated on a product-market basis. Pioneered in the aerospace industry, the matrix structure was developed to combine the stability of the functional structure with the flexibility of a project organization. The matrix structure is very useful when the external environment (especially the technological and market aspects) is very complex and changeable. It does, however, result in conflicts revolving around duties, authority, and resource allocation.

Conglomerate Structure

A variant of a divisional structure organized by product, the conglomerate structure is typically an assemblage of separate firms having different products in different markets but operating together under one corporate umbrella. The divisions are independent of each other but share a dependence on central headquarters for financial resources and corporate planning. Its chief advantages to the corporation lie in the limitation of liability, a possible reduction in taxes, and, for the various divisions, the appearance of autonomy.[4] In addition, risks are spread over many different segments of the marketplace. The disadvantages of conglomerate structure derive from its heavy legalistic and financial orientation. In order to keep the legal advantages, the corporation cannot easily combine divisions to generate operating or marketing synergy. The investment orientation at the corporate level can easily prevent top management from understanding divisional problems in any sense other than financial. Furthermore, the ability to sell off a troubled division can lead to a short-run strategic orientation concerned only with the year-end bottom line.

An understanding of how the corporation is structured can be very useful in developing strategic plans. If the structure is compatible with a particular change in strategy, it is a corporate strength. If the structure is not compatible with either a present or a potential strategy, it is a definite weakness and will act to constrain strategy formulation. Data General, for example, has had some serious problems because its growth strategy was incompatible with its centralized decision-making structure. Opportunities were not grasped quickly enough because all decisions had to be approved by the president.[5]

5.2 CULTURE

A corporation's culture is the collection of beliefs, expectations, and values shared by the corporation's members and transmitted from one generation of employees to another. These form norms (rules of conduct) that define acceptable behavior of people from top management to the operative employee. Myths and rituals, often unrecorded, emerge over time to emphasize certain norms or values and to explain why a certain aspect of the culture is important. Like the retelling of the vision and perseverance of the founder(s) of the corporation, the myth is often tied closely to the corporate mission.

Corporate culture shapes the behavior of people in the corporation. Analysts Schwartz and Davis point this out: "Apparently, the well-run corporations of the world have distinctive cultures that are somehow responsible for their ability to create, implement, and maintain their world leadership positions."[6] Since these cultures have a powerful influence on the behavior of managers, they may strongly affect a corporation's ability to shift its strategic direction. For example, in 1975, the CEOs of two major oil companies changed the strategy of their respective firms from concentration in oil to diversification. They did so because they believed that their current business could neither support long-term growth nor deal with serious political threats. The strategy was announced, and elaborate implementation plans were developed and put into action. As of 1980, however, both companies were again firmly concentrating in oil after five years of floundering in attempts to acquire and build new businesses. Both CEOs had been replaced. As *Business Week* reported, "Each of the CEOs had been unable to implement his strategy, not because it was theoretically wrong or bad but because neither had understood that his company's culture was so entrenched in the traditions and values of doing business as oilmen that employees resisted—and sabotaged—the radical changes that the CEOs tried to impose."[7]

Schwartz and Davis have developed a method to assess the current culture of a corporation (or a division). They examine boss-subordinate, peer, and interdepartmental relationships in terms of such critical tasks as innovating, decision making, communicating, organizing, monitoring, appraising, and rewarding.[8] Table 5.1 is an illustration of the culture in the international banking division of a major money-center bank. The data were gathered from a series of individual and small-group interviews. Executives and managers were asked to describe the survival rules of how "the game is played" as if they were coaching a new member of the organization. The result was a collection of norms (risk assessments) that people followed if they expected to be a successful part of the firm. These formed the culture of the division.

Schwartz and Davis summarize these characteristics as follows:

> The resulting summary of the international banking division culture characterized individual area managers as feudal barons. Each had been in place from five to seven years. As long as their profit contribution goals were met, they operated with almost complete autonomy. To preserve that autonomy, their concern for short-term performance was paramount. Planning and decision making were undisciplined, excessively personalized, and focused on each individual deal. Subordinates were highly averse to taking risks. So many people were involved in signing off on a loan decision that it was difficult to hold anyone truly accountable for results.
>
> There was, furthermore, a veneer of mannerliness and colleagueship that inhibited frank and honest confrontations to resolve conflicts in the bank's best interest. Information, jealously guarded, was used to manipulate and control adversaries. Political intrigues abounded, with advancement often going to people most loyal to immediate supervisors. As a result of these cultural aspects of our composite division, innovation was risky and received little support. Anything the area manager decided to address was quickly picked up by subordinates. Opportunism was more important than strategy. Not surprisingly, the organization very quickly fell into second place behind more innovative, effective competitors.[9]

**Table 5.1 SUMMARY OF CULTURAL RISK ASSESSMENT
(International Banking Division)**

RELATIONSHIPS	CULTURE SUMMARY
Company-wide	Preserve your autonomy. Allow area managers to run the business as long as they meet the profit budget.
Boss-subordinate	Avoid confrontations. Smooth over disagreements. Support the boss.
Peer	Guard information; it is power. Be a gentleman or lady.
Interdepartment	Protect your department's bottom line. Form alliances around specific issues. Guard your turf.

TASKS	CULTURE SUMMARY
Innovating	Consider it risky. Be a quick second.
Decision making	Handle each deal on its own merits. Gain consensus. Require many sign-offs. Involve the right people. Seize the opportunity.
Communicating	Withhold information to control adversaries. Avoid confrontations. Be a gentleman or lady.
Organizing	Centralize power. Be autocratic.
Monitoring	Meet short-term profit goals.
Appraising and rewarding	Reward the faithful. Choose the best bankers as managers. Seek safe jobs.

SOURCE: H. Schwartz and S. M. Davis, "Matching Corporate Culture and Business Strategy," *Organizational Dynamics*, vol. 10, no. 1 (Summer 1981), p. 38. Copyright © 1981 by AMACOM, a division of American Management Association. All rights reserved. Reprinted by permission.

An understanding of a corporation's (or division's) culture is thus imperative if the firm is to be managed strategically. A change in mission, objectives, strategies, or policies is not likely to be successful if it is in opposition to the accepted culture of the corporation. As was true for structure, if the culture is compatible with the change, it is an internal strength. But if the corporate culture is not compatible with the change, it is, under circumstances of a changing environment, a serious weakness. This does not mean that a manager should *never* consider a strategy that runs counter to the established culture. However, if such a strategy is to be seriously considered, top management must be prepared to attempt to change the culture as well, a task that will take much time, effort, and persistence.

5.3 RESOURCES

William Newman, an authority in strategic management, points out that a practical way to develop a master strategy of the corporation is to "pick particular roles or niches that are appropriate in view of competition and the company's resources."[10] Company resources are typically considered in terms of financial, physical, and human resources, as well as organizational systems and technological capabilities. Because these resources have functional significance, we can discuss them under commonly accepted functional headings, as depicted in Table 5.2. These resources, among others, should be audited to ascertain internal strengths and weaknesses.

Corporate-level strategy formulators must be aware of the many contributions each functional area can make to divisional and corporate performance. Functional resources include not only the people in each area but also that area's ability to formulate and implement under corporate guidance functional objectives, strategies, and policies. Thus they include the knowledge of analytical concepts and procedural techniques common to each area and the ability of the people in the area to utilize them effectively. These are some of the most valuable and well-known concepts and techniques: market segmentation, product life cycle, capital budgeting, financial leverage, technological competence, operating leverage, learning curve analysis, job analysis, and job design. There are many others, of course, but these are the basic ones. If used properly, these resources can improve overall strategic management.

Marketing

The primary task of the marketing manager from a corporation's point of view is to regulate the level, timing, and character of demand in a way that will help the corporation achieve its objectives.[11] The manager must therefore be especially concerned with the market position and marketing mix of the firm.

Market position deals with the question, "Who are our customers?" It refers to the selection of specific areas for marketing concentration, and can be expressed in terms of market, product, and geographical locations. Through market research, corporations are able to practice market segmentation with various products or services so that a family

Table 5.2 A TYPICAL FUNCTIONAL AREA RESOURCE PROFILE

	R&D ENGINEERING (Conceive/Design/ Develop)	MANUFACTURING (Produce)	MARKETING (Distribute/ Sell/Service)	FINANCE (Finance)	MANAGEMENT (Plan/Organize/ Control)
FOCUS OF FINANCIAL DEPLOYMENTS	$ for basic research; $ for new product development; $ for product improvements; $ for process improvements.	$ for plant; $ for equipment; $ for inventory; $ for labor.	$ for sales and promotion; $ for distribution; $ for service; $ for market research.	$ for S.T. cash management; $ for raising L.T. funds; $ for allocating L.T. funds;	$ for planning system; $ for control system; $ for management development.
PHYSICAL RESOURCES	Size, age, and location of R&D facilities; Size, age, and location of development facilities.	Number, location, size, and age of plants; Degree of automation; Degree of integration; Type of equipment.	Number and location of sales offices; Number and location of warehouses; Number and location of service facilities.	Number of lock boxes; Number of major lenders; Dispersion of stock ownership; Number and types of computers.	Location of corporate headquarters.
HUMAN RESOURCES	Number, types, and ages of key scientists and engineers; Turnover of key personnel.	Number, types, and ages of key staff personnel and foremen; Turnover of key personnel.	Number, types, and ages of key salesmen; Marketing staff; Turnover of key personnel.	Number, types, and ages of key financial and accounting personnel; Turnover of key personnel.	Number, types, and ages of key managers and corporate staff; Turnover of key personnel.

(Continued)

Table 5.2 (*Cont.*)

	R&D ENGINEERING (Conceive/Design/Develop)	MANUFACTURING (Produce)	MARKETING (Distribute/Sell/Service)	FINANCE (Finance)	MANAGEMENT (Plan/Organize/Control)
ORGANIZATIONAL SYSTEMS	System to monitor technological developments; System to control conceptual/design/development process	Nature and sophistication of • purchasing system • production scheduling and control system • quality control system	Nature and sophistication of • distribution system • service system • pricing and credit staff • market research staff	Type and sophistication of • cash management system • financial markets forecasting system • corporate financial models • accounting system	Nature of organizational culture and values; Sophistication of planning and control systems; Delegation of authority; Measurement of reward systems.
TECHNOLOGICAL CAPABILITIES	Number of patents; Number of new products; Percent of sales from new products; Relative product quality.	Raw materials availability; Trends in total constant dollars per-unit costs for • raw materials and purchased parts • direct labor and equipment; Productivity; Capacity utilization; Unionization.	Trends in total constant dollars per-unit costs for • sales and promotion • distribution and service; Percent retail outlet coverage; Key account advantages; Price competitiveness; Breadth of product line; Brand loyalty; Service effectiveness.	Credit rating; Credit availability; Leverage; Price/Earnings ratio; Stock price; Cash flow; Dividend payout.	Corporate image prestige; Influence with regulatory and governmental agencies; Quality of corporate staff; Organizational synergies.

SOURCE: C. W. Hofer and D. Schendel, *Strategy Formulation: Analytical Concepts* (St. Paul, Minn.: West Publishing Co., 1978), p. 148. Copyright © 1978 by West Publishing Co. All rights reserved. Reprinted by permission.

of products does not directly compete with each other. For example, Procter and Gamble Company positions Crest as a toothpaste for young children, whereas it positions Gleem as an adult toothpaste.

The *marketing mix* refers to the particular combination of key variables under the corporation's control that can be used to affect demand and to gain competitive advantage. These variables are *product*, *place*, *promotion*, and *price*. Within each of these four variables are several subvariables, listed in Table 5.3, which should be analyzed in terms of their effect upon divisional and corporate performance.

One of the most useful concepts in marketing insofar as strategic management is concerned is that of the *product life cycle*. As depicted in Table 5.4, the product life cycle is a graph showing time plotted against the dollar sales of a product as it moves from introduction through growth and maturity to decline. Table 5.4 lists the functional strategic objective at each developmental stage, as well as appropriate approaches for each stage in terms of design, pricing, promotion, and distribution. This concept enables a marketing manager to examine the marketing mix of a particular product or group of products given its position in its life cycle.

Finance

The job of the financial manager is the management of funds. The manager must ascertain the best *sources* of funds, *uses* of funds, and *control* of funds. Cash must be raised from internal or external financial sources

Table 5.3 MARKETING MIX VARIABLES

PRODUCT	PLACE	PROMOTION	PRICE
Quality	Channels	Advertising	List price
Features	Coverage	Personal selling	Discounts
Options	Locations	Sales promotion	Allowances
Style	Inventory	Publicity	Payment periods
Brand name	Transport		Credit terms
Packaging			
Sizes			
Services			
Warranties			
Returns			

SOURCE: Philip Kotler, *Marketing Management: Analysis, Planning, and Control*, 4th ed. (Englewood Cliffs, N.J.: Prentice-Hall, 1980), p. 89. Copyright © 1980 by Prentice-Hall, Inc. Reprinted by permission.

Table 5.4 DYNAMIC COMPETITIVE STRATEGY AND THE MARKET LIFE CYCLE.

	MARKET DEVELOPMENT (Introductory period for high learning products only)	RAPID GROWTH (Normal introductory pattern for a very low learning product)	COMPETITIVE TURBULENCE	SATURATION (MATURITY)	DECLINE
STRATEGY OBJECTIVE	Minimize learning requirements; locate and remedy offering defects quickly; develop widespread awareness of benefits; and gain trial by early adopters.	To establish a strong brand market and distribution niche as quickly as possible.	To maintain and strengthen the market niche achieved through dealer and consumer loyalty.	To defend brand position against competing brands and product category against other potential products, through constant attention to product-improvement opportunities and fresh promotional and distribution approaches.	To milk the offering dry of all possible profit.
OUTLOOK FOR COMPETITION	None is likely to be attracted in the early, unprofitable stages.	Early entrance of numerous aggressive emulators.	Price and distribution squeezes on the industry, shaking out the weaker entrants.	Competition stabilized, with few or no new entrants and market shares not subject to substantial change in the absence of a substantial perceived improvement in some brand.	Similar competition declining and dropping out because of decrease in consumer interest.
PRODUCT DESIGN OBJECTIVE	Limited number of models with physical product and offering designs both focused on minimizing learning requirements. Designs cost-and-use engineered to appeal to most receptive segment. Utmost attention to quality control and quick elimination of market-revealed defects in design.	Modular design to facilitate flexible addition of variants to appeal to every new segment and new use-system as fast as discovered.	Intensified attention to product improvement, tightening up of line to eliminate unnecessary specialties with little market appeal.	A constant alert for market pyramiding opportunities through either bold cost- and price-penetration of new markets or major product changes. Introduction of flanker products. Constant attention to possibilities for product improvement and cost cutting. Reexamination of necessity of design compromises.	Constant pruning of line to eliminate any items not returning a direct profit.

PRICING OBJECTIVE	A price line for every taste, from low-end to premium models. Customary trade discounts. Aggressive promotional pricing, with prices cut as fast as costs decline due to accumulated production experience. Intensification of sampling.		Increased attention to market-broadening and promotional pricing opportunities.	Defensive pricing to preserve product category franchise. Search for incremental pricing opportunities, including private label contracts, to boost volume and gain an experience advantage.	Maintenance of profit-level pricing with complete disregard of any effect on market share.
PROMOTIONAL GUIDELINES *Communications Objectives*	a) Create widespread awareness and understanding of offering benefits. b) Gain trial by early adopters.	Create and strengthen brand preference among trade and final users. Stimulate general trial.	Maintain consumer franchise, and strengthen dealer ties.	Maintain consumer and trade loyalty, with strong emphasis on dealers and distributors. Promotion of greater use frequency.	Phase out, keeping just enough to maintain profitable distribution.
Most valuable media mix	In order of value: Publicity. Personal Sales. Mass communications.	Mass media. Personal sales. Sales promotions, including sampling. Publicity.	Mass media. Dealer promotions. Personal selling to dealers. Sales promotions. Publicity.	Mass media. Dealer-oriented promotions.	Cut down all media to the bone—use no sales promotions of any kind.
DISTRIBUTION POLICY	Exclusive or selective, with distributor margins high enough to justify heavy promotional spending.	Intensive and extensive, with dealer margins just high enough to keep them interested. Close attention to rapid resupply of distributor stocks and heavy inventories at all levels.	Intensive and extensive, and a strong emphasis on keeping dealer well supplied, but with minimum inventory cost to him/her.	Intensive and extensive, with strong emphasis on keeping dealer well supplied, but at minimum inventory cost to him/her.	Phase out outlets as they become marginal.
INTELLIGENCE FOCUS	To identify actual developing use-systems and to uncover any product weaknesses.	Detailed attention to brand position, to gaps in model and market coverage, and to opportunities for market segmentation.	Close attention to product improvement needs, to market-broadening chances, and to possible fresh promotion themes.	Intensified attention to possible product improvements. Sharp alert for potential new inter-product competition and for signs of beginning product decline.	Information helping to identify the point at which the product should be phased out.

Note: Strictly speaking, this is the cycle of the category market, and only a high-learning introduction passes through all the phases indicated above. The term, *product life cycle*, is sometimes applied indiscriminately to both brand cycles and category cycles. Most new brands are only emulative of other products already on the market, have a much shorter life cycle than the product category, and must follow a strategy similar to any low-learning product.

SOURCE: C. R. Wasson, *Dynamic Competitive Strategy and Product Life Cycles*, 3rd ed. (Austin, Tex.: Austin Press, 1978), pp. 256–257. Copyright © 1978 by Chester R. Wasson. Reprinted by permission.

and allocated for different uses. The flow of funds in the operations of the corporation must be monitored. Benefits must be given to the sources of outside financing in the form of returns, repayments, or products and services. All these tasks must be handled in a way that complements and supports overall corporate strategy.

From a strategic point of view, the financial area should be analyzed to see how well it deals with funds. The mix of externally generated short-term and long-term funds in relation to the amount and timing of internally generated funds should be appropriate to corporate objectives, strategies, and policies. The concept of *financial leverage* (the ratio of total debt to total assets) is very useful in describing the use of debt to increase the earnings available to common stockholders.[12] Financial leverage can be used to boost earnings per share. Although interest paid on debt reduces taxable income, the higher debt means there are fewer stockholders to share the profits. There are fewer stockholders because the corporation finances its activities by selling bonds or notes instead of stock. The debt, however, gives the firm a higher break-even point than it would have if the firm financed from internally generated funds only. High leverage may therefore be perceived as a corporate strength in times of prosperity and ever-increasing sales, or as a weakness in times of a recession and dropping sales. This is because leverage acts to magnify the effect on earnings *per share* of an increase or decrease in dollar sales.

The knowledge and use of *capital budgeting* techniques is an important financial resource. A good finance department will be able to analyze and rank possible investments in such fixed assets as land, buildings, and equipment in terms of additional outlays a corporation must make as well as the additional receipts that will result. Then it can rank investment proposals on the basis of some accepted criteria (for example, years to payback investment, rate of return, time to break-even point, etc.) and make a decision.

Break-even analysis is an analytical technique for studying the relations among fixed costs, variable costs, and profits. It is a device for determining the point at which sales will just cover total costs. Figure 5.2 shows a basic break-even chart for a hypothetical company. The chart is drawn on a unit basis, with volume produced shown on the horizontal axis and with costs and revenues measured on the vertical axis. Fixed costs are $40,000, as represented by the horizontal line; variable costs are $1.20 per unit. Total costs rise by $1.20, the amount of the variable costs, for each additional unit produced past $40,000, and the product is sold at $2.00 per unit. The total revenue line is a straight line increasing directly with production. As is usual, the slope of the total revenue line is steeper than that of the total cost line because, for every unit sold, the firm receives $2.00 of revenue for every $1.20 paid out for labor and material. Up to the break-even point (the intersection of the total revenue and total cost lines), the firm suffers losses. After that point, the firm

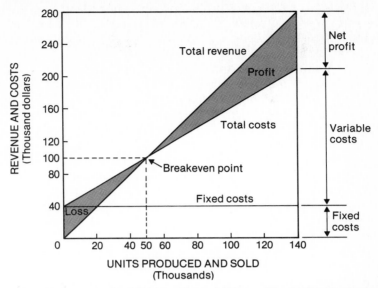

SOURCE: J. F. Weston and E. F. Brigham, Managerial Finance, 7th ed., (Hinsdale, Ill.: The Dryden Press, 1981), p. 226. Copyright © 1981 by The Dryden Press, a division of Holt, Rinehart & Winston, Publishers. Copyright © 1962, 1969, 1972, 1977, 1978 by Holt, Rinehart & Winston. Reprinted by permission of Holt, Rinehart & Winston, CBS College Publishing.

Figure 5.2   *Break-even chart.*

earns profits at an increasing amount as volume increases. In this in-stance, the break-even point for the firm is at a sales and cost level of $100,000 and a production level of 50,000 units.

Research and Development

The R&D manager is responsible for suggesting and implementing a corporation's technological strategy in light of corporate objectives and policies. The manager's job therefore involves (1) choosing among alter-native new technologies to use within the corporation, (2) developing methods of embodying the new technology in new products and pro-cesses, and (3) deploying resources so that the new technology can be successfully implemented.[13]

The term "research and development" is used to describe a wide range of activities. In some corporations R&D is conducted by scientists in well-equipped expensive laboratories where the focus is on theoretical problem areas. In other firms, R&D is heavily oriented toward marketing and is concerned with product or product-packaging improvements. In still other firms, R&D takes on an engineering orientation concentrating on quality control, the manufacturing of design specifications, and the development of improved production equipment. Most corporations will have a mix of basic, applied, and engineering R&D. The balance of these types of research is known as the *R&D mix* and should be appropriate to corporate strategy.

A corporation's R&D unit should be evaluated for *technological competence* in both the development and use of innovative technology. Not only should the corporation make a consistent research effort (as measured by reasonably constant corporate expenditures that result in usable innovations), it should also be proficient in managing research personnel and integrating their innovations into its day-to-day operations.

Corporations operating in technology-based industries must be willing to make substantial investments in R&D. For example, the computer and pharmaceutical industries spend an average of 6.4% and 4.9% respectively of their sales dollars for R&D. As shown in Table 5.5, other industries, such as metals and mining, may spend less than one percent. If a corporation is unwilling to invest the large amount of money necessary for its own research and development, it may be able to purchase or lease the equipment, techniques, or patents necessary to stay abreast of the competition. Japanese corporations, for instance, used this approach to make extensive use of integrated circuit modules developed and manufactured in the United States for their large-scale entry into the electronic calculators market.[14]

Those corporations that do purchase an innovative technology must, nevertheless, have the technological competence to make good use of it. Unfortunately, some corporations introduce the latest technology into their processes without adequately assessing the competence of their organization to handle it. For example, the U.S. Navy contracted with Tano Corporation to replace the existing manually operated propulsion controls of five amphibious assault vessels, (at a cost of $5 million per ship) with new automatic, computer-controlled, electro-pneumatic systems. When in place the systems failed to operate as planned. A few months after installation, the Navy was forced to spend $30 million to have Tano take out the new automatic systems on all five ships and to replace them with the previously used manual systems. According to an executive from Tano, the removal was "a very unfortunate situation for us. We assumed that a certain level of technicians would be on the ships to operate this equipment. They weren't."[15]

Manufacturing

The primary task of the manufacturing manager is to develop and operate a system that will produce the required number of products or services, with a certain quality, at a given cost, within an allotted time. However, manufacturing operations vary significantly depending on the type of product made. In very general terms, operations may be intermittent or continuous. In *intermittent systems*, the item normally goes through a sequential process, but the work and sequence of the process vary. At each center, the tasks determine the details of processing and the time required for them: "Work flows through the system in batches or special orders and commonly waits for a time before being processed at service facilities required by the products."[16] In contrast, *continuous systems* are those laid out as lines on which products can be assembled or processed. An example is an automobile assembly line.

The type of manufacturing system used by a corporation determines divisional or corporate strategy. It makes no sense, for example, to plan to increase sales by saturating the market with low priced products if the corporation's manufacturing process was designed as an intermittent "job shop" system that now produces one-time-only products to a customer's specifications. Conversely, a plan to produce a number of specialty products may not be economically feasible if the manufacturing process was designed to be a mass-producing, continuous system using low-skilled labor or robots.

Continuous systems are popular because they allow a corporation to take advantage of manufacturing *operating leverage*. According to Weston and Brigham, "The degree of operating leverage is the percentage change in operating income that results from a percentage change in units sold."[17] For example, a highly labor-intensive firm has little automated machinery and thus a small amount of fixed costs. It has a fairly low break-even point, but its variable cost line has a relatively steep slope. Since most of the costs associated with the product are variable (many employees earning piece rate wages), its variable costs are higher than those of automated firms. Its advantage over other firms is that it can operate at low levels and still be profitable. Once it reaches break-even, however, the huge variable costs as a percentage of total costs keep the profit per unit at a relatively low level. Its low operating leverage prevents it from gathering the huge profits possible from a high amount of sales. In terms of strategy, this firm should look for a niche in the marketplace where it can produce and sell a reasonably small quantity of goods.

In contrast, a capital-intensive firm has a lot of money invested in automated processes and highly sophisticated machinery. Its labor force is relatively small but highly skilled, earning salaries rather than piece-rate wages. Consequently, it has a high amount of fixed costs. It also has a relatively high break-even point, but its variable cost line rises slowly. Its advantage over other firms is that once it reaches break-even, its profits rise faster than do those of less automated firms. In terms of strategy, this firm needs to find a high-demand niche in the marketplace where it can produce and sell a large quantity of goods. Its high operating

Table 5.5   1980 R&D INDUSTRY EXPENDITURES

INDUSTRY		SALES (Million Dollars)	PROFITS (Million Dollars)	R&D EXPENSES			
				(Million Dollars)	Percent of Sales	Percent of Profits	Dollars per Employee
Aerospace	[14]	45,092	1,642	2,045	4.5	124.6	3,026
Appliances	[10]	9,511	267	168	1.8	63.1	921
Automotive:							
Cars, Trucks	[6]	113,161	(4,573)	4,501	4.0	(98.4)	3,264
Parts, Equipment	[14]	15,726	425	292	1.9	68.9	1,127
Building Materials	[21]	14,017	573	159	1.1	27.9	939
Chemicals	[43]	89,877	4,847	2,161	2.4	44.6	2,478
Conglomerates	[16]	67,675	3,143	1,197	1.8	38.1	1,141
Containers	[5]	15,115	510	116	0.8	22.9	617
Drugs	[23]	43,629	4,206	2,157	4.9	51.3	3,466
Electrical	[24]	46,645	2,658	1,311	2.8	49.3	1,703
Electronics	[69]	27,929	1,446	805	2.9	55.7	1,584
Food & Beverage	[39]	86,732	3,337	502	0.6	15.6	530
Fuel	[18]	380,536	22,828	1,506	0.4	6.6	1,774

Informational Processing:							
Computers	[20]	53,258	5,307	3,400	6.4	64.1	3,979
Office Equipment	[12]	13,217	880	562	4.3	63.9	2,659
Peripherals, Services	[32]	5,151	239	301	5.9	126.2	3,060
Instruments	[61]	14,169	771	591	4.2	76.8	2,142
Leisure Time	[21]	19,005	1,429	799	4.2	56.0	2,879
Machinery:							
Farm, Construction	[18]	24,376	1,165	668	2.7	57.4	2,462
Machine Tools, Industrial, Mining	[64]	30,208	1,590	491	1.6	30.9	1,061
Metals & Mining	[14]	24,173	2,039	215	0.9	10.6	1,001
Miscellaneous Manufacturing	[85]	45,178	2,607	930	2.1	35.7	1,303
Oil Service & Supply	[18]	29,059	2,646	470	1.6	17.8	1,007
Paper	[18]	32,550	1,947	271	0.8	13.8	809
Personal & Home Care Products	[23]	28,541	1,746	524	1.8	30.0	1,847
Semiconductors	[8]	10,232	635	617	6.0	97.2	2,378
Steel	[7]	29,438	941	165	0.6	17.6	477
Telecommunications	[6]	63,969	6,967	614	1.0	8.8	559
Textiles, Apparel	[17]	10,186	281	50	0.5	17.8	236
Tires, Rubber	[12]	22,989	246	413	1.8	168.4	1,176
Tobacco	[4]	9,530	707	31	0.3	4.4	340
All-Industry Composite	[744]	1,420,858	73,493	28,064	2.0	38.2	1,834

Note: Numbers in brackets represent the number of corporations in that industry grouping.

SOURCE: Adapted from "R&D Scoreboard," *Business Week* (July 6, 1981), pp. 60–75.

leverage makes it an extremely profitable and competitive firm once it reaches its high break-even point. Changes in the level of sales have a magnified (leveraged) impact on profits. In times of recession, however, it is likely to suffer huge losses. During an economic downturn, the firm with less automation and thus less leverage is more likely to survive comfortably, since a drop in sales primarily affects variable costs. It is easier to lay off labor than machines.

A conceptual framework that many large corporations have used for a manufacturing strategy is the *learning* (or experience) *curve*.[18] The concept applied to business is that production costs decline by some fixed percentage as production increases. A learning curve is simply a line showing the relationship between unit production time and the number of consecutive units of production.[19] The learning curve concept is commonly used in estimating the production costs of (1) a product never before made with the present techniques and processes or (2) current products produced by newly introduced techniques or processes.

The learning curve concept is based upon three assumptions:

1. The amount of time required to complete a given task or unit of a product will be less each time the task is undertaken.
2. Unit time will decrease at a decreasing rate.
3. The reduction in time will follow a specific and predictable pattern, such as an exponential function.[20]

Learning curves were first applied in the airframe industry, where each of these assumptions was found to hold true. While many firms have used learning curves extensively, an unquestioning acceptance of the industry norm (such as 80% for the airframe industry) is very risky.[21] The learning curve for a given industry may not hold for a specific corporation for a variety of reasons. Differences in equipment, plant size, methods, and product design, among others, may cause two firms to have very different curves. Procedural differences reflected in the development of the learning percentage itself may result in different percentages, depending upon whether the rate is based upon a single product or an entire product line.[22]

Human Resource Management

The primary task of the manager of human resources is to improve the match between individuals and jobs. The quality of this match influences job performance, employee satisfaction, and employee turnover.[23] Consequently, human resource management (HRM) is concerned with the selection and training of new employees, appraisal of employee performance, the assessment of employees' promotion potential, and recruitment and personnel planning for the future. HRM is also highly involved in wage and salary administration, labor negotiations, job design, and employee morale.

A good HRM department should be competent in the use of attitude surveys and other feed-back devices to assess employee satisfaction with their jobs and with the corporation as a whole. HRM managers should also be knowledgeable in *job analysis* and competent in its use. Job analysis is a means of obtaining information for job descriptions about what needs to be accomplished by each job in terms of quality and quantity. Up-to-date job descriptions are essential not only for proper employee selection, appraisal, training, and development; wage and salary administration; and labor negotiations—but also for summarizing the human resources of a corporation in terms of employee-skill categories. Just as a corporation must know the number, type, and quality of its manufacturing facilities, it also must know the kinds of people its employs and the skills they possess. This knowledge is essential for the formulation and implementation of corporate strategy. The best strategies are meaningless if employees do not have the skills to carry them out or if jobs cannot be designed to accommodate the available workers.

Human resource departments have found that to reduce employee dissatisfaction and unionization efforts (or conversely, to improve employee satisfaction and existing union relations), they must consider the *quality of work life* (QWL). Partially a reaction to the traditionally heavy emphasis upon technical and economic factors in job design, QWL emphasizes the human dimension of work.[24] Corporations such as General Motors, General Foods, Procter and Gamble, Cummins Engine, and Shell Canada, Ltd., have been actively involved in improving QWL through extensive job and plant redesigning.[25] In general, quality of work life is "the degree to which members of a work organization are able to satisfy important personal needs through their experiences in the organization."[26] A high QWL is characterized by the following:[27]

☐ Adequate and fair compensation.

☐ A safe and healthful environment.

☐ The development of human potential through meaningful work.

☐ Growth and security in future job assignments.

☐ Social integration of the work force.

☐ Constitutionality (that is, ensuring that the worker is treated with dignity and that the worker's rights are respected).

☐ Absence of undue job stress.

☐ Social relevance of the organization and its products and services.

Because the quality of work life has an effect upon employee performance, satisfaction, and turnover, HRM has become increasingly concerned with *job design*. The design of a particular job is influenced by many factors, including technology, working conditions, unions, and managerial style (among others); and, as a result, many different techniques are used to improve job design. As depicted in Fig. 5.3, these techniques range from job engineering (scientific management) and goal setting (management by objectives) to job enlargement and enrichment.

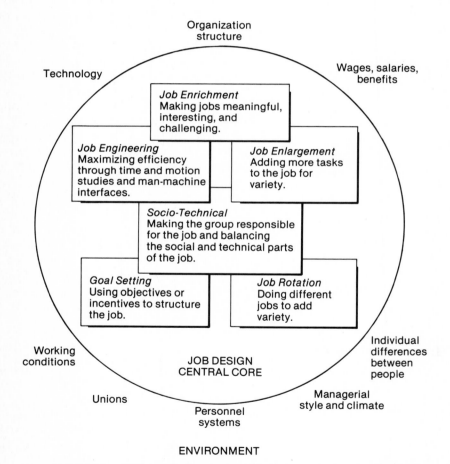

SOURCE: D. Hellriegel and J. Slocum, Jr. *Organizational Behavior* (St. Paul, Minn.: West Publishing Co., 1979), p. 432. Copyright © 1979 by West Publishing Company. All rights reserved. Reprinted by permission.

Figure 5.3   *The dimensions of job design.*

5.4 SUMMARY AND CONCLUSION

Before strategy formulation can begin, top management needs to assess its internal corporate environment for strengths and weaknesses. It must have an in-depth understanding of the internal strategic factors, such as the corporation's structure, culture, and resources.

A corporation's *structure* is its anatomy. It is often described graphically with an organization chart. Corporate structures range from the simple structure of an owner-manager operated business to the complex series of structures of a large conglomerate. If compatible with present and potential strategies, a corporation's structure is a great internal strength. Otherwise, it may be a serious weakness that will either prevent a good strategy from being implemented properly or reduce the number of strategic alternatives available to a firm.

A corporation's *culture* is the collection of beliefs, expectations, and values shared by its members. A culture produces norms that shape the behavior of employees. Top management must be aware of this culture and include it in its assessment of strategic factors. Those strategies that run counter to an established corporate culture are likely to be doomed by the poor motivation of the workforce. If a culture is antagonistic to a strategy change, the implementation plan will also have to include plans to change the culture.

A corporation's *resources* include not only such generally recognized assets as people, money, and facilities, but also those analytical concepts and procedural techniques known and in use within the functional areas. Since most top managers view their corporations in terms of functional activities, it is simplest to assess resource strengths and weaknesses by functional area. Each area should be audited in terms of financial, physical, and human resources, as well as its organization and technological competencies and capabilities. Just as the knowledge of key functional concepts and techniques is a corporate strength, its absence is a weakness.

DISCUSSION QUESTIONS

1. In what ways can a corporation's structure act as an internal strength or weakness to those formulating corporate strategies?
2. Why should top management be aware of a corporation's culture?
3. What kind of internal factors help determine whether a firm should emphasize the production and sales of a large number of low-priced products or a small number of high-priced products?
4. What is the difference between operating and financial leverage? What are their implications to strategic planning?
5. Why is technological competence important in strategy formulation?

NOTES

1. R. N. Osborn, J. G. Hunt, and L. R. Jauch, *Organization Theory: An Integrated Approach* (New York: John Wiley & Sons, 1980), p. 274.

2. R. H. Miles, *Macro Organizational Behavior* (Santa Monica, Calif.: Goodyear Publishing, 1980), pp. 28–34.

3. Osborn, Hunt, and Jauch, pp. 288–289.

4. Osborn, Hunt and Jauch, p. 293.

5. "Data General's Management Trouble," *Business Week* (February 9, 1981), pp. 59–61.

6. H. Schwartz and S. M. Davis, "Matching Corporate Culture and Business Strategy," *Organizational Dynamics* (Summer 1981), p. 30.

7. "Corporate Culture," *Business Week* (October 27, 1980), p. 148.

8. Schwartz and Davis, p. 36.

9. Schwartz and Davis, pp. 39–40.

10. W. H. Newman, "Shaping the Master Strategy of Your Firm," *California Management Review*, vol. 9, no. 3 (1967), p. 77.

11. P. Kotler, *Marketing Management*, 4th ed. (Englewood Cliffs, N.J.: Prentice-Hall, 1980), p. 22.

12. J. F. Weston and E. F. Brigham, *Managerial Finance*, 7th ed. (Hinsdale, Ill. Dryden Press, 1981), pp. 555-569.

13. M. A. Maidique and P. Patch, "Corporate Strategy and Technological Policy," (Boston: Intercollegiate Case Clearing House, no. 9-769-033, 1978, rev. March 1980), p. 3.

14. Y. N. Chang and F. Campo-Flores, *Business Policy and Strategy* (Santa Monica, Calif.: Goodyear Publishing, 1980), p. 294.

15. "Navy Scraps $6 Million Computer Systems Sailors Couldn't Operate," (Charlottesville, Va.) *Daily Progress* (April 22, 1981), p. B11.

16. E. S. Buffa, *Modern Production/Operations Management*, 6th ed. (New York: John Wiley & Sons, 1980), p. 487.

17. J. F. Weston and E. F. Brigham, *Managerial Finance*, 7th ed. (Hinsdale, Ill.: Dryden Press, 1981), p. 231.

18. E. S. Buffa, p. 48.

19. R. B. Chase and N. J. Aquilano, *Production and Operations Management*, rev. ed. (Homewood, Ill.: Richard D. Irwin, Inc., 1977), p. 526.

20. W. J. Fabrycky and P. E. Torgersen, *Operations Economy: Industrial Applications of Operations Research* (Englewood Cliffs, N.J.: Prentice-Hall, 1966), p. 100.

21. Chase and Aquilano, p. 526.

22. Chase and Aquilano, p. 531.

23. H. G. Heneman, D. P. Schwab, J. A. Fossum, and L. D. Dyer, *Personnel/Human Resource Management* (Homewood, Illinois: Richard D. Irwin, Inc., 1980), p. 7.

24. E. F. Huse, *Organization Development and Change*, 2nd ed. (St Paul, Minn.: West Publishing Co., 1980), p. 236.

25. Huse, pp. 237–244.

26. J. L. Suttle, "Improving Life at Work—Problems and Perspectives," *Improving Life at Work: Behavioral Science Approaches to Organizational Change*, eds. J. R. Hackman and J. L. Suttle (Santa Monica, Calif.: Goodyear Publishing, 1976), p. 4.

27. Huse, pp. 237–238.

STRATEGY FORMULATION

PART III

STRATEGIC MANAGEMENT MODEL

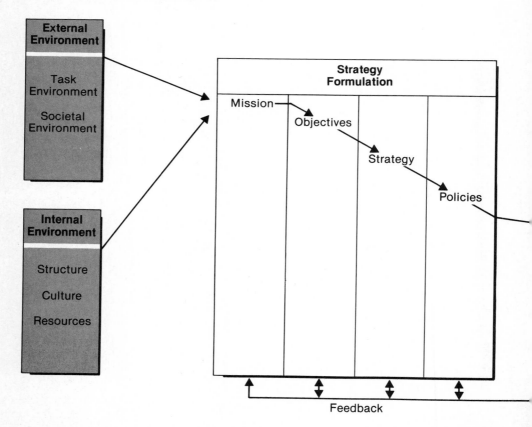

STRATEGY FORMULATION: SITUATION ANALYSIS

CHAPTER 6

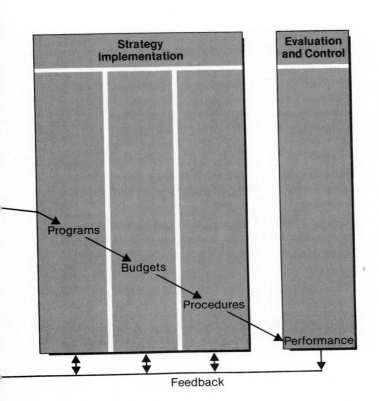

Strategy formulation is often referred to as strategic planning or long-range planning. Regardless of the term used, the process is primarily analytical, not action-oriented. The basic Strategic Management Model, shown first in Chapter 1, reflects the distinction between strategy formulation and strategy implementation. As shown in the model, the formulation process is concerned with developing a corporation's *mission, objectives, strategy*, and *policies*. In order to do this, corporate strategy makers must scan both the *external* and *internal environments* for needed information on strategic factors.

The Strategic Management Model does *not* show *how* the formulation process occurs. It merely describes the key *input variables* (internal and external environments) and the key *output factors* (mission, objectives, strategy, and policies). One purpose of Chapters 6 and 7, therefore, is to provide a more detailed discussion of the key activities in the process in order to supplement the Strategic Management Model.

In Chapter 2, a strategic decision-making process was introduced as a graphic representation of the strategic audit. It is also included in this chapter as Fig. 6.1.

The first six steps commonly found in strategy formulation are a series of interrelated activities:

1. *Evaluation* of (a) the corporation's current performance results in terms of return on investment, profitability, etc., and (b) the corporation's current mission, objectives, strategies, and policies.

2. *Examination* and *evaluation* of the corporation's strategic managers— board of directors and top management.

3. *Scanning* of the *external* environment to locate strategic opportunities and threats.

4. *Scanning* of the *internal* corporate environment to determine strategic strengths and weaknesses.

5. *Analysis* of the strategic factors (a) to pinpoint problem areas and (b) to review and revise the corporate mission and objectives as necessary.

6. *Generation, evaluation*, and *selection* of the best alternative strategy appropriate to the analysis conducted in step 5.

Situation analysis is the first part of the strategy formulation process. Beginning with an evaluation of current performance and ending with the review and possible revision of mission and objectives, the process includes steps one through five. These steps are discussed in this chapter. Step six, the generation, evaluation, and selection of the best alternative strategy, is discussed in chapter seven.

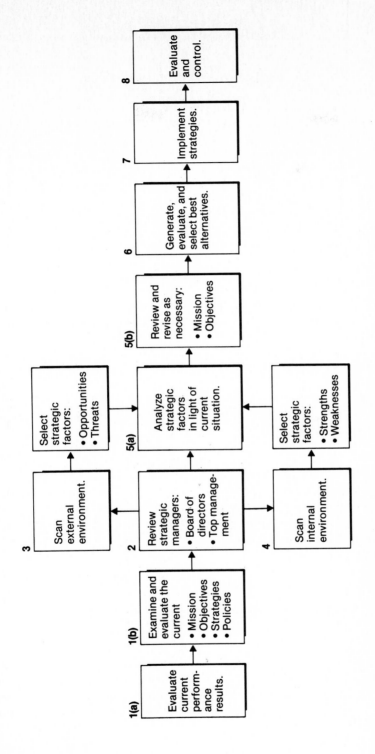

NOTE: Steps 1 through 6 are *strategy formulation*.
Step 7 is *strategy implementation*.
Step 8 is *evaluation and control*.

Figure 6.1 *Strategic decision-making process.*

6.1 EVALUATION OF
CURRENT RESULTS

After much research in the area, Henry Mintzberg found that strategy formulation is typically not a regular, continuous process: "It is most often an irregular, discontinuous process, proceeding in fits and starts. There are periods of stability in strategy development, but also there are periods of flux, of groping, of piecemeal change, and of global change."[1] This view of strategy formulation as an irregular process may be explained by the tendency of most people to continue on a particular course of action until something goes wrong. In a business corporation, the stimulus for a strategy review lies, in most instances, in current performance results.

Performance results are generally periodic measurements of developments that occur during a given time period. At the corporate level, for example, the board and top management would be most concerned with overall measurements such as return on investment (ROI), profits after taxes, and earnings per share. The measurements for the current year would be compared to similar measurements from previous years to see whether a trend exists. At the business or divisional level, the manager might be concerned with the return on division assets or the net contribution to corporate profits. At the functional level, various managers would be concerned with total sales and market share, plant efficiency, or number of new patents.

Current performance results are compared with current objectives (desired results). If the results are equal to or greater than current objectives, most strategic managers are likely to assume that current strategies and policies are appropriate, as is. In this instance, only incremental changes to present objectives and strategy are likely to be recommended. The strategy formulation process may thus end rather abruptly with a summary statement suggesting that the corporation continue doing what it's already doing—only do it a little better next year. This is basically what occurred at Coca Cola Company a few years ago. Hugh Schwarz, director of corporate planning for Coca Cola, stated

> If a person is happy with the present situation, he will not want to change. The very success of The Coca Cola Company works against its planning for change.[2]

If, however, the results of performance are less than what is desired, the formulation process begins in earnest. People at all levels are urged by the board and top management to question present objectives, strategies, and policies. Even the mission may be questioned. Are we aiming too high? Do our strategies make sense? Environmental scanning of both internal and external variables begins. What went wrong? Why? Questions such as these prompt top management to review the corporation's mission, objectives, strategies, and policies. As discussed in Illustrative Example 6.1, General Foods Corporation and Montgomery Ward and Company both use a deteriorating situation to stimulate a strategy review.

Evaluation of Mission

The breadth or narrowness of the corporate mission has an important effect upon performance. The definition of the corporate mission determines the broad limits of a company's growth.[3] For example, amusement parks traditionally defined themselves as in-place carnivals. Floundering in the 1950s, many went bankrupt. The success of Disneyland in the 1960s caused many parks such as Cedar Point, Inc. in Sandusky, Ohio to redefine themselves as "theme" parks with entertainment "packages" of shows, rides, and nationally known performers. With the aging of the American population, that mission is being further broadened to include a wider spectrum of entertainment.[4]

The concept of a corporate mission implies that throughout a corporation's many activities there should be a *common thread* or unifying theme, and that those corporations with such a common thread are better able to direct and administer their many activities.[5] In acquiring

Illustrative Example 6.1
EVALUATING CURRENT PERFORMANCE RESULTS: GENERAL FOODS AND MONTGOMERY WARD

GENERAL FOODS CORPORATION

James Ferguson, CEO of General Foods, noticed in 1981 increasing stagnation in several of General Foods' businesses, such as cereals and pet foods. Even though General Foods' earnings had been increasing at an average annual rate over the last five years of 17%, it had come at the expense of product innovation and diversification. The corporation generated only enough new products between 1974 and 1980 to add $375 million to revenues in the 1980–81 fiscal year. Executive vice-president Philip Smith commented, "Against a mass of $7 billion [estimated sales for the fiscal year ending March 31, 1981], $375 million is an inadequate addition." General Foods' top management reported that it wanted to make its businesses grow at a rate of two to three percent over time rather than the industry average of one percent per year. As a result, it began to develop a series of strategies focusing on diversification and growth.

(Continued)

MONTGOMERY WARD AND COMPANY

Since 1976, Montgomery Ward has been sliding downhill. Excluding stores in its discount division, it has slipped from having 432 stores in 1976 to 360 stores in 1981. It is not even represented in many metropolitan markets. Although 1980 sales totaled $5.5 billion, Ward reported losses of $210 million in the previous five quarters. Only interest-free loans of $355 million from Mobil Corporation, which owns Marcor Inc., has kept Wards solvent. "We need a refurbishing of our approach to the business," stated Charles Wagner, a recently retired Executive Vice-President.

Ward's new President, Stephen L. Pistner, must make Montgomery Ward profitable once again. To set the corporation on a new course, he initiated planning discussions to identify Ward's present and future niche in retailing. Pistner wants to create for Wards an entirely new kind of merchandising entity that will be successful throughout the coming decade.

SOURCES: "Changing the Culture at General Foods," *Business Week* (March 30, 1981), pp. 136–140. S. Weiner, "Much of Old Montgomery Ward May Go as Pistner Seeks Profitability, New Image," *Wall Street Journal* (June 15, 1981), p. 23.

new firms or in developing new products, such a corporation looks for "strategic fit," that is, the likelihood that new activities will mesh with present ones in such a way that the corporation's overall effectiveness and efficiency will be increased. There may be common distribution channels or similar customers, warehousing economies or the mutual use of R&D, better use of managerial talent or any of a number of possible synergistic effects.[6]

Evaluation of Objectives

As pointed out in Chapter 4, each group in a corporation's task environment will have its own way of measuring the corporation's performance. Stockholders may want dividends and price appreciation, whereas unions want good wages, stability of employment, and opportunities for advancement. Customers, distributors, creditors, suppliers, local communities, and other governments, to name only a few, have their own criteria to judge the corporation. The objectives and the priorities attached to them by the corporation are one way to recognize these outside forces and to deal with them in a logical fashion. Some of the possible objectives a corporation might pursue are the following:

☐ Profitability (Net profits)

☐ Efficiency (Low costs, etc.)

☐ Growth (Sales, size of facilities, etc.)

- ☐ Utilization of resources (ROE or ROI)
- ☐ Contributions to owners (Dividends)
- ☐ Contributions to customers (Quality/Price)
- ☐ Contributions to employees (Stability of employment)
- ☐ Contributions to society (Taxes paid, participation in charities)
- ☐ Market leadership (Market share)
- ☐ Technological leadership (Innovations)
- ☐ Survival (Avoiding bankruptcy)
- ☐ Personal needs of top management (Using the firm for personal purposes)

It is likely, however, that many small corporations have no formal objectives—simply vague, verbal ones. It is even more likely that even though a corporation has specified, written objectives, they will not be ranked on the basis of priority.

Evaluation of Strategies and Policies

Just as a number of firms have no formal objectives, many CEOs have "unstated, incremental, or intuitive strategies that have never been articulated or analyzed. . . ."[7] If pressured, these executives may state that they are following a certain strategy. This stated or "explicit" strategy is one with which few could quarrel, such as the development and acquisition of new product lines. Further investigation, however, may reveal the existence of a very different "implicit" strategy, such as the building of a large empire so that everyone will be impressed by the dynamic CEO! Often the only way to spot the implicit strategies of a corporation is to look not at what top management says, but at what it does. Implicit strategies can be derived from examining corporation policies, programs approved (and disapproved), and authorized budgets. Programs and divisions favored by budget increases and staffed by managers who are considered to be on the fast promotion track reveal where the corporation is putting its money and its energy.

It is, nevertheless, not always necessary for strategic planning to be a formal process for it to be effective. Small corporations, for example, may plan informally, yet continuously. The president and a handful of top managers may get together frequently to resolve strategic issues and plan their next steps. They need no formal, elaborate planning system, for "The number of key executives involved in such decisions is usually small, and they are located close enough for frequent, casual get-togethers."[8]

In large, multi-divisional corporations, however, the planning of strategy can become quite complex. A formalized system is needed to ensure that a hierarchy of objectives and strategy exists. Otherwise, top management becomes isolated from developments in the divisions and lower-level managers lose sight of the corporate mission.

6.2 EVALUATION OF STRATEGIC MANAGERS

As discussed in Chapter 3, the interaction of a corporation's board with its top management is likely to reflect one of four basic styles of strategic management: chaos, entrepreneurial, marionette, and partnership. Firms like Adolph Coors Company, Cannon Mills Company, and Tandy Corporation have for years been so dominated by their founders to the extent that their boards probably operated passively as an instrument of the founder. Once the founder dies and an outsider is brought in to head the firm, however, the board may take a more active role in representing the interests of the family. In such instances, the new CEO may be quite constrained by the board in terms of strategic options.

The strategic management style of such a corporation may thus change abruptly from entrepreneurial (where the founder dominates the board) to marionette management (where the board, made up of the founder's family and friends, dominates top management and makes the significant decisions).

In many instances where the board is only moderately involved in strategic management, the CEO has a free hand to set the direction of the corporation. Then the success or failure of a corporation's strategy must be evaluated in light of the CEO's managerial style. For example, Robert Wilson, past CEO at Memorex Corporation, had a reputation of being a cost-cutter with a "heavy-handed management style." He tended to emphasize short-term payoffs.[9] In contrast, Stephen Pistner, who took over the job of President of Montgomery Ward in 1981, had a reputation of being a strategic planner who "drives right for the meat of a situation" and builds strong management teams.[10] The management style of Edson De Castro, president of Data General, is reported to have a strong effect on the firm's strategic management. His keeping of most of the strategic decision making authority to himself enabled the corporation to succeed as a small firm by reacting quickly to new technology and shifts in market. As Data General grew larger, however, De Castro became a bottleneck by continuing to require that pricing, marketing, and hiring decisions receive his approval before being carried out.[11]

Henry Mintzberg has pointed out that a corporation's objectives and strategies are strongly affected by top management's view of the world.[12] This view determines the approach or "mode" to be used in strategy formulation. He names three basic modes: entrepreneurial, adaptive, and planning.

□ *Entrepreneurial mode.* Strategy makers focus on opportunities. Problems are secondary. Strategy is guided by the founder's own vision of direction and is exemplified by large, bold decisions. The dominant goal is growth of the corporation.

□ *Adaptive mode.* Sometimes referred to as "muddling through," this strategy-formulation mode is characterized by reactive solutions to existing problems, rather than a proactive search for new opportunities. Much bargaining goes on concerning priorities of objectives. Strategy is fragmented and is developed to move the corporation forward in incremental steps.

□ *Planning mode.* Analysts assume major responsibilities for strategy formulation. Strategic planning includes both the proactive search for new opportunities and the reactive solution of existing problems. Systematic comprehensive analysis is used to develop strategies that integrate the corporation's decision making processes.

In the *entrepreneurial* mode, top management believes that the environment is a force to be used and controlled. In the *adaptive* mode, it assumes the environment is too complex to be completely comprehended. In the *planning* mode, it works on the assumption that systematic scanning and analysis of the environment can provide the knowledge necessary to influence the environment to the corporation's advantage. The specific planning mode used reflects top management's perception of the corporation's environment. If we categorize a corporation's top management according to one of these three planning modes, we can better understand how and why key decisions are made. Then if we look at these decisions in light of the corporation's mission, objectives, strategies, and policies, we can then determine whether the dominant planning mode is appropriate.

In addition, strategy-making modes may change as a corporation increases in size and complexity, or changes top management personnel. Tandy Corporation, for example, has changed from the entrepreneurial mode characteristic of the reign of its founder Charles Tandy to the more adaptive mode under his successor, Phil North. If Tandy Corporation continues to be successful, North's successor may move toward a more planning-oriented mode.[13]

6.3 SCANNING THE EXTERNAL ENVIRONMENT

At the point in the strategy formulation process where the external environment is scanned, strategic managers must examine both the societal and task environments for those strategic factors that are likely to strongly influence their corporation's success—factors that are, in other words, opportunities and threats. Long-run developments in the economic, technological, political-legal, and socio-cultural aspects of the societal environment tend to strongly affect a corporation's activities by asserting more immediate pressures on the corporation's task environment. Such societal issues as consumerism, governmental regulations, environmental pollution, energy cost and availability, inflation-fed wage demands, and heavy foreign competition tend to emerge from groups in the firm's task environment.

The important point to remember at this stage of strategy formulation is that managers should closely monitor only those factors that might have strategic relevance to the corporation.

> When firms attempt to collect and assimilate voluminous amounts of data, they may experience information overload, become bogged down in detail, and fail to see the forest for the trees. They fail to identify and address many critical strategic issues that significantly affect their performance, responding instead to much irrelevant stimuli. This results in an inappropriate allocation of the firm's finite resources.[14]

Some of the most important variables to monitor in a corporation's societal environment were listed in Fig. 4.2. These ranged from life-style changes to GNP trends, to federal support of R&D, to local tax laws.

One attempt to pinpoint the relevant strategic factors in a corporation's task environment was made by the PIMS (Profit Impact of Market Strategy) Program of the Strategic Planning Institute. This research program, which surveyed many corporations between 1971 and 1975, revealed that twenty-eight factors explained about 75% of the ROI variations among the businesses.[15] The PIMS Program, therefore, defined key strategic factors as "those descriptors of a business' strategic position which have exhibited a consistent and strong relationship with return on investment over a wide range of business samples and time periods."[16] The twenty-eight factors are placed in five categories: attractiveness of environment, competitive position, differentiation from competitors, effectiveness of investment use, and discretionary budget expenditures.[17] The PIMS Program thus combined strategic factors from both the internal and external environments. A limitation of PIMS, however, is that its conclusions do not necessarily apply to all corporations and all situations. For example, PIMS concludes that the combination of high marketing and high R&D expenditures depresses a corporation's ROI, but this has not been true of Hewlett-Packard.

6.4 SCANNING THE INTERNAL ENVIRONMENT

Before top management can properly address what possible future strategies are appropriate for the corporation, it must assess its own internal situation—the environment within the firm itself. Strategic decisions should not be made until top management understands the strengths and weaknesses in the division and functional areas. Examples of two corporations in which internal weaknesses have seriously hurt the implementation of reasonable strategies are given in Illustrative Example 6.2.

Key internal variables that affect strategy formulation are the corporation's structure, culture, and resources. These were discussed in detail in Chapter 5.

6.5 ANALYSIS OF STRATEGIC FACTORS

The analysis of the strategic factors in the strategic decision making process calls for an integration and evaluation of data collected earlier from the scanning of the internal and external environments. External strategic factors are those opportunities and threats found in the present and future task and societal environments. Internal strategic factors are those important strengths and weaknesses within the corporation's divisional and functional areas. Step 5(a) in Fig. 6.1 requires that top management attempt to find a "strategic fit" between external opportunities and internal strengths.

Illustrative Example 6.2
INTERNAL WEAKNESSES AFFECT STRATEGIC MANAGEMENT AT RAMADA INNS AND COORS

RAMADA INNS CORPORATION

In December 1979, Ramada acquired the Las Vegas Tropicana, a hotel-casino. Soon thereafter, it began construction of what was planned to be the most luxurious casino in Atlantic City. Up to this time Ramada had had very little experience in running a gambling operation. Consequently it retained many of the Las Vegas casino employees hired by previous management. Soon, however, it learned that the poor profit performance of its Las Vegas operation during 1980 and 1981 was a result of more than $30 million in alleged thefts by employees and uncollectable accounts receivable. A New Jersey gambling official stated that these problems "indicate a question of management ability" to run a gambling operation and could seriously effect Ramada's request for a gambling license for its Atlantic City casino.

(Continued)

ADOLPH COORS COMPANY

In 1978, Coors planned an expensive marketing program designed to stop competitors from encroaching on its territory and to expand Coors nationally. Three years later, however, Coors was still having problems keeping its territory. Its market share in California, for example, dropped from 35.8% in 1976 to 22.5% in 1980. Net income in 1980 dropped 70% on a 2% rise in volume. It continued to drop in the first quarter of 1981. Industry observers believe that Coors's difficulties stem from serious conflicts within the marketing department regarding the allocation of advertising money. In addition, top management cannot agree on marketing strategy. "The problem with these guys is that they still don't have their act together," says Robert S. Weinberg, president of R. S. Weinberg and Associates, a St. Louis–based brewing industry consulting firm. In commenting on Coors's planned brewery in Virginia, Weinberg states, "it would be walking into a hornet's nest when its own backyard isn't in order."

SOURCES: J. Drinkhall and J. Andrew, "Ramada Inns' Gambling Operations Beset by Thefts and Mounting Costs," *Wall Street Journal* (August 18, 1981), pp. 17 and 21. L. Schuster, "Internal Conflicts Inhibiting Coors Move to the Big Time," *Wall Street Journal* (July 10, 1981), pp. 29 and 38.

Finding a Niche

William Newman suggests that a corporation should seek to obtain a "propitious niche" in its strategy formulation process.[18] This niche is a corporation's specific competitive role. It should be so well-suited to the firm's internal and external environment that other corporations are not likely to challenge or dislodge it.

The Ramada Inns Corporation, presented in Illustrative Example 6.2, is an example of a firm that failed to note that its lack of managerial expertise in running a gambling operation constituted a strategic internal weakness. Because of this weakness, it was unable to exploit an environmental opportunity, and the niche was filled by established Las Vegas casinos, which were easily able to transfer their corporate skills to Atlantic City. Procter and Gamble, in contrast, appears to be attempting to apply its internal strengths in marketing and in "desorbate technology" to the slightly declining fruit juice market (see Illustrative Example 6.3). It may be hoping to find in the present market a propitious niche that will grow quickly in the near future and transform the entire market, much as it did with Crest toothpaste and "fluoride technology" in the 1960s.

Portfolio Analysis

The business portfolio is the most recommended approach to aid the integration and evaluation of environmental data. All corporations, except the simplest and smallest, are involved in more than one business. Even

Illustrative Example 6.3 _____
PROCTER AND GAMBLE LOOKS FOR ITS NICHE IN FRUIT JUICES

In 1981, Procter and Gamble purchased the citrus processing business of Ben Hill Griffin, Inc., a family-owned company based in Frostproof, Florida. This appeared to be an extension of P&G's August 1980 acquisition of the non-Canadian soft drink business of Crush International, Ltd. Although the fruit-juice market is relatively static in sales, analysts believe that P&G may be thinking of applying its new "desorbate technology" to the juice business. This technology is a process patented by P&G that allows the extraction of more of a fruit's natural flavor.

SOURCE: M. Yao, "P&G Is Buying Ben Hill Griffin Citrus Business," *Wall Street Journal* (August 19, 1981), p. 5.

though a corporation sells only one product, it may benefit from handling separately a number of distinct product-market segments. Procter and Gamble, for example, managed Prell Liquid and Prell Concentrate as two separate brands for a number of years because of their appeal to two separate and distinct market segments.

Portfolio analysis recommends that each product, strategic business unit (SBU), or division be considered separately for purposes of strategy formulation.[19] The determination of a multi-industry or multi-product corporation's current portfolio involves five sequential activities.[20]

1. Selection of the appropriate portfolio matrix.
There are a number of matrixes available to reflect the variables under consideration in a portfolio. SBUs or products can be compared for growth rate in sales, relative competitive position, stage of product/market evolution, market share, and industry attractiveness. The simplest such matrix is the four-cell square developed by the *Boston Consulting Group* as depicted in Fig. 6.2.

Each of the corporation's SBUs or products is plotted on the matrix according to both the growth rate of the industry in which it competes and its relative market share. A corporation's relative competitive position is defined as its market share in the industry divided by that of the largest other competitor. The line separating areas of high and low relative competitive position is set at 1.5 times. Relative strengths of this magnitude are needed to ensure the dominant position needed to be a star or cash-cow. On the other hand, a product or SBU should be 1 times or less to

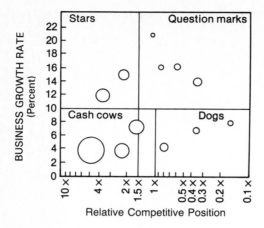

SOURCE: B. Hedley, "Strategy and the Business Portfolio," *Long Range Planning* (February 1977), p. 12. Reprinted by permission.

Figure 6.2   *The BCG portfolio matrix.*

ensure its dog status.[21] The business growth rate is the percentage of market growth—that is, the percentage of increased sales of a particular product or SBU classification of products. Each product or SBU is represented in Fig. 6.2 by a circle. The area of the circle represents the relative significance of each SBU or product to the corporation in terms of assets used or sales generated.

Once a corporation's current position has been plotted on a matrix, a projection can be made of its future position, assuming no changes in strategy. Present and projected matrixes can thus be used to assist in the identification of major strategic issues facing the corporation.

> Ideally, one would hope that the company in Figure [6.2] would develop along the following lines. For the *stars*, the key objectives should be the maintenance of market share; current profitability should be accorded a lower priority. For the *cash cows*, however, current profitability may well be the primary goal. *Dogs* would not be expected to be as profitable as the *cash cows*, but would be expected to yield cash. Some *question marks* would be set objectives in terms of increased market share; others, where gaining dominance appeared too costly, would be managed instead for cash.[22]

The use of BCG-type portfolios has been criticized for a number of reasons:

□ The use of highs and lows is too simplistic. Middle positions are needed.

□ Growth rate is only one aspect of industry attractiveness.

□ Market share is only one aspect of overall competitive position.[23]

A more complicated matrix is that developed by General Electric (see Fig. 6.3). It includes nine cells based on long-term industry attractiveness and business strength/competitive position. Referred to as the *GE Business Screen*, the two variables include much more data than do the two

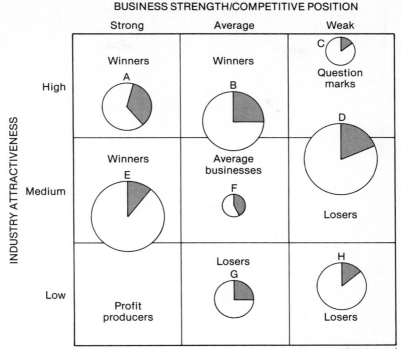

BUSINESS STRENGTH/COMPETITIVE POSITION

SOURCES: Adapted by permission from *Strategic Management in GE*, Corporate Planning and Development, General Electric Corporation; also adapted from C. W. Hofer and D. Schendel, *Strategy Formulation: Analytical Concepts* (St. Paul, Minn.: West Publishing Co., 1978), p. 83. Copyright © 1978 by West Publishing Company. All rights reserved.

Figure 6.3 *General Electric's business screen.*

variables in the BCG matrix. For example, at GE, industry attractiveness is defined as a composite projection of—among other characteristics— market size, market growth rate, competitive diversity, competitive structure, and profitability.[24] Business strengths or competitive position can be a combination of, among others, market share, profitability, technological position, image in marketplace, and calibre of management. As with the BCG matrix, the individual products or SBUs are plotted on the GE Screen. The area of the circles is in proportion to the size of the industry. The pie slices within the circles depict the market share of each product or SBU.[25]

As depicted in Fig. 6.3, each product or SBU is identified by a letter. As with the BCG matrix, the corporation's present and future positions can be plotted and used to identify some strategic issues facing the firm. One shortcoming of GE's Business Screen is that it cannot effectively depict the positions of new products or SBUs in new industries.

In response to this limitation, Hofer developed a fifteen-cell matrix called the *Product/Market Evolution Portfolio Matrix*. Products or SBUs

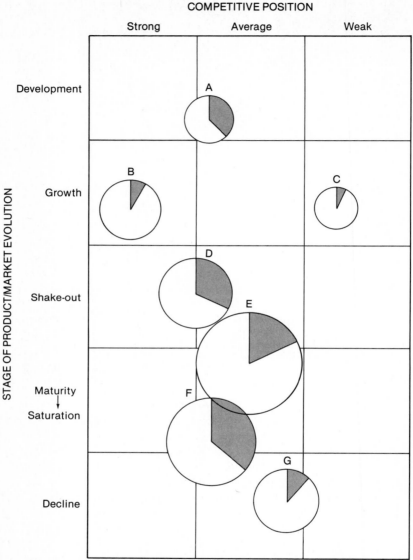

SOURCES: C. W. Hofer and D. Schendel, *Strategy Formulation: Analytical Concepts* (St. Paul, Minn.: West Publishing Co., 1978), p. 34. From C. W. Hofer, "Conceptual Constructs for Formulating Corporate and Business Strategies," (Boston: Intercollegiate Case Clearing House, no. 9-378-754, 1977), p. 3. Copyright © 1977 by Charles W. Hofer. Reprinted by permission.

Figure 6.4   *Product/market evolution portfolio matrix.*

are plotted in terms of their competitive positions and their stages of product/market evolution. As with the GE Business Screen, the circles represent the sizes of the industries involved with the pie wedges representing the market shares of the firm's SBUs or products. Present and future matrixes can be developed to identify strategic issues. In Fig. 6.4, for example, one could ask why product or SBU B does not have a greater share of the market given its strong competitive position.[26]

Of the three portfolio matrixes depicted in Figs. 6.2 (Boston Consulting Group), 6.3 (General Electric Business Screen), and 6.4 (Product/Market Evolution), one should be selected for use throughout the portfolio analysis of a corporation or SBU. For the purposes of this chapter, we will assume that the analysis is of a large multi-industry corporation with several loosely related SBUs. In this instance, the GE-type business screen will be most useful.

2. *Assessment of industry attractiveness.* The assessment of an industry by a corporation's management involves four steps:

a) Select general criteria to rate the industry. These criteria should be key aspects of the industry, such as its potential for sales growth and likely profitability. Table 6.1 lists fifteen criteria for one specific industry.

b) Weight each criterion according to management's perception of the criterion's importance to achieving corporate objectives. For example, because the key criterion of the corporation in Table 6.1 is profitability, it receives the highest weight, 0.20.

c) Rate the industry on each of these criteria from 1 (very unattractive) to 5 (very attractive). For example, if an industry is facing a long-term decline in profitability, this criterion should be rated 2 or less.

d) Multiply the weight for each criterion by its rating to get a weighted score. These scores are then added to get the weighted score for the industry as a whole.

3. *Assessment of business strength/competitive position.* The assessment of an SBU's business strength or competitive position also involves four steps:

a) Identify the SBU's key factors for success in the industry. Table 6.2 lists seventeen such factors for a specific industry.

b) Weight each success factor (market share, for instance) in terms of its relative importance to profitability or some other measure of success within the industry. For example, since market share was believed to have a relatively small impact on most firms in the industry of Table 6.2, this success factor was given a weight of only 0.10.

c) Rate the SBU on each of the factors from 1 (very weak competitive position) to 5 (very strong competitive position). For example, as the products of the SBU of Table 6.2 have very high market share, it received a rating of 5.

**Table 6.1   AN EXAMPLE OF AN
INDUSTRY ATTRACTIVENESS
ASSESSMENT MATRIX**

ATTRACTIVENESS CRITERIA	WEIGHT*	RATING**	WEIGHTED SCORE
Size	0.15	4	0.60
Growth	0.12	3	0.36
Pricing	0.05	3	0.15
Market diversity	0.05	2	0.10
Competitive structure	0.05	3	0.15
Industry profitability	0.20	3	0.60
Technical role	0.05	4	0.20
Inflation vulnerability	0.05	2	0.10
Cyclicality	0.05	2	0.10
Customer financials	0.10	5	0.50
Energy impact	0.08	4	0.32
Social	GO	4	—
Environmental	GO	4	—
Legal	GO	4	—
Human	0.05	4	.20
	1.00		3.38

*Some criteria may be of a GO/NO GO type. For example, many *Fortune 500* firms probably would decide not to invest in industries that are viewed negatively by our society, such as gambling, even if it were both legal and very profitable to do so.
**1 (very unattractive) through 5 (highly attractive).
SOURCE: C. W. Hofer and D. Schendel, *Strategy Formulation: Analytical Concepts* (St. Paul, Minn.: West Publishing Co., 1978), p. 73. Copyright © 1978 by West Publishing Company. All rights reserved. Reprinted by permission.

d) Multiply the weight of each factor by its rating to get a weighted score. These scores are then added to provide a weighted score for the SBU as a whole.

4. *Plotting a corporation's current portfolio position.* Once industry attractiveness and business strengths are calculated for each SBU, the SBUs should be plotted on a matrix like the one illustrated in Fig. 6.3. This matrix will show the corporation's current portfolio situation. This situation can be then contrasted with an ideal portfolio. Figure 6.5 depicts what Hofer and Schendel consider to be such a portfolio. It is considered ideal because it includes primarily winners, with enough winners and profit producers to finance the growth of developing (or potential) winners. In reality, however, even a successful firm would probably have a few question marks and perhaps a small loser.

Table 6.2   AN EXAMPLE OF A BUSINESS STRENGTH/ COMPETITIVE POSITION ASSESSMENT MATRIX FOR AN SBU

KEY SUCCESS FACTORS	WEIGHT	RATING**	WEIGHTED SCORE
Market share	0.10	5	.50
SBU growth rate	X*	3	—
Breadth of product line	.05	4	.20
Sales distribution effectiveness	.20	4	.80
Proprietary and key account advantages	X	3	—
Price competitiveness	X	4	—
Advertising and promotion effectiveness	.05	4	.20
Facilities location and newness	.05	5	.25
Capacity and productivity	X	3	—
Experience curve effects	.15	4	.60
Raw materials cost	.05	4	.20
Value added	X	4	—
Relative product quality	.15	4	.60
R&D advantages/position	.05	4	.20
Cash throw-off	.10	5	.50
Caliber of personnel	X	4	—
General image	.05	5	.25
	1.00		4.30

*For any particular industry, there will be some factors that, while important in general, will have little or no effect on the relative competitive position of firms within that industry. It is usually better to drop such factors from the analysis than to assign them very low weights.

**1 (very weak competitive position) through 5 (very strong competitive position).

SOURCE: C. W. Hofer and D. Schendel, *Strategy Formulation: Analytical Concepts* (St. Paul, Minn.: West Publishing Co., 1978), p. 76. Copyright © 1978 by West Publishing Company. All rights reserved. Reprinted by permission.

5. Plotting the firm's future portfolio position. An assessment of the current situation is complete only when the present portfolio is projected into the future. Assuming the present corporate and SBU strategies continue unchanged, top management should assess the probable impact likely changes to the corporation's task and societal environments will have on both future industry attractiveness and SBU competitive position. They should ask themselves, do future matrixes show an improving or deteriorating portfolio position? Is there a performance gap between projected and desired portfolios? If the answers are yes, there is a *strategic gap* that should be the stimulus to review the corporation's current mission, objectives, strategies, and policies.

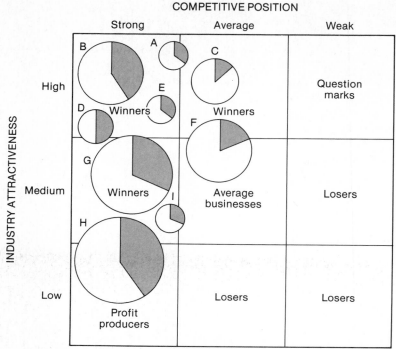

SOURCES: C. W. Hofer and D. Schendel, *Strategy Formulation: Analytical Concepts* (St. Paul, Minn.: West Publishing Co., 1978), p. 83. Copyright © 1978 by West Publishing Company. All rights reserved. Reprinted by permission.

Figure 6.5   *An ideal multi-industry corporate portfolio**

6.6 REVIEW OF MISSION AND OBJECTIVES

A reexamination of a corporation's current mission and objectives must be done before alternative strategies can be generated and evaluated. The seriousness of this step is emphasized by Tregoe and Zimmerman.

> When making a decision, there is an almost universal tendency to concentrate on the alternatives—the action possibilities—rather than on the objectives we want to achieve. This tendency is widespread because it is much easier to deal with alternative courses of action that exist right here and now than

---

*It is impossible to identify the orientation (i.e., growth, profit, or balance) of an ideal portfolio based solely on the information contained in the GE business screen, because the screen does not reflect all the information needed to do so. For instance, SBUs B, C, F, G, and H could be developing winners in very large markets or established winners in smaller markets. Likewise, SBUs A, D, E, and I could represent either developing potential winners in large markets or established winners in small markets. In the majority of instances, however, the pattern of SBU sizes and postions depicted in this figure would correspond to a balanced, ideal portfolio.

to really think about what we want to accomplish in the future. Projecting a set of values forward is hard work. The end result is that we make choices that set our objectives for us, rather than having our choices incorporate clear objectives.[27]

Problems in corporate performance may derive from an inappropriate statement of mission, which may be too narrow or too broad. If the mission does not provide a common thread for a corporation's businesses, managers may be unclear about where the corporation is heading. Objectives and strategies may be in conflict with each other. Divisions may be competing against one another, rather than against outside competition—to the detriment of the corporation as a whole. According to Lorange, "Rapid changes in the environment suggest that the definition of businesses should be reviewed frequently, so that the relevance of the business definitions can be maintained."[28]

An example of a recent revision of a corporation's mission statement is that by American Telephone and Telegraph (AT&T). The revised mission was published in AT&T's 1980 annual report to stockholders and has important implications for future corporate strategy:

> No longer do we perceive that our business will be limited to telephony or, for that matter, telecommunications. Ours is the business of information handling, the knowledge business. And the market that we seek is global.

A corporation's objectives may also be inappropriately stated. They may either focus too much on short-term operational goals or be so general that they provide little real guidance. Consequently, objectives should be constantly reviewed to ensure their usefulness.

6.7 SUMMARY AND CONCLUSION

This chapter describes the key activities involved in the process of formulating strategy. Following the strategic decision making process introduced in Chapter 2, formulation is described as being composed of six distinct steps. Situation analysis incorporates five steps beginning with the evaluation of current performance results and ending with the review and revision of mission and objectives. Step six—the generation, evaluation, and selection of the best alternative strategy—is discussed in the next chapter.

Step 1—the evaluation of current performance results and the review of the corporation's mission, objectives, strategies, and policies—deals with the initial stimulus to start the formulation process. *Step 2*, the review of strategic managers, includes an evaluation of the competencies, level of involvement, and performance of the corporation's top management and board of directors. *Step 3*, scanning the external environment, focuses on collecting information, selecting strategic factors, and forecasting future events likely to affect the corporation's strategic decisions. *Step 4*, scanning the internal environment, deals with the assessment of internal strengths and weaknesses in terms of structure, culture, and resources. *Step 5(a)*, analysis of strategic factors in light of the current situation, proposes portfolio analysis as a technique to locate a business' propitious niche. Matrixes developed by the Boston Consulting Group, General Electric, and Hofer, are described as three ways to compare business strengths with industry attractiveness. *Step 5(b)*, review and revision of the mission and objectives, completes the situation analysis by forcing a strategic manager to reexamine corporate purpose and objectives before initiating alternative strategies.

DISCUSSION QUESTIONS

1. Does strategy formulation need to be a regular continuous process? Explain.
2. Is it necessary that a corporation have a "common thread" running through its many activities in order to be successful? Why or why not?
3. What set of objectives might a typical university have?
4. What is likely to happen to an SBU that loses its propitious niche?
5. What value has portfolio analysis in the consideration of strategic factors?

NOTES

1. H. Mintzberg, "Planning on the Left Side and Managing on the Right," *Harvard Business Review* (July–August 1976), p. 56.
2. P. Lorange, *Implementation of Strategic Planning* (Englewood Cliffs, N.J.: Prentice-Hall, 1982), p. 130.
3. B. E. Gup, *Guide to Strategic Planning* (New York: McGraw-Hill, 1980), p. 12.
4. M. D. Frank, "Amusement Parks Ease Off Thrill Ride Image As Boom Slows," (Charlottesville, Va.) *Daily Progress* (June 28, 1981), p. E5.
5. H. I. Ansoff, *Corporate Strategy* (New York: McGraw-Hill, 1965), pp. 104–108.
6. A. A. Thompson and A. J. Strickland, *Strategy and Policy*, rev. ed. (Plano, Texas: Business Publications, 1981), p. 37.
7. K. R. Andrews, "Directors' Responsibility for Corporate Strategy," *Harvard Business Review* (November–December 1980), p. 30.
8. F. R. Vancil and P. Lorange, "Strategic Planning in Diversified Companies," *Harvard Business Review* (January–February 1975), p. 81.
9. "Memorex Tries a Turnaround Again," *Business Week* (January 19, 1981), pp. 78–83.

10. S. Weiner, "Much of Old Montgomery Ward May Go As Pistner Seeks Profitability, New Image," *Wall Street Journal* (June 15, 1981), p. 23.

11. "Data General's Management Trouble," *Business Week* (February 9, 1981), pp. 59–61.

12. H. Mintzberg, "Strategy-Making in Three Modes," *California Management Review* (Winter 1973), pp. 44–53.

13. J. Kirkpatrick, "Tandy Corp. Survives Loss of Legendary Entrepreneur," (Charlottesville, Va.) *Daily Progress* (July 8, 1981), p. B14.

14. N. H. Snyder, "Environmental Volatility, Scanning Intensity and Organization Performance," *Journal of Contemporary Business* (September 1981), p. 15.

15. B. T. Gale, D. F. Heany, and D. J. Swire, *The Par ROI Report: Explanation and Commentary on Report* (Cambridge, Mass.: Strategic Planning Institute, 1977), p. iii.

16. Gale, Heany, and Swire, p. 6.

17. Gale, Heany, and Swire, p. 9.

18. W. H. Newman, "Shaping the Master Strategy of Your Firm," *California Management Review*, vol. 9, no. 3 (1967), pp. 77–88.

19. B. Hedley, "Strategy and the Business Portfolio," *Long Range Planning* (February 1977), p. 9.

20. Much of this discussion is adapted from C. W. Hofer and D. Schendel, *Strategy Formulation: Analytical Concepts* (St. Paul: West Publishing Co., 1978), pp. 30–34 and 71–81.

21. Hedley, pp. 12–13.

22. Hedley, p. 13.

23. Hofer and Schendel, pp. 31–32.

24. W. K. Hall, "SBUs: Hot, New Topic in the Management of Diversification," *Business Horizons* (February 1978), p. 20.

25. Hofer and Schendel, pp. 32–33.

26. Hofer and Schendel, pp. 33–34.

27. B. B. Tregoe and J. W. Zimmerman, "The New Strategic Manager," *Business* (May–June 1981), p. 19.

28. Lorange, p. 211.

STRATEGIC MANAGEMENT MODEL

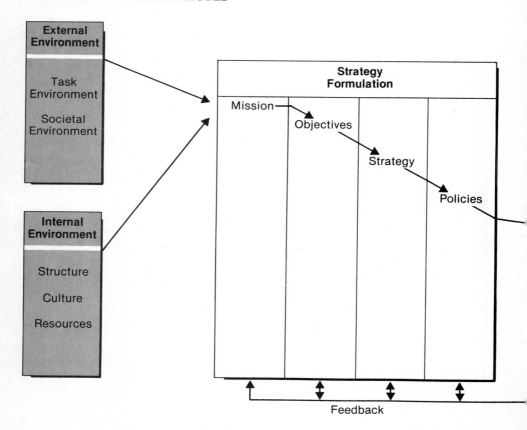

STRATEGY FORMULATION: STRATEGIC ALTERNATIVES

CHAPTER 7

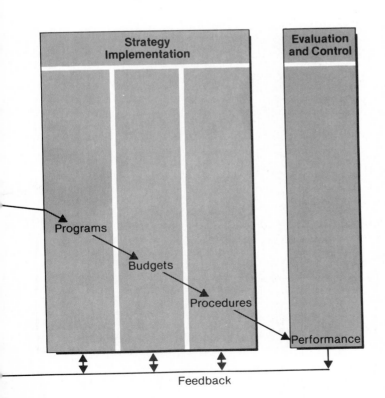

A key part of strategy formulation is the development of alternative courses of action that specify means by which the corporate mission and objectives are to be accomplished. As was explained in Chapter 6 and depicted in Fig. 6.1, the generation, evaluation, and selection of an appropriate strategic alternative is the sixth step of the strategic decision making process. Once the best strategy is selected, appropriate policies must be established to define the ground rules for implementation. The purposes of this chapter, therefore, are (a) to explain the many alternative strategies available at the corporate, divisional, and functional levels of the corporation; (b) to suggest criteria to use in the evaluation of these strategies; (c) to explain how an optimal strategy is selected; and (d) to suggest how strategy is translated into policies.

7.1 ALTERNATIVE STRATEGIES

There is no one set of strategies that can be used at all levels of a corporation. Most likely, a company will need to have both corporate and functional-level strategies. If it is in many different industries, the corporation will also have to develop divisional or SBU strategies for its families of related products or businesses.

Corporate Strategies

Prefaced by the broad question, "What should our corporation be like in the future?" the following are questions that top management should ask itself in order to develop strategic alternatives:[1]

1. Should we stay in the same business(es)?
2. Should we leave this business entirely or just some parts of it by merging, liquidating, and/or selling part of our corporation?
3. Should we become more efficient or effective in the business(es) we are presently in?
4. Should we try to grow in this business by (a) increasing our present size and market or (b) acquiring corporations in similar businesses?
5. Should we try to grow primarily by expanding into other businesses?
6. Should we use different strategies in different parts of the corporation?

If question 1 is answered yes, top management will probably choose a *stability* strategy. If question 2 or 3 is yes, *retrenchment* is a likely strategy. If either question 4 or 5 is yes, a *growth* strategy is appropriate. If question 6 is yes, top management should adopt a *combination* of strategies.

An analysis by Glueck of the strategic choices of 358 executives over a period of 45 years found the following frequency of usage of the four overall strategies:[2]

Stability: 9.2%
Growth: 54.4%
Retrenchment: 7.5%
Combination: 28.7%

Stability strategies. The "stability" family of strategies is appropriate for a successful corporation operating in a reasonably predictable environment. Epitomized by a steady-as-she-goes philosophy, these strategies involve no major changes. A corporation concentrates its resources on its present businesses in order to build upon and improve its competitive advantage. It retains the same mission and similar objectives; it simply increases its level of achievement by approximately the same percentage each year. Its main strategic decisions concern improving the performance of functional areas. Some stability strategies are as follows:

No-change strategy. A corporation continues on its course only with an adjustment for inflation in its objectives. Rarely articulated as a definite strategy, the success of a no-change strategy depends on a lack of change in a corporation's internal or external environments. This strategy may evolve from a lack of interest in or need to engage in hard strategic analysis. After all, if everything is going along fine, why change anything?

Profit strategy. The profit strategy involves the sacrifice of future growth for present profits. The result is often short-term success coupled to long-term stagnation. By reducing expenditures for R&D, maintenance, or advertising, short-term profits increase and are reflected in the stockholders' dividends. If a corporation has a number of "cash cow" divisions, they can be "milked" of more cash than they spend. George Allen made this strategy famous in the National Football League during the 1970s with his slogan, "The future is now!" By trading off future draft choices in return for over-the-hill players who he hoped could get the Washington Redskins into the next year's Super Bowl, he, in effect, robbed Peter to pay Paul.

Pause strategy. After a period of prolonged fast growth, a corporation may become inefficient or unmanageable. The adding of new divisions through acquisition or internal development can stretch management and resources thin. A pause strategy involves reducing the levels of a corporation's objectives so that it is able to consolidate its resources. This strategy is generally thought of as temporary—a way to get a corporate house in order. For example, after acquiring more than 150 companies and selling off about 75 of them since 1952, W. R. Grace and Company turned to consolidating organizationally its myriad holdings in chemicals, natural resources, and consumer goods.[3]

Proceed-with-caution strategy. This strategy results from a specific decision to proceed slowly because of important factors developing in the external environment. Top management may feel that a growth strategy is no longer feasible given, for instance, a sudden scarcity of needed raw materials, new governmental regulations, or a poor economic climate.

Growth strategies.   These strategies are extremely popular because most executives tend to equate growth with success. Those corporations that are in dynamic environments *must* grow in order to survive. Growth means greater sales and a chance to take advantage of the learning curve to reduce the per unit cost of products sold, thereby increasing profits. This becomes extremely important if a corporation's industry is growing quickly and competitors are engaging in price wars in order to gain larger shares of the market. Those firms that have not reached "critical mass" (that is, gained the necessary economy of large-scale production) will face large losses unless they can find and fill a small, but profitable niche.

Growth is a very seductive strategy for two key reasons:

□ A growing firm can cover up mistakes and inefficiencies more easily than can a stable one. A growing flow of revenue into a highly leveraged corporation can create a large amount of "organization slack"[4] (unused resources) that can be used to quickly resolve problems and conflicts between departments and divisions.

□ There are more opportunities for advancement, promotion, and interesting jobs in a growing firm. Growth, per se, is exciting and ego enhancing for CEOs. A corporation tends to be seen as a "winner" or "on the move" by the marketplace and by potential investors.

Vertical integration strategy. This is the strategy of a corporation that enters one or more businesses that are necessary to the manufacture and distribution of its own products but that were previously purchased from other companies. These can range from the obtaining of raw materials to the merchandising of the product. *Backward* integration is the corporation's entry into the business of supplying some of its present raw materials. Henry Ford I achieved this when he built his own steel mill to supply Ford's assembly lines. *Forward* integration is the entry of the corporation into the business of distributing its product by entering marketing channels closer to the ultimate consumer. This is common in the tire industry where manufacturers, such as Firestone and Goodyear, own and manage their own retail outlets. More recently, Digital Equipment has been opening retail stores in order to market its home computers.

Vertical integration is also quite common in the oil, rubber, basic metal, automobile, and forest products industries. The advantages lie in better control of raw materials and distribution channels. Although backward integration is usually more profitable than forward integration,[5] it can reduce a corporation's strategic flexibility by an encumbrance of expensive assets that may be hard to sell.[6]

Horizontal integration strategy. The acquisition by a corporation of another corporation in the same industry is called horizontal integration. The term is applied primarily to those corporations that predominantly operate in one industry, such as Ford or Pan American Airlines. Since the acquiring firm is thus buying a competitor, such a transaction is liable to antitrust suits. The corporation's objective may be to become more efficient through larger economies of scale, to enter another geographic market, or simply to reduce competition for supplies and customers. Renault's acquisition of American Motors is one example of horizontal integration. If Pan American, for example, acquires another international airline (such as TWA), it would be integrating horizontally. The same would be true if Ford purchased Chrysler Corporation.

Diversification strategy. This is the strategy of adding *different* products or divisions to the corporation. There are two types of diversification—concentric and conglomerate.

Concentric diversification is the addition to a corporation of *related* products or divisions. The corporation's lines of business still possess some "*common thread*" that serves to relate them in some manner. The point of commonality may be similar technology, customer usage, distribution, managerial skills, or product similarity. An example of concentric diversification would be Pan American Airlines' purchase of National Airlines' domestic routes to complement its international business. Another example is Texas Instruments' application of its integrated circuit technology to wrist watches as well as calculators.

Conglomerate diversification, in contrast to concentric diversification, is the addition to the firm of *unrelated* products or divisions. Rather than focusing on having a common thread throughout their corporation, top managers who adopt this strategy are primarily concerned with a return on investment criterion: Will it increase the corporation's level of profitability? The addition may, however, be justified in terms of strategic fit. A cash-rich corporation with few opportunities for growth in its industry may, for example, move into another industry where opportunities are great, but cash hard to find. An example of this strategy was the purchase of cash-poor Piedmont Aviation stock by cash-rich Norfolk and Western Railway.[7] Another instance of conglomerate diversification might be the purchase by a corporation with a seasonal and, therefore, uneven cash flow of a firm in an unrelated industry with complementing seasonal sales that will level out the cash flow.

Mergers, acquisitions, and joint ventures. Corporations may engage in strategic mergers, acquisitions, and joint ventures in order to attain *synergy* (the 2 + 2 = 5 effect). Two corporations so involved are able to achieve more by working together than they could by acting separately. Different types of synergy are possible:

1. *Sales synergy* exists when many products use the same distribution channels.
2. *Operating synergy* exists when many products use the same manufacturing facilities and personnel, thereby distributing the overhead among more products.
3. *Management synergy* exists when managerial skills and abilities can be transferred from one corporation or industry to solving problems in another.
4. *Technological synergy* exists when R&D personnel and techniques can be combined for greater effectiveness.

A *merger* is a transaction involving two or more corporations in which stock is exchanged, but from which only one corporation survives. Mergers are usually between firms of somewhat similar size and are usually "friendly." The resulting firm is likely to have a name quite different from its composite firms. One example is the merging of North Central Airlines and Southern Airways to form Republic Airlines.

An *acquisition* is the purchase of a corporation that is completely absorbed as an operating subsidiary or division of the acquiring corporation. An example is the acquisition by U. S. Steel of Marathon Oil. Acquisitions are usually between firms of different sizes and can be either "friendly" or "unfriendly." A friendly acquisition usually begins with the acquiring corporation discussing its desires with the other firm's top management. In return for fair consideration after acquisition, the top management of the firm to be acquired agrees to work for the acquisition. Friendly acquisitions are thus very similar to mergers. Unfriendly acquisitions, in contrast, are often called "takeovers." The acquiring firm ignores the other firm's top management or board of directors and simply begins buying up the other firm's stock until it owns a controlling interest. The takeover target, in response, begins defensive maneuvers, such as buying up its own stock, calling in the Justice Department to initiate an anti-trust suit in order to stop the acquisition, or looking for a friendly merger partner (as Conoco did with DuPont when Seagram's began to buy Conoco's stock). Slang terms are very popular in mergers and acquisitions. For example, a "pigeon" (highly vulnerable target) or "sleeping beauty" (more desirable than a pigeon) may take a "cyanide pill" (taking on a huge long-term debt on the condition that the debt falls due immediately upon the firm's acquisition) in order to avoid being "raped" (forcible hostile takeover sometimes accompanied by looting the target's profitability) by a "shark" (extremely predatory takeover artist) using "hired guns" (lawyers, merger and acquisition specialists, and certain investment bankers).[8] For an interesting application of a "takeover" strategy, see Illustrative Example 7.1.

Illustrative Example 7.1
USE OF TAKEOVER STRATEGY AT
TYCO LABORATORIES, INC.

Tyco Laboratories, Inc., a miniconglomerate based in New Hampshire, has adopted an interesting growth strategy. The stated aim of Tyco's president, Joseph S. Gaziano, is to make Tyco grow through acquisitions. Gaziano, according to Lynch, "...likes to muse that Tyco one day might be as well known as International Telephone and Telegraph Co.—with Mr. Gaziano ranked right up there with his idol, former ITT chieftain Harold Geneen."

Tyco usually begins by buying the stock of another corporation on the open market. If the other firm objects, Mr. Gaziano becomes very aggressive. He once appeared at a takeover target's stockholders meeting and loudly demanded a meeting with the CEO. As in the case of his attempt to acquire Leeds and Northrup, he sometimes promises to fire the top executives, so his demand was tantamount to a threat. In 1979, Tyco acquired some shares of Trane Company, an air-conditioner manufacturer, for $43 each. So fearful was Trane of Gaziano's takeover tactics, it paid Tyco $50 per share to get its shares back. At the time, Trane's common stock was trading at less than $40 a share.

Tyco's attempt to acquire Ludlow Corporation took two and a half years to complete. Ludlow, a packaging and furniture concern, fought Tyco's advances at every step. At the beginning of his takeover attempt, Mr. Gaziano cited Ludlow's $22 million in cash as a reason for the bid. In order to avoid Tyco's grasp, Ludlow used the cash to acquire a packaging concern—a decision that has resulted in lower profits for Ludlow.

So far, Mr. Gaziano's use of the takeover strategy has been extremely profitable. Even in those attempts when a second bidder wins a takeover battle by paying a higher price, Tyco is able to sell the acquired stock at a much higher price than it paid for it. On three takeover attempts that failed, Tyco earned approximately $15 million.

SOURCE: M. C. Lynch, "Tyco's Successful Acquisition Still Leaves Questions About Gaziano's Grand Design," *Wall Street Journal* (August 27, 1981), p. 21.

A *joint venture* is the strategy of forming a temporary partnership or consortium for the purpose of gaining synergy. Joint ventures occur because the corporations involved do not wish to or cannot legally merge permanently. They are especially popular in international undertakings because of financial and political-legal constraints. The Alaskan pipeline, for example, involved many different companies because no one corporation could afford to build such a pipeline alone. General Electric formed a joint venture with France's national engineering firm Société Nationale d'Étude et de Construction de Moteur d'Aviation (SNECMA) so that SNECMA could use GE's technology and GE could gain direct access to the Common Market,[9] from which it was excluded. Joint ventures are a convenient way for a privately owned and a publicly owned (state-owned) corporation to work together. Joint ventures are further discussed in Chapter 10.

Mergers, acquisitions, and joint ventures are often combined with vertical and horizontal integration, and with diversification. As mentioned earlier, Henry Ford I vertically integrated backward by using his own and Ford Motor's cash to build a steel mill for his River Rouge Plant, and Texas Instruments diversified concentrically into digital watches by expanding its own integrated circuit operations. In contrast, many corporations, such as DuPont, Pepsico, and Philip Morris, grew externally: DuPont vertically integrated by acquiring Conoco to assure oil supplies for the manufacture of its petroleum-based synthetics; Philip Morris diversified in the acquisition of Miller Brewing Company so that it could apply its marketing expertise to another industry.

Concentration strategy. A corporation may choose to grow by concentrating all of its resources in the development of a single product or product line, single market, or single technology. Corporations such as Xerox, McDonald's, Polaroid, and Caterpillar that concentrate their efforts on a single product are able to stay ahead of competitors who dilute their effort in many industries. These firms can organize on a functional or geographical basis with no need for divisions. The very real advantages inherent in a concentration strategy may have been one reason why many large multi-industry, multiproduct corporations have begun to reorganize themselves around strategic business units. Such concentration allows the corporation to put more time, energy, and resources into developing innovative product strategies through market penetration, market development, and product development.

Investment strategy. This growth strategy is sometimes referred to as "grow to sell out." It is a way to maximize stockholder investment when the corporation is sold at an attractive price. An entrepreneur may successfully build a corporation for the purpose of selling it just at the point when competition becomes heavy and when further growth would require giving up control. The corporation is therefore viewed as an investment not only by the stockholders, but also by top management and the board of directors.

Retrenchment strategies. This group of strategies is relatively unpopular because retrenchment seems to imply failure—that something has gone wrong with previous strategies. With these strategies there *is* a great deal of pressure to improve performance. As with the coaches of losing football teams, the CEO is typically under pressure to do something quickly or be fired.

Turnaround strategy. This strategy emphasizes improving operational efficiency. It is appropriate when a corporation's problems are pervasive, but not yet critical. Analogous to going on a diet, a turnaround strategy includes two phases. The first phase is *contraction*, the initial effort to reduce size and costs. It typically involves a general cutback in personnel and all noncritical expenditures. Hiring stops, and across-the-board reductions in R&D, advertising, training, supplies, and services are usual. The second phase is *consolidation*, the development of a program to stabilize the leaner corporation. An in-depth audit is conducted in order to identify areas where long-run improvements can be made in corporate efficiency. Plans are developed to streamline the corporation by reducing unnecessary overhead and to make functional activities "cost-effective." Financial expenditures in all areas must be justified on the basis of their contribution to profits. This is a crucial time for the corporation. If the consolidation phase is not conducted in a positive manner, many of the best people will leave the organization. If, however, all employees are encouraged to get involved in productivity improvements, the corporation may likely emerge from this strategic retrenchment period a much stronger and better organized company. For an example of an effective use of the turnaround strategy, see Illustrative Example 7.2.

Divestment strategy. Divestment is appropriate when corporate problems can be traced to the poor performance of an SBU or product line or when a division or SBU is a "misfit," unable to synchronize itself with the rest of the corporation. Still another appropriate situation is that of a division's needing more resources to be competitive than a corporation is willing to provide. Some corporations, however, select divestment instead of the more painful turnaround strategy. With divestment, top management is able to do one of two things: (1) select a scapegoat to blame for all of the corporation's problems, or (2) generate a lot of cash in the sale, which can be used to reduce debt and buy time. The second rationale may explain why Pan American chose to sell the most profitable parts of its corporation, the Pan Am Building in New York and Intercontinental Hotels, while keeping its money-losing airline.[10]

Illustrative Example 7.2 _____
TURNAROUND STRATEGY
AT FIRESTONE

When John J. Nevin became president of Firestone Tire & Rubber Co. late in 1979, the company was in desperate trouble, an industrial dinosaur trapped by obsolete plants, a bloated payroll, and a mountain of debt.

To save the company, Nevin attacked it with a cleaver. He closed seven of its seventeen plants in the United States and Canada, trimmed the number of employes by about 25%, reduced the product line, abandoned some foreign operations, and sold off a money-losing subsidiary to raise cash.

The result was a dramatic turnaround. For the nine months that ended July 31, 1981, Firestone reported net income of $121 million, against a loss of $98 million for the same period a year earlier. Debt, which was crippling the company, had been cut in half, from $1100 million in 1980 to about $550 million in 1981. The remaining plants were operating at nearly 90% capacity, up from 57%.

Firestone, third largest tire company in the world and second largest in the United States, with total 1980 sales of $4850 million, has reached the point where it appears assured of surviving the shakeout that analysts say is coming in the stagnant world tire market; and Nevin has turned his attention to improving the company's performance. In June 1981, he submitted to Firestone's directors a "strategic plan" that called for raising the company's credit rating, for achieving a return on equity of 9% in 1982 and 15% in 1985, and for diversifying to reduce Firestone's dependence on the tire business.

Nevin is proud that his performance at Firestone has drawn high grades from the Wall Street analysts he professes to ignore. The only subject on which he says he feels defensive was his decision to lay off more than 25,000 workers.

"We were at the brink of economic disaster," he said. "The issue was not whether to keep those jobs, the issue was only when to stop taking the losses. There was no one in this world who could have saved those jobs. You could have risked the jobs of the other 80,000 people in this company by trying to hang on for another year or two, and this company had gotten into a lot of trouble by doing that."

SOURCE: T. W. Lippman, "Nevin Plans Drive to Top for Firestone," *Washington Post* (September 13, 1981), pp. F1 and F7.

Captive company strategy. Rarely discussed as a separate strategy, the captive strategy is similar to divestment; but instead of selling off divisions or product lines, the corporation reduces the scope of some of its functional activities and becomes "captive" to another firm. In this manner, it reduces expenses and achieves some security through its relationship with the stronger firm. An agreement is reached with a key customer that in return for a large number of long-run purchases, the captive company will guarantee delivery at a favorable price. Since 75% or more of its product is sold to a single purchaser, the captive company can reduce its marketing expenditures and develop long-run production schedules that reduce costs. If supplies ever become a problem for the captive company, it can call on its key customer to help put pressure on a reluctant supplier.

Liquidation strategy. A strategy of last resort when other retrenchment strategies have failed, an early liquidation may serve stockholder interests better than an inevitable bankruptcy. To the extent that top management identifies with the corporation, liquidation is perceived as an admission of failure. Pride and reputation are liquidated as well as jobs and financial assets. Even when things are going terribly, there is a strong temptation for top management to avoid liquidation in the hope of a miracle. It is for this reason that a corporation needs a strong board of directors who can safeguard stockholder interests by telling top management when to quit.

Combination strategies. These strategies can be composed of any number of variations of the preceding strategies. The main focus is on the conscious use of several overall strategies (stability, growth, retrenchment) in several SBUs at the same time or at different times in the future.[11] One example of such a strategy is given in Illustrative Example 7.3.

Evaluation of corporate strategies. Before the selection of a particular corporate strategy, top management must critically analyze the pros and cons of each feasible alternative in light of the corporation's situation. The tendency to select the most obvious strategy can sometimes lead to serious trouble in the long run. The orientation of most top management toward growth strategies has resulted in a high value being placed on acquisitions and mergers as preferred alternatives. A survey of chief financial officers found that the major motive for acquiring another firm was to generate fast growth.[12] Nevertheless, it is estimated that because of poor planning, high prices, mismanaged consolidation, or bad luck, one-third of all acquisitions are ultimately failures.[13] The explanation may lie in top management's overestimating the benefits to be derived or from valuing too highly their own skills in managing a new business.

A number of techniques are available to aid strategic planners in estimating the likely effects of strategic changes. One of these was derived from the research project on the profit impact of market strategies (PIMS), which was discussed in Chapter 6. From the analysis of data from a large number of business corporations, key factors were identified in regression equations to explain large variations in ROI, profitability, and cash flow.

Illustrative Example 7.3 ———
NORFOLK AND WESTERN
RAILWAY USES A
COMBINATION STRATEGY

Norfolk and Western Railway, a well-known carrier of coal, vertically integrated a number of years ago by acquiring some coal mines in West Virginia. N&W managers jokingly state that one reason N&W has been so profitable at a time when other railroads have suffered is that it is really in the coal business. "We keep our fuel usage low. We haul empty cars up the mountains, fill the cars with coal, and coast all the way down to the pier," explained one middle manager. In addition to this backward integration of buying a number of its suppliers, N&W is attempting to integrate forward by building its own automated facility at Hampton Roads, Virginia for unloading its coal onto cargo ships.

In 1980, N&W agreed to merge with Southern Railway. This merger between two very profitable railroads was to take place in 1982. Meanwhile, during 1981, N&W purchased 8.2% (650,000 shares) of North Carolina–based Piedmont Aviation, Inc. A carrier operating in eighteen states, Piedmont serves 43 airports including Roanoke, Virginia, N&W's headquarters. Piedmont was low on capital, with $10 million in cash. N&W, in contrast, had $221.7 million in cash as of June 30, 1981. Although Piedmont had rebuffed N&W's offers to merge, analysts expected N&W to continue efforts to acquire control.

Also in 1981, N&W announced that it had signed a letter of intent to sell its Delaware and Hudson Railway subsidiary to Guilford Transportation Industries, Inc., a holding company belonging to Timothy Mellon. Mellon is apparently attempting to put together a New England rail system. The D&H is an 1,800 mile system stretching from Montreal to Washington, D.C. and from New York City to Buffalo, New York. Previously, the D&H had been opposed to N&W's merger with Southern Railway unless the D&H was included in the merger, and the State of New York had been supporting the D&H position in Interstate Commerce Commission proceedings. However, a D&H spokesperson reported that the company was "generally pleased" with N&W's plans to sell its 1,000 shares of D&H stock to Mellon's corporation. In 1968, the N&W had been forced by the ICC, as a condition of an earlier N&W merger, to acquire the D&H. Apparently displeased with the D&H for a number of years, N&W wrote the stock value down to $500,000 in 1978 and took a $13.7 million loss on its books. Since 1978, N&W has excluded D&H's losses in its consolidated income statement, but has included them in its consolidated tax returns. It was rumored that the sale of the D&H to Guilford Transportation was for N&W's book value, only $500,000.

SOURCE: J. D. Williams, "N&W Railway Buys 8.2% Stake in Piedmont Air," *Wall Street Journal* (September 2, 1981), p. 2.

As part of PIMS, reports are prepared for a participating corporation's business units showing how its expected level of ROI is influenced by each factor. A second report shows how ROI can be expected to change, both in the short and long runs, if particular changes are made in its strategy.[14]

In deciding upon retrenchment strategies, the Altman bankruptcy indicator, or "Z-value," is likely to be of some assistance. Developed by Edward Altman, the formula combines five ratios by weighting them according to their importance to a corporation's financial strength (see Illustrative Example 7.4). GTI Corporation successfully used the Altman formula to avoid bankruptcy. The selection of a turnaround strategy hinged upon the CEO's ability to bring each of the five ratios into the favorable range to increase GTI's Z-value.[15]

Business (SBU) Strategies

Sometimes referred to as division strategy, business strategy focuses on improving the competitive position of a corporation's products or services within the specific industry or market segment that the division serves. It is a strategy developed by a division to complement the overall corporate strategy. Although many business strategies appear to be similar to corporate strategies, they differ in terms of their orientation to a specific market and to a specific line of business or product.

Directional policy matrix (DPM). Originally developed by Shell, the directional policy matrix has become very popular with European corporations, such as Rolls Royce. It is an example of portfolio analysis used for generating alternative strategies. As with the GE Business Screen, the DPM has two axes and nine cells. One axis is entitled "business sector prospects" (industry attractiveness). The other is labeled "company's competitive capabilities" (business strengths). Figure 7.1 is an example of the matrix, with the axes' names modified.

Depending on the cell in which a division or product is placed, the matrix recommends one of the following eight strategies:

1. *Disinvestment.* Products falling in this area will probably be losing money—not necessarily every year; but losses in bad years will outweigh the gains in good years. It is unlikely that any activity will surprise management by falling within this area because its poor performance should already be known.

2. *Phased withdrawal.* A product with an average to weak position with low unattractive market prospects, or a weak position with average market prospects is unlikely to be earning any significant amounts

Illustrative Example 7.4 _____
THE ALTMAN
BANKRUPTCY FORMULA

Edward I. Altman developed a formula to predict a company's likelihood of going bankrupt. His system of multiple discriminate analysis is used by stockholders to determine if the corporation is a good investment. The formula was developed from a study of 33 manufacturing companies with assets averaging $6.4 million that had filed Chapter X bankruptcies. These were paired with 33 similar but profitable firms with assets between $1 million and $25 million. The formula is:

$$Z = 1.2x_1 + 1.4x_2 + 3.3x_3 + 0.6x_4 + 1.0x_5$$

where

x_1 = Working capital divided by total assets.

x_2 = Retained earnings divided by total assets.

x_3 = Earnings before interest and taxes divided by total assets.

x_4 = Market value of equity divided by book value of total debt.

x_5 = Sales divided by total assets.

Z = Overall index of corporate fiscal health.

The range of the Z-value for most corporations is −4 to +8. According to Altman, financially strong corporations have Z values above 2.99. Corporations in serious trouble have Z values below 1.81. Those in the middle are question marks that could go either way. The closer a firm gets to bankruptcy, the more accurate the Z-value is as a predictor.

SOURCE: M. Ball, "Z Factor: Rescue by the Numbers," *Inc.* (December 1980), p. 48. Reprinted with the permission of *Inc.* Magazine, December 1980. Copyright © 1980 by INC. Publishing Company, Boston.

of cash. The indicated strategy is used to realize the value of the assets on a controlled basis in order to make resources available for employment elsewhere.

3. *Cash generator.* A typical situation in this matrix area is that of a product moving towards the end of its life cycle, which is being replaced in the market by other products. No finance should be allowed for expansion; and the product, so long as it is profitable, should be used as a source of cash for other areas. Every effort should

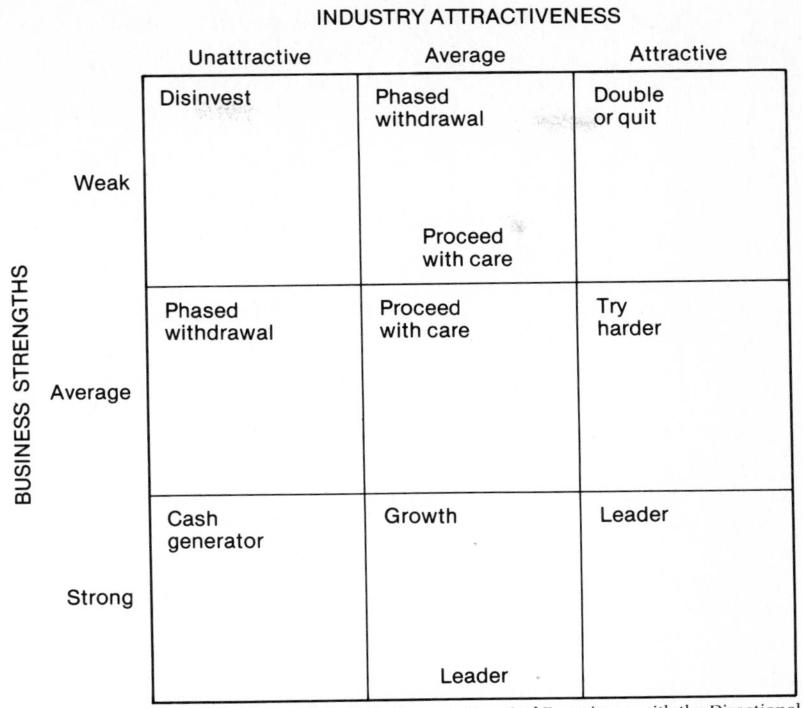

INDUSTRY ATTRACTIVENESS

	Unattractive	Average	Attractive
Weak	Disinvest	Phased withdrawal Proceed with care	Double or quit
Average	Phased withdrawal	Proceed with care	Try harder
Strong	Cash generator	Growth Leader	Leader

BUSINESS STRENGTHS

SOURCE: Adapted from D. E. Hussey, "Portfolio Analysis: Practical Experience with the Directional Policy Matrix," *Long Range Planning*, vol. 11 (August 1978), p. 3. Reprinted by permission.

Figure 7.1   *Directional policy matrix.*

be made to maximize profits, because activity concerning the product has no long-term future.

4. *Proceed with care.* In this position, some investment may be justified, but major investments should be made with extreme caution.

5. *Growth.* Investment should be made to allow the product to grow with the market. In general, the product will generate sufficient cash to be self-financing and will not be making demands on other corporate cash resources.

6. *Double or quit.* Tomorrow's breadwinners among today's R&D projects may come from this area. Putting the strategy simply, those with the best prospects should be selected for full backing and development. The rest should be abandoned.

7. *Try harder.* The implication is that the product can be moved towards the leadership box by judicious application of resources. In these circumstances the division may wish to make available resources in excess of what the product can generate for itself.

8. *Leader.* The strategy should be to maintain a leading position. At certain stages this may imply that resources to expand capacity may be required, but that the cash required need not be met entirely from funds generated by the product, although its earnings should be above average.[16]

The Directional Policy Matrix can help a division develop appropriate alternative strategies. It is *not*, however, a push-button technique, but should be used with common sense and in conjunction with other methods. Portfolio analysis by its nature tends to be somewhat simplistic. It may, for example, rule out what might be the very profitable strategy of being a minority producer in certain markets.

Porter's competitive strategies.   Porter, an authority on business level strategies, proposes three generic strategies for outperforming other corporations in a particular industry: overall cost leadership, differentiation, and focus.[17]

1. *Overall cost leadership.* This strategy requires "aggressive construction of efficient-scale facilities, vigorous pursuit of cost reductions from experience, tight cost and overhead control, avoidance of marginal customer accounts, and cost minimization in areas like R&D, service, sales force, advertising, and so on."[18] Having a low cost position gives an SBU a defense against rivals. Its lower costs allow it to continue to earn profits during times of heavy competition.

2. *Differentiation.* This strategy involves the creating of a product or service that is perceived throughout its industry as being unique. It may be accomplished through design or brand image, technology, features, dealer network, or customer service. Differentiation is a viable strategy for earning above-average returns in a specific business because the resulting brand loyalty lowers customer sensitivity to price.

3. *Focus.* Similar to the corporate strategy of concentration, this business strategy focuses on a particular buyer group, product line segment, or geographic market. The value of the strategy derives from the belief that an SBU that focuses its efforts is better able to serve its narrow strategic target more effectively or efficiently than can its competition. Focus does, however, necessitate a trade-off between profitability and overall market share.

Before selecting one of these strategies for a particular corporate business or SBU, it is important to assess its feasibility in terms of divisional strengths and weaknesses. Porter lists some of the commonly required skills and resources, as well as organizational requirements, in Table 7.1.

**Table 7.1   REQUIREMENTS FOR GENERIC
                 COMPETITIVE STRATEGIES**

GENERIC STRATEGY	COMMONLY REQUIRED SKILLS AND RESOURCES	COMMON ORGANIZATIONAL REQUIREMENTS
Overall cost leadership	Sustained capital investment and access to capital.	Tight cost control.
		Frequent, detailed control reports.
	Process engineering skills.	Structured organization and responsibilities
	Intense supervision of labor.	
	Products designed for ease in manufacture.	Incentives based on meeting strict quantitative targets.
	Low-cost distribution system.	
Differentiation	Strong marketing abilities.	Strong coordination among functions in R&D, product development, and marketing.
	Product engineering.	
	Creative flair.	
	Strong capability in basic research.	Subjective measurement and incentives instead of quantitative measures.
	Corporate reputation for quality or technological leadership.	
	Long tradition in the industry or unique combination of skills drawn from other businesses.	Amenities to attract highly skilled labor, scientists, or creative people.
	Strong cooperation from channels.	
Focus	Combination of the above policies directed at the particular strategic target.	Combination of the above policies directed at the particular strategic target.

SOURCE: M. E. Porter, *Competitive Strategy* (New York: Free Press, 1980), pp. 40–41. Copyright © 1980 by The Free Press, a division of Macmillan Publishing Co., Inc. Reprinted by permission.

Functional-Area Strategies

The principal focus of functional-area strategy is to maximize corporate and divisional resource productivity. Given the constraints of corporate and divisional strategies, functional-area strategies are developed to pull together the various activities and competencies of each function to improve performance. For example, a manufacturing department would be very concerned with developing a strategy to reduce costs and to improve the quality of its output. Marketing, in comparison, would typically be concerned with developing strategies to increase sales. A functional area receiving a great deal of attention recently in terms of strategy is that of technology (R&D). Those corporations that are dependent on technology for their success are becoming increasingly concerned with developing new R&D strategies that complement business-area strategies.[19]

Some of the many possible alternative functional strategies were listed in Table 5.2 in Chapter 5 and included in this chapter in the decision tree depicted in Fig. 7.2. These are some of the many functional-area strategy decisions that need to be made if corporate and divisional strategies are to be implemented properly by functional managers.

Strategies to Avoid

There are a number of strategies used at various levels that are very dangerous. They may be considered by managers because of a poor analysis or lack of creativity.[20]

1. *Follow the leader*. Imitating the strategy of a leading competitor may seem good, but it ignores a firm's particular strengths and weaknesses.

2. *Hit another home run*. If a corporation is successful because it pioneered an extremely successful product, it has a tendency to search for another super product that will ensure growth and prosperity. Like betting on "long shots" at the horse races, the probability of finding a second winner is slight.

3. *Arms race*. Entering into a spirited battle with another firm for increased market share may increase sales revenue, but will probably be more than offset by increases in advertising, promotion, R&D, and manufacturing costs.

4. *Do everything*. When faced with a number of interesting opportunities, there may be a tendency to take all of them. At first, a corporation may have enough resources to develop each into a project, but it soon runs short as the many projects demand large infusions of time, money, and energy.

5. *Losing hand*. A corporation may have invested so much in a particular strategy that top management is unwilling to accept the fact that the strategy is not successful. Believing that it has "too much invested to quit," the corporation continues to throw good money after bad.

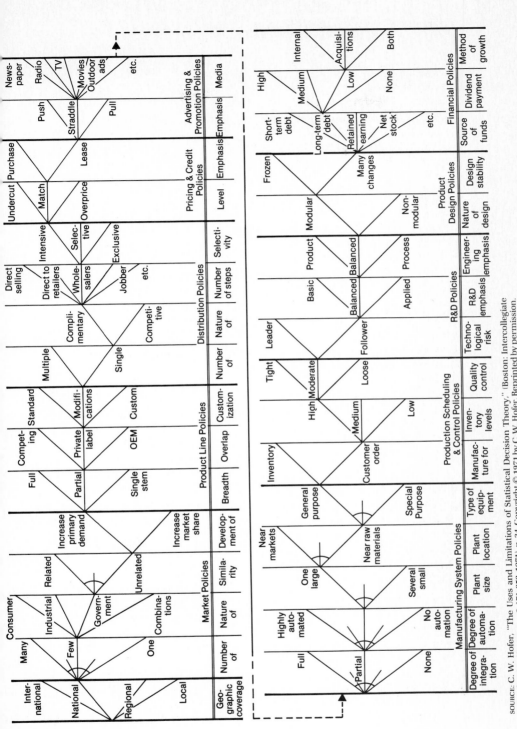

Figure 7.2 *Functional strategy decision tree.*

SOURCE: C. W. Hofer, "The Uses and Limitations of Statistical Decision Theory," (Boston: Intercollegiate Case Clearing House, no. 9-171-653, 1971), p. 34. Copyright © 1971 by C. W. Hofer. Reprinted by permission.

161

7.2 SELECTION OF
THE BEST STRATEGY

Once potential strategic alternatives have been identified and evaluated in terms of their pros and cons, top management must select one to implement. By this point, it is likely that a number of alternatives will have emerged as feasible. How is the decision made to determine the "best" strategy?

Choosing among a set of acceptable alternative strategies is often not easy. Each alternative is likely to have its proponents as well as critics. Steiner and Miner suggest using the twenty questions listed below before selecting one strategy over another. Perhaps the most important criterion to use is the ability of each alternative to satisfy agreed-upon objectives with the least use of resources and with the fewest number of negative side effects. It is therefore important to develop a tentative implementation plan in order to address the probable difficulties management is likely to face. Is the alternative worth the probable short-term as well as long-term costs?

Regardless of the pros and cons of each alternative, the actual decision will probably be influenced by a number of subjective factors that are difficult to quantify. Some of these factors are management's attitude toward risk, pressures from the external environment, influences from the corporate culture, and the personal needs and desires of key managers.

TWENTY QUESTIONS TO USE
IN EVALUATING STRATEGY

1. Does the strategy conform with the basic mission and purpose of the corporation? If not, a new competitive arena may be entered with which management is not familiar.

2. Is the strategy consistent with the corporation's external environment?

3. Is the strategy consistent with the internal strengths, objectives, policies, resources, and personal values of managers and employees? A strategy may not be completely in tune with all of these, but major dissonance should be avoided.

4. Does the strategy reflect the acceptance of minimum potential risk, balancing it against the maximum potential profit consistent with the corporation's resources and prospects?

5. Does the strategy fit a niche in the corporation's market not now filled by others? Is this niche likely to remain open long enough for the corporation

to return capital investment plus the required level of profit? (Niches have a habit of filling up fast.)

6. Does the strategy conflict with other corporate strategies?

7. Is the strategy divided into substrategies that interrelate properly?

8. Has the strategy been tested with appropriate criteria (such as consistency with past, present, and prospective trends) and by the appropriate analytical tools (such as risk analysis, discounted cash flows, and so on)?

9. Has the strategy been tested by developing feasible implementation plans?

10. Does the strategy really fit the life cycles of the corporation's products?

11. Is the timing of the strategy correct?

12. Does the strategy pit the product against a powerful competitor? If so, re-evaluate carefully.

13. Does the strategy leave the corporation vulnerable to the power of one major customer? If so, reconsider carefully.

14. Does the strategy involve the production of a new product for a new market? If so, reconsider carefully.

15. Is the corporation rushing a revolutionary product to market? If so, reconsider carefully.

16. Does the strategy imitate that of a competitor? If so, reconsider carefully.

17. Is it likely that the corporation can get to the market first with the new product or service? (If so, this is a great advantage. The second firm to market has much less chance of high returns on investment than the first.)

18. Has a really honest and accurate appraisal been made of the competition? Is the competition under- or overestimated?

19. Is the corporation trying to sell abroad something it cannot sell in the United States? (This is not usually a successful strategy.)

20. Is the market share likely to be sufficient to assure a required return on investment? (Market share and return on investment generally are closely related but differ from product to product and market to market.) Has this relationship of market and product been calculated?

SOURCE: Adapted from G. A. Steiner and J. B. Miner, *Management Policy and Strategy* (New York: Macmillan, 1977), pp. 219–221. Copyright © 1977 by Macmillan Publishing Co. Reprinted by permission.

Management's Attitude toward Risk

The attractiveness of a particular alternative is partially a function of the amount of risk it entails. The risk is composed not only of the *probability* that the strategy will be effective, but also of the amount of *assets* the corporation must allocate to that strategy, and the length of *time* the assets will be unavailable for other uses. The greater the amount of assets involved and the longer they are tied up, the more likely top management will demand a higher probability of success. This may be one reason why innovations seem to occur more often in small firms than in large, established corporations. The small firm managed by an entrepreneur is willing to accept greater risk than would a large firm of diversified ownership. It is one thing to take a chance if you are the primary stock-holder. It is something else if throngs of widows and orphans depend on your corporation's monthly dividend checks for living expenses.

Decision style. The decision style of top management and the board of directors will heavily affect the way a decision is made. Thompson points out that there are two basic variables to each decision: (1) preferences about possible outcomes (the amount of agreement about the key objectives to be met), and (2) beliefs about cause/effect relationships (the amount of certainty that a specific means will cause a specific end.)[21] These are depicted graphically in Fig. 7.3.

If there is total agreement among top management and the board about the corporation's mission and key objectives, one of two decision styles is likely to be used—computational or judgmental. A *computational* style is appropriate in those situations when there is a high degree of

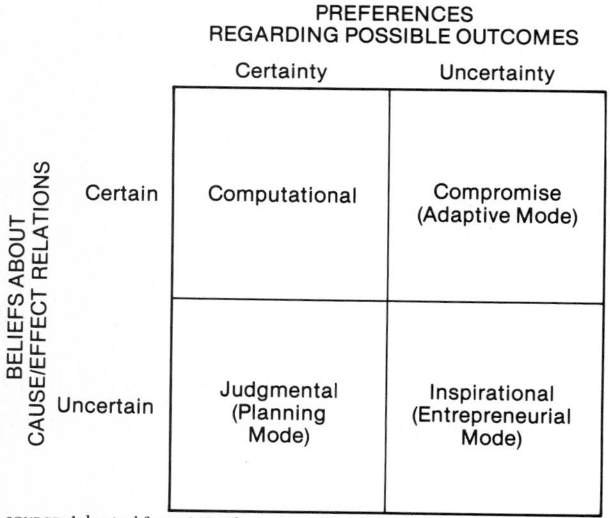

SOURCE: Adapted from J. D. Thompson, *Organizations in Action* (New York: McGraw-Hill, 1967), p. 134. Copyright © 1967 by McGraw-Hill, Inc. Reprinted by permission.

Figure 7.3   *Four basic decision styles* .

certainty about cause/effect relationships. The "best" alternative in this situation is either "obvious" or can be programmed on a computer using quantitative techniques. A *judgmental* style is typically used when there is no clear-cut connection between cause and effect. The ability of a specific strategy to achieve specific objectives is considered in terms of probabilities. Executive judgment is called for. This decision making style is most likely to epitomize strategy makers who operate in what Mintzberg calls a "planning mode."

If, however, there is little agreement about the mission and key objectives of the corporation, one of two decision styles is likely to be used—compromising or inspirational. A *compromising* style is appropriate in those situations where there is a high degree of certainty about cause/effect relationships. The selection of the "best" strategy boils down to a compromise regarding which objectives top management and the board are willing to pursue. This style is characteristic of what Mintzberg calls the "adaptive mode." An *inspirational* style is likely to be used not only when there is no clear-cut connection between strategy and the accomplishment of objectives, but also when there is no agreement about which objective has priority. This style is characteristic of Mintzberg's "entrepreneurial mode." In this mode the founder of a corporation makes strategic decisions based on the personal need to achieve a vague goal such as success. To outsiders, such decisions may appear to be arbitrary and capricious.

Pressures from the External Environment

The attractiveness of a strategic alternative will be affected by its perceived compatibility with the key elements in a corporation's task environment. These elements are typically concerned with certain aspects of a corporation's activities. Creditors want to be paid on time. Unions exert pressure for comparable wages and employment security. Governments and interest groups demand social responsibility. Stockholders want dividends. All of these pressures must be considered in the selection of the best alternative.

As previously stated in Chapter 4, most strategy makers will probably lean toward satisfying pressures from groups in their corporation's task environment in the following order:

1. Customers
2. Stockholders
3. Employees
4. Local Community

5. Society in General

6. Suppliers

7. Government[22]

Questions to raise in attempting to assess the importance to the corporation of these pressures are the following:

1. Which groups are most crucial for corporate success?

2. How much of what they want are they likely to get under this alternative?

3. What are they *likely* to do if they don't get what they want?

4. What is the probability that they will do it?

By ranking the key elements in a corporation's task environment and asking these questions, strategy makers should be better able to choose strategic alternatives that minimize external pressures.

Pressures from the Corporate Culture

As pointed out in Chapter 5, the norms and values shared by the members of a corporation do affect the attractiveness of certain alternatives. If a strategy is incompatible with the corporate culture, the likelihood of its success will be very low. There will be much footdragging and even sabotage as employees fight to resist a radical change in corporate philosophy.

Precedents from the past tend to restrict the kinds of objectives and strategies that can be seriously considered. The "aura" of the founding father of a corporation lingers long past his lifetime because his values have been imprinted on the corporation's members. According to Cyert and March,

> Organizations have memories in the form of precedents, and individuals in the coalition are strongly motivated to accept the precedents as binding. Whether precedents are formalized in the shape of an official standard operating procedure or are less formally stored, they remove from conscious consideration many agreements, decisions, and commitments that might well be subject to renegotiation in an organization without a memory.[23]

In considering a strategic alternative, the strategy makers must assess its compatibility with the corporate culture. To the extent that there is little fit, management must decide if it should (1) take a chance on ignoring the culture, (2) manage around the culture by changing the implementation plan, (3) try to change the culture to fit the strategy, or (4) change the strategy to fit the culture.[24] If the culture will be strongly opposed to a possible strategy, it is foolhardy to ignore the culture.

Further, a decision to proceed with a particular strategy without being committed to changing the culture or managing around the culture (both very tricky and time consuming) is dangerous. Nevertheless, restricting a corporation to only those strategies that are completely compatible with its culture may eliminate from consideration the most profitable alternatives.

Needs and Desires of Key Managers

Even the most attractive alternative may not be selected if it is contrary to the needs and desires of important top managers. A person's ego may be tied to a particular proposal to the extent that all other alternatives are strongly lobbied against. Key executives in operating divisions, for example, may be able to influence other people in top management in favor of a particular alternative so that objections to it are ignored.

An example of such a situation was described by John DeLorean when he was at Pontiac Division of General Motors in 1959. At that time, General Motors was developing a new rear-engined auto called Corvair. Ed Cole, the General Manager of Chevrolet Division, was very attracted to the idea of building the first modern, rear-engine American automobile. A number of engineers, however, were worried about the safety of the car and made vigorous attempts to either change the "unsafe" suspension system or keep the Corvair out of production. "One top corporate engineer told me that he showed his test results to Cole but by then he said, 'Cole's mind was made up.'"[25] By this time, there had developed quite a bit of documented evidence that the car should not be built as designed. However, according to DeLorean,

> ... Cole was a strong product voice and a top salesman in company affairs. In addition, the car, as he proposed it, would cost less to build than the same car with a conventional rear suspension. Management not only went along with Cole, it also told the dissenters in effect to "stop these objections. Get on the team, or you can find someplace else to work." The ill-fated Corvair was launched in the fall of 1959.
>
> The results were disastrous. I don't think any one car before or since produced as gruesome a record on the highway as the Corvair. It was designed and promoted to appeal to the spirit and flair of young people. It was sold in part as a sports car. Young Corvair owners, therefore, were trying to bend their cars around curves at high speeds and were killing themselves in alarming numbers.[26]

In only a few years, General Motors was inundated by lawsuits over the Corvair. Ralph Nader soon published a book primarily about the Corvair called *Unsafe at any Speed*, launching his career as a consumer advocate.

Strategic Choice Model

A technique found to be useful in methodically comparing various strategic alternatives is that of the Strategic Choice Model developed by Snyder.[27] As shown in Table 7.2, the model incorporates both the alternatives under consideration and the decision criteria considered most relevant by the strategic managers using the model.

The specific alternatives, criteria, and numbers given in Table 7.2 are those for a specific computer corporation and, of course, will vary depending upon the corporation and situation under consideration. The choice model is developed by going through the following seven steps:

1. List the feasible alternatives on the vertical axis. (Six are given in Table 7.2—for example, personal home computers and software development.)

2. List important internal and external considerations (decision criteria) along the horizontal axis. Although it is not done in Table 7.2, internal consistency can be subdivided into separate columns showing internal consistency with each functional area. Likewise, external consistency can be subdivided into external consistency with each element in the task environment. Obviously, other criteria in addition to those given in Table 7.2 can be listed for any particular situation.

3. Weight each decision criterion listed on the horizontal axis from 1 to 5 according to its importance to the firm. For example, the strategists who prepared Table 7.2 believed that long-run return on investment was more important than was short-run return. Thus, short-run return was weighted 3 and long-run return was rated 5.

4. Evaluate each feasible alternative in terms of its effect on each criterion listed on the horizontal axis. The effect may be positive, neutral, or negative. Use a scale ranging from -5 (negative effect) to $+5$ (positive effect). The numerical weight of each criterion for each alternative is the left side of each "equation" at the intersection of each row and column. For example, in Table 7.2 software development is thought to have a positive effect $(+4)$ on the corporation's short-run return and an extremely positive effect $(+5)$ on its long-run return.

5. Multiply the numerical weight for each criterion in the horizontal axis (calculated in step 3) by the numerical weight on the left side of each equation (calculated in step 4). The resulting product of each multiplication is recorded on the right side of each "equation." For example, the value of software development on short-run return is $3 \times 4 = 12$.

6. Sum the products for each row. Record that total in the column on the far right. For example, we find the sum of the products for the "personal home computers" alternative by adding thus: $20 + 20 + 9 + 25 + 12 + 20 = 106$.

Table 7.2 STRATEGIC CHOICE MODEL

ALTERNATIVES	WEIGHTED DECISION CRITERIA						TOTAL OF MULTIPLIED WEIGHTS
	Internal Consistency (5×)	External Consistency (4×)	Short Run Return (3×)	Long Run Return (5×)	Marketability (4×)	Investment Feasibility (5×)	
Personal home computers	4 = 20	5 = 20	3 = 9	5 = 25	3 = 12	4 = 20	106
Software development	5 = 25	5 = 20	4 = 12	5 = 25	5 = 20	4 = 20	122
Expansion/ retail stores	4 = 20	3 = 12	3 = 9	5 = 25	3 = 12	3 = 15	93
Management consulting	3 = 15	5 = 20	2 = 6	5 = 25	3 = 12	2 = 10	88
Computer networking	5 = 25	4 = 16	4 = 12	5 = 25	5 = 20	5 = 25	123
Communications satellite	2 = 10	4 = 16	1 = 3	5 = 25	2 = 8	3 = 15	77

SOURCE: N. H. Snyder, "A Strategic Choice Model," a Working Paper (Charlottesville, Va.: McIntire School of Commerce, University of Virginia), 1982.

7. Find the "best" alternative; it has the highest numerical total. Given the decision criteria and weights stated in Table 7.2, "computer networking" is the best alternative. If the corporation has the resources to develop more than one alternative at a time, the model is of use in establishing the priority of each selected alternative.

7.3 DEVELOPMENT OF POLICIES

The selection of the best strategic alternative is not the end of strategy formulation. Policies must now be established to define the ground rules for implementation. As defined earlier, policies are broad guidelines for making decisions. They flow from the selected strategy to provide guidance for decision making throughout the organization. Corporate policies are broad guidelines for divisions to follow in order to comply with corporate strategy. These policies are interpreted and implemented through each divisions' own objectives and strategies. Divisions may then develop their own policies that will be guidelines for their functional areas to follow.

Policies tend to be rather long lived and may even outlast the particular strategy that caused their creation. Interestingly, these general policies, such as "We are an equal opportunity employer" or "Research and development should get first priority on all budget requests," can become, in time, part of a corporation's culture. Such policies may make the implementation of specific strategies easier. They may also restrict top management's strategic options in the future. It is for this reason that a change in strategy should be followed quickly by a change in policies. It is one way to manage the corporate culture.

7.4 SUMMARY AND CONCLUSION

This chapter has focused on the last stage of the strategy formulation process: generating, evaluating, and selecting the best strategic alternative. It also has discussed the development of policies for implementing strategies.

There are three main kinds of strategies: corporate, business (divisional), and functional. Corporate strategies fall into four main families: stability, growth, retrenchment, and a combination of these. Epitomized by a steady-as-she-goes philosophy, *stability* strategies are (1) no change, (2) profit, (3) pause, and (4) proceed with caution. The very popular *growth* strategies are (1) vertical integration, (2) horizontal integration, (3) diversification, (4) merger, acquisition, and joint ventures, (5) concentration, and (6) investment. *Retrenchment* strategies are generally unpopular because they imply failure. They include (1) turnaround, (2) divestment, (3) captive company, and (4) liquidation. *Combination* strategies are composed of a number of these strategies.

Business or divisional strategies are described as the logical result of portfolio analysis. The Directional Policy Matrix suggests eight recommended strategies based upon a division's or product line's situation in terms of industry attractiveness and business strengths. Porter's three generic competitive strategies—*overall cost leadership, differentiation,* and *focus*—are also suggested. Functional-area strategies are described briefly in terms of their effect upon maximizing corporate and divisional resource productivity.

The selection of the best strategic alternative will probably be affected by a number of factors. Among them are management's attitude toward risk, pressures from the external environment, influences from the corporate culture, and the personal needs and desires of key managers. A Strategic Choice Model is recommended as a means of comparing feasible alternatives.

Corporate policies operate as broad guidelines for divisions to follow in order to assure their compliance with corporate strategy. Divisions may then generate their own internal policies for their functional areas to follow. These policies define the ground rules for strategy implementation and serve to align corporate activities in the new strategic direction.

DISCUSSION QUESTIONS

1. Is the profit strategy really a stability strategy? Why or why not?
2. Why is growth the most frequently used corporate-level strategy?
3. How does horizontal integration differ from concentric diversification?
4. In what situations at the corporate level might Porter's generic competitive strategies be useful?
5. What are the advantages and disadvantages of Snyder's Strategic Choice Model?

NOTES

1. W. F. Glueck, *Business Policy and Strategic Management,* 3rd ed. (New York: McGraw-Hill, 1980), p. 199.
2. Glueck, p. 290. Glueck uses the term "stable growth" instead of "stability."

3. J. F. Berry, "Amazing Grace and Unbelievers," *Washington Post* (December 6, 1981), pp. F1 and F3.

4. R. M. Cyert and J. G. March, *A Behavioral Theory of the Firm* (Englewood Cliffs, N.J.: Prentice-Hall, 1963).

5. J. Vesey, "Vertical Integration: Its Effects on Business Performance," *Managerial Planning* (May–June 1978), pp. 11–15.

6. R. H. Hayes and W. J. Abernathy, "Managing Our Way to Economic Decline," *Harvard Business Review* (July–August 1980), pp. 72–73.

7. J. D. Williams, "N&W Railway Buys 8.2% Stake in Piedmont Air," *Wall Street Journal* (September 2, 1981), p. 2.

8. P. M. Hirsch, "Ambushes, Shootouts, and Knights of the Roundtable: The Language of Corporate Takeovers" (Paper presented to the 40th Meeting of the Academy of Management, Detroit, Mich., August 1980.)

9. G. W. Weiss, Jr., "The General Electric–SNECMA Jet Engine Development Program," (Boston: Intercollegiate Case Clearing House, no. 9-380-739, 1980).

10. D. Brand, "Pan Am to Sell Its Hotel Chain to Grand Met," *Wall Street Journal* (August 24, 1981), p. 6.

11. Glueck, pp. 229–231.

12. H. K. Baker, T. O. Miller, and B. J. Ramsperger, "An Inside Look at Corporate Mergers and Acquisitions," *MSU Business Topics* (Winter 1981), p. 51.

13. T. Petzinger, Jr., "To Win a Bidding War Doesn't Ensure Success of Merged Companies," *Wall Street Journal* (September 1, 1981), pp. 1 and 19.

14. S. Schoeffler, R. D. Buzzell, and D. F. Heany, "Impact of Strategic Planning on Profit Performance," *Harvard Business Review* (March–April 1974), pp. 144–145.

15. M. Ball, "Z Factor: Rescue by the Numbers," *Inc.* (December 1980), pp. 45–48.

16. D. E. Hussey, "Portfolio Analysis: Practical Experience with the Directional Policy Matrix," *Long Range Planning* (August 1978), pp. 3–4.

17. M. E. Porter, *Competitive Strategy* (New York: Free Press, 1980), pp. 34–46.

18. Porter, p. 35.

19. A. L. Frohman and D. Bitondo, "Coordinating Business Strategy and Technical Planning," *Long Range Planning* (December 1981) pp. 58–67.

20. A. A. Thompson, Jr., and A. J. Strickland, III, *Strategy and Policy* (Plano, Tex.: Business Publications, 1981), pp. 106–107.

21. J. D. Thompson, *Organizations In Action*, (New York: McGraw-Hill, 1967), p. 134.

22. S. N. Brenner and E. A. Molander, "Is the Ethics of Business Changing?" *Harvard Business Review* (January–February 1977), p. 69.

23. R. M. Cyert and J. G. March, "A Behavioral Theory of Organizational Objectives," *Management Classics*, eds. M. T. Matteson and J. M. Ivancevich (Santa Monica, Calif.: Goodyear Publishing, 1977), p. 114.

24. H. Schwartz and S. M. Davis, "Matching Corporate Culture and Business Strategy," *Organizational Dynamics* (Summer 1981), p. 43.

25. J. P. Wright, *On a Clear Day You Can See General Motors*, (Grosse Point, Mich.: Wright Enterprises, 1979), p. 54.

26. Wright, p. 55.

27. N. H. Snyder, "A Strategic Choice Model," a Working Paper (Charlottesville, Va.: McIntire School of Commerce, University of Virginia, 1982).

STRATEGY IMPLEMENTATION AND CONTROL

PART IV

STRATEGIC MANAGEMENT MODEL

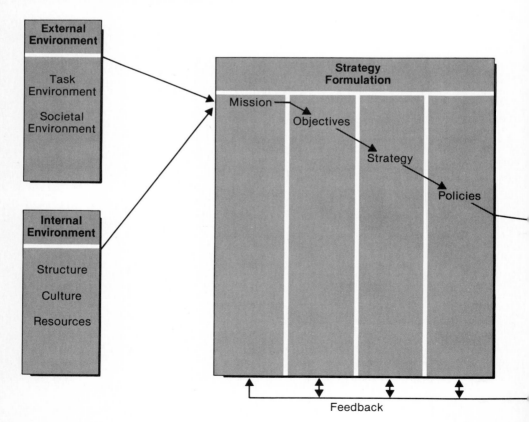

STRATEGY IMPLEMENTATION

CHAPTER 8

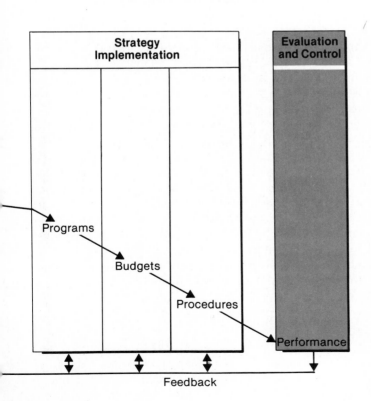

O nce a strategy and a set of policies have been formulated, the focus of strategic management shifts to implementation. Corporate strategy makers must consider these three questions:

Who are the people who will carry out the strategic plan?

What must be done?

How are they going to do what is needed?

These questions and others like them should have been addressed initially when the pros and cons of strategic alternatives were analyzed. They must also be addressed now before appropriate implementation plans can be made. Unless top management is able to answer these basic questions in a satisfactory manner, it is unlikely that even the best planned strategy will have the desired results.

8.1 *WHO* IMPLEMENTS STRATEGY?

Depending on how the corporation is organized, those who implement corporate strategy may be a different set of people from those who formulate it. In most large, multi-industry corporations, the implementers will be everyone in the organization except top management and the board of directors. Vice-presidents of functional areas and directors of divisions or SBUs will work with their subordinates to put together large-scale implementation plans. From these plans, plant managers, project managers, and unit heads will put together plans for their specific plants, departments, and units. As a result, every operational manager down to the first-line supervisor will be involved in some way in implementing corporate, divisional, and functional strategies.

It is important to note that many of the people in the corporation who are crucial to successful strategy implementation probably had little, if anything, to do with the development of the corporate strategy. As a result, they may be entirely ignorant of the vast amount of data and work that went into the formulation process. Unless changes in mission, objectives, strategies, and policies and their importance to the corporation are communicated clearly to all operational managers, there may be a lot of resistance and footdragging. In those instances when top management formulates strategy that goes counter to the corporation's culture, lower-level managers may even sabotage the implementation. These managers may hope to cause top management to abandon its new plans and return to the old ways.

8.2 *WHAT* MUST BE DONE?

The managers of divisions and functional areas work with their fellow managers to develop *programs*, *budgets*, and *procedures* for the implementation of strategy. A *program* is a statement of activities or steps needed to accomplish a single-use plan, the purpose of which is to make the strategy action-oriented. For example, top management may have chosen forward vertical integration as its best strategy for growth. The corresponding divisional strategy might be to purchase existing retail outlets from another firm rather than to build and develop its own outlets. Various programs—such as the following—would have to be developed to integrate the new stores into the corporation:

1. An advertising program ("Jones Surplus is now a part of Ajax Continental. Prices are lower. Selection is better.")
2. A training program for newly hired store managers as well as for those Jones Surplus managers the corporation has chosen to keep.
3. A program to develop reporting procedures that will integrate the stores into the corporation's accounting system.
4. A program to modernize the stores and to prepare them for a "grand opening."

Once these and other programs are developed, the budget process begins. A *budget* is a statement of a corporation's programs in terms of dollars. The detailed cost of each program is listed for planning and control purposes. Planning a budget is the last real check a corporation has on the feasibility of its selected strategy. An ideal strategy may be found to be completely impractical only after specific implementation programs are costed in detail. A good example was President Reagan's attempt in 1981 to implement his strategy of reducing taxes, increasing defense spending, and balancing the federal budget without hurting the poor or the old. In theory, everyone agreed. In practice, conflict reigned. No one in Congress was willing to cut Social Security, the school lunch program, or any of a number of other social programs.

Once program, divisional, and corporate budgets are approved, procedures must be developed to guide the employees in their day-to-day actions. Sometimes referred to as Standard Operating Procedures, *procedures* are a system of sequential steps or techniques specified to perform a particular task or job. They typically detail the various activities that must be carried out to complete a corporation's programs. In the case of the corporation that decided to acquire another firm's retail outlets, new operating procedures must be established for, among others, in-store promotions, inventory ordering, stock selection, customer relations, credits and collections, warehouse distribution, pricing, paycheck timing, grievance handling, and raises and promotions. These procedures ensure that the day-to-day store operations will be consistent over time (that is, next week's work activities will be the same as this week's) and consistent among stores (that is, each store will operate in the same manner as the others). McDonald's, for example, has done an excellent job of developing very detailed procedures (and policing them!)

to ensure that its policies are carried out to the letter in every one of its retail outlets.

8.3 *HOW* IS STRATEGY TO BE IMPLEMENTED?

Up to this point, both strategy formulation and implementation have been discussed in terms of planning. Programs, budgets, and procedures are simply more detailed plans for the eventual implementation of strategy. The total management process includes, however, several additional activities crucial to implementation, such as organizing, staffing, directing, and controlling. Before *plans* can lead to actual performance, top management must ensure that the corporation is appropriately *organized*, programs are adequately *staffed*, and activities are being *directed* toward achieving desired objectives. These activities are reviewed briefly in this chapter. Top management must also ensure that there is progress toward objectives according to plan; this is a *control* function that will be discussed in Chapter 9.

Organizing

It is very likely that a change in corporate strategy will cause some sort of change in the way a corporation is structured and in the kind of skills needed in particular positions. In a classic study of large American corporations, such as DuPont, General Motors, Sears Roebuck, and Standard Oil, Chandler concluded that changes in corporate strategy lead to changes in organization structure. He also concluded that American corporations follow a pattern of development from one kind of structural arrangement to another as they expand. According to him, these structural changes occur because inefficiencies caused by the old structure have, by being pushed too far, become too obviously detrimental to live with: "The thesis deduced from these several propositions is then that structure follows strategy and that the most complex type of structure is the result of the concatenation (linking together) of several basic strategies."[1] Chandler therefore proposed the following as the sequence of what occurs:

1. New strategy is created.
2. New administrative problems emerge.
3. Economic performance declines.
4. New appropriate structure is invented.
5. Profit returns to its previous level.

Structure follows strategy. Chandler found that in their early years, corporations such as DuPont tend to have a centralized organizational structure that is well suited to their producing and selling a limited range of products. As they add new product lines, purchase their own sources of supply, and create their own distribution networks, they become too complex for highly centralized structures. In order to remain successful, this type of successful organization needs to shift to a decentralized structure with several semi-autonomous divisions.

In his book, *My Years with General Motors*, Alfred P. Sloan detailed how General Motors conducted such structural changes in the 1920s.[2] He saw decentralization of structure as centralized policy determination coupled with decentralized operating management. Once a strategy was developed for the total corporation by top management, the individual divisions, such as Chevrolet, Buick, etc., were free to choose how they would implement that strategy. Patterned after DuPont, GM found the decentralized multidivisional structure to be extremely effective in allowing the maximum amount of freedom for product development. Return on investment was used as a financial control.

Research generally supports Chandler's proposition that structure follows strategy.[3] Figure 8.1, for example, is an advertisement used by International Harvester to announce how its retrenching strategy was to be reflected in a leaner corporate structure. There is some evidence, however, that a change in strategy may not necessarily result in a corresponding change in structure if the corporation has very little competition. If a firm occupies a monopolistic position, with tariffs in its favor or close ties to a government, it can raise prices to cover internal administrative inefficiencies. This is an easier path for these firms to take than going through the pain of corporate reorganization.[4]

Although it is agreed that organizational structure must vary with different environmental conditions, which, in turn, affect an organization's strategy, there is no agreement about an optimal organizational design.[5] What was appropriate for DuPont and General Motors in the 1920s may not be appropriate today. Successful firms in particular industries do, however, tend to organize themselves in a similar fashion. For example, automobile manufacturers tend to emulate General Motors' decentralized division concept, whereas consumer-goods producers tend to emulate the brand-management concept pioneered by Procter and Gamble Company.

Organic and mechanistic structure. Research by Burns and Stalker concluded that a "mechanistic" structure with its emphasis on the centralization of decision making and bureaucratic rules and procedures appears to be well suited to organizations operating in a reasonably stable environment. In contrast, however, they found that successful firms operating in a constantly changing environment, such as those in the electronics and aerospace industries, find that a more "organic" structure, with the decentralization of decision making and flexible procedures, is more appropriate.[6] Studies by Lawrence and Lorsch support this conclusion. They found that successful firms in a reasonably stable environ-

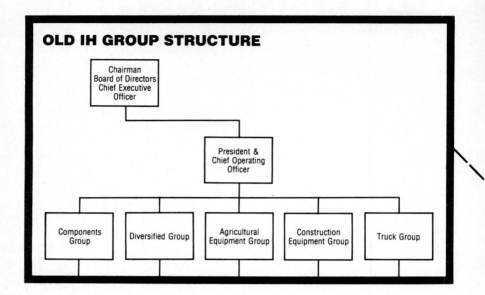

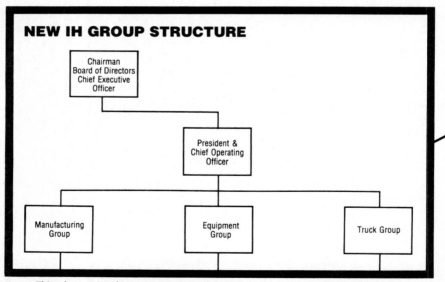

SOURCE: This ad was printed in major newspapers during the week of September 7, 1981, and is reprinted here courtesy of International Harvester Company, Chicago.

Figure 8.1   *An example of a change in structure following a change in strategy.*

Corporate Reorganization is the first step in IH's 3-year plan

Make no mistake about it.

Despite any current problems IH may be having, we're still a company with major strengths. Even during the difficult economic times facing American business today, we've been increasing our market penetration in nearly every major product category. Entire product lines are being redesigned for greater competitiveness, and new products are being introduced at a record rate.

As a matter of fact, about 50% of IH sales are from products that are less than four years old.

To build on these strengths, and better position IH for the future, a major reorganization is taking place, effective September 9. These charts will show you the major changes at a glance.

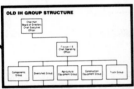

OLD IH GROUP STRUCTURE

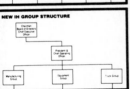

NEW IH GROUP STRUCTURE

What it means is simple: we've eliminated the duplication of many services, skills and facilities that were required to support five free-standing groups. We've merged the groups into compatible marketing and engineering structures where the people who sell our products and the people who design our products can work best together. And we've centralized our manufacturing operations.

That makes our entire corporation leaner, streamlines the structure, but most important, organizes IH in a way that concentrates on the basics of our business. Our operating structure now consists of three groups: The Manufacturing Group; The Truck Group; and The Equipment Group, which consists of the Agricultural and Construction Equipment product lines.

- New organization concentrates on basic strengths of IH businesses

- Manufacturing and support functions centralized for more efficiency, ending duplication

- Over $100 million additional annual savings from these changes

- Other cost reductions ahead of schedule: inventories reduced nearly $400 million in last nine months

- Annual operating costs reduced over $800 million since 1977

- Record 51 new products introduced in 1981

27 North American plants will now report to the head of the newly-created Manufacturing Group, rather than to the heads of our old groups. That will mean greater efficiencies in plant and people utilization, and less costly overlap. It also means Manufacturing can respond more rapidly to changes in the market. Both our Truck Group and Equipment Group will concentrate on marketing, sales, product planning and engineering, which is where we've always had strength. Functions such as data processing, engineering services, communications, and human resources, which had been spread among the groups, will now be centralized.

This reorganization is the first step in a 3-year plan designed to make IH significantly more cost effective by trimming overcapacity, eliminating unprofitable product lines, and cutting over $100 million from overhead costs on an annualized basis.

Capital improvements

A major part of the plan is to make IH the least-cost producer in each of its businesses. To achieve that, a number of steps are being taken. In the period 1979-81, IH will have spent about one billion dollars on capital improvements, up 83% from $547 million in the previous three fiscal years. These improvements include automated transfer lines, robots, computerized shop floor monitoring systems, and other state-of-the-art methods.

Cutting costs

Cost reduction programs are another big factor in our 3-year plan. Programs already in place have produced major savings since 1977. Our worldwide workforce has been reduced 25% by closing inefficient facilities and selling off product lines that didn't fit our long-term business goals. In the first nine months of 1981, inventories have already been cut by almost $400 million, putting us ahead of our schedule. By 1983, major system changes and efficiencies will have cut inventories by one billion dollars.

To help solve liquidity problems, a financial restructuring program is being worked out with over 200 banks in the U.S. and overseas.

Where do we go from here?

IH is planning for improved profitability. The efficiencies we're building into IH with this reorganization will make it a stronger company in each of the next three years.

IH continues to produce products that are basic to human needs. There will always be a market for these products. Today's actions will help make IH more profitable at serving those markets.

IH has been the kind of company that reflected the best of the strengths of the American free enterprise system in the past. And we mean to build on those strengths in the future.

We're building on our strengths.

ment, such as the container industry, coordinate activities primarily through fairly centralized corporate hierarchies, which place some reliance on direct contact by managers as well as on paper-work directives. Successful firms in more dynamic environments, such as the plastics industry, coordinate activities through integrative departments and permanent cross-functional teams as well as through the hierarchical contact and paper work.[7] These differences in the use of structural integrating devices are detailed in Table 8.1. The container industry is most stable; foods, intermediate; plastics, the least stable and subject to the most change.

Strategic business units. Another recently developed method of structuring a large and complex business corporation was developed in 1971 by GE. Referred to as strategic business units or SBUs, organizational groups composed of discrete, independent product-market segments served by the firm were identified and given primary responsibility and authority to manage their own functional areas. Recognizing that its structure of decentralized operating divisions was not working efficiently (massive sales growth was not being matched by profit growth), GE's top management decided to reorganize. They restructured nine groups and forty-eight divisions into forty-three strategic business units, many of which crossed traditional group, divisional, and profit center lines. For example, food preparation appliances in three separate divisions were merged into a single SBU serving the "housewares" market.[8] The concept is, thus, to decentralize on the basis of strategic elements rather than on the basis of size or span of control.

Table 8.1 INTEGRATING MECHANISMS IN THREE DIFFERENT INDUSTRIES

	PLASTICS	FOOD	CONTAINER
Percent new products in last 20 years	35%	15%	0%
Integrating devices	Rules. Hierarchy. Goal setting. Direct contact. Teams at 3 levels. Integrating departments.	Rules. Hierarchy. Goal setting. Direct contact. Task forces. Integrators.	Rules. Hierarchy. Goal setting. Direct contact.
Percent integrators/ managers	22%	17%	0%

SOURCE: J. Galbraith, *Designing Complex Organizations* (Reading, Mass.: Addison-Wesley, 1973), p. 111. Copyright © 1973 by Addison-Wesley Publishing Co. Reprinted by permission.

General Electric was so pleased with the results of its experiment in organizational design that it reported " ... the system helped GE improve its profitability, and return on investment has been rebuilt to a healthier level. In the last recession, General Electric's earnings dropped much less than the overall decline for the industry generally."[9] As a result, other firms such as General Foods, Mead Corporation, Union Carbide, and Armco Steel, have implemented the strategic business unit concept.[10] General Foods introduced the concept by organizing certain products on the basis of menu segments like breakfast food, beverage, main meal, dessert, and pet foods. Hall contends that the SBU approach to the management of diversified corporations is the "hot" method of organizing for the 1980s, much as the decentralized operating division method was for the 1950s.[11]

Organizing for high technology. Those corporations that emphasize the latest technology as part of their missions, objectives, and strategies are finding that their structure tends to lag behind their technology. Keen suggests there is a lag time before a technology can be fully exploited because more change is expected than a system can handle. An infrastructure needs to be built within a corporation to deal with the implications and impact of rapid technological change.[12] Frohman makes a similar argument: "Many aspects of an organization—from technical talent to reward systems, from climate to equipment—affect the payoff a company will receive from its investments in technology."[13] He contends that corporations that exploit technology will have three conditions in common:

1. A majority of top management have technical education and work experience.
2. Managers allocate funds among projects that support and maintain the corporation's technological leadership.
3. The decision making systems and structure of the corporation ensure that (a) there is a close connection between business and technological decision making, and (b) other systems within the corporation are congruent with the technological system.[14]

It has even been suggested that a corporation with a high-technology SBU may need to establish a separate mini-Board of Directors for that SBU! These board members, because they would have high-technology expertise, would be better able than the typical corporate board to provide guidance in strategic matters regarding the SBU. With its influence *vis-à-vis* the corporate board, an SBU board would be more likely to focus the corporate board's attention on technological considerations.

Stages of corporate development. A key proposition of Chandler's was that successful corporations tend to follow a pattern of structural development as they grow and expand. Further work by Thain, Scott, and Tuason specifically delineate three distinct structural stages.[15]

Stage I is typified by the entrepreneur, who founds the corporation to promote an idea (product or service). The entrepreneur tends to make all the important decisions personally, and is involved in every detail and phase of the organization. The Stage I corporation has a structure allowing the entrepreneur to directly supervise the activities of every employee (see Fig. 8.2). The corporation in Stage I is thus characterized by little formal structure. Planning is usually short range or fire fighting in nature. The typical managerial functions of planning, organizing, directing, staffing, and controlling are usually performed to a very limited degree, if at all. The greatest strengths of a Stage I corporation are its flexibility and dynamism. The drive of the entrepreneur energizes the corporation in its struggle for growth. Its greatest weakness is its extreme reliance on the entrepreneur to decide general strategies as well as detailed procedures. If the entrepreneur falters, the corporation usually flounders. This was the case with the Ford Motor Company in the 1930s and early 1940s until Henry Ford II took over control of the corporation during World War II and moved it away from the Stage I company built by his grandfather.

At *Stage II*, the entrepreneur is replaced by a team of managers with functional specializations (see Fig. 8.2). The transition to this state requires a substantial managerial style change for the chief officer of the corporation, especially if the chief officer was the Stage I entrepreneur. Otherwise, having additional staff members yields no benefits to the corporation. At this juncture, the corporate strategy favors protectivism by trying to dominate the industry, often through vertical or horizontal integration. The great strength of a Stage II corporation lies in its concentration and specialization in one industry. Its great weakness is that all of its eggs are in one basket.[16] Until its recent diversification, Coca Cola was a Stage II corporation.

The *Stage III* corporation focuses on internal operating efficiencies. These corporations grow by diversifying their product lines and expanding to cover wider geographical areas. These corporations move to a divisional structure with a central headquarters (see Fig. 8.2). Headquarters attempts to coordinate the activities of its operating divisions through performance and results-oriented control and reporting systems, and by stressing corporate planning techniques. The divisions are not tightly controlled, but are held responsible for their own performance results. Therefore, to be effective, there has to be a decentralized decision process. The greatest strength of a Stage III corporation is its almost unlimited resources. Its most significant weakness is that it is usually so large and complex that it tends to become relatively inflexible.[17] General Electric, DuPont, and General Motors are Stage III corporations.

These three stages of corporate development are summarized in depth by Thain in Tables 8.2 and 8.3.

STAGE I: ENTREPRENEURIAL

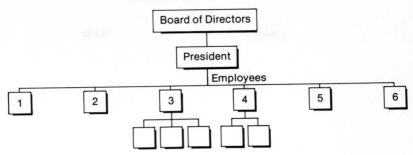

STAGE II: FUNCTIONALLY ORGANIZED

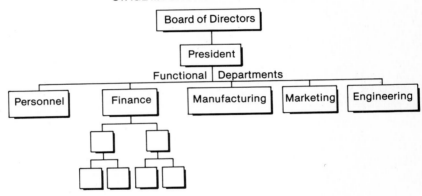

STAGE III: DIVERSIFIED AND DECENTRALIZED

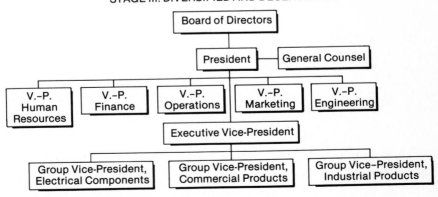

Figure 8.2 *Stages of corporate development.*

Table 8.2 KEY FACTORS IN TOP MANAGEMENT PROCESS IN STAGE I, II, AND III COMPANIES

FUNCTION	STAGE I	STAGE II	STAGE III
1. Size-up: Major problems	Survival and growth dealing with short-term operating problems.	Growth, rationalization, and expansion of resources, providing for adequate attention to product problems.	Trusteeship in management and investment and control of large, increasing, and diversified resource. Also, important to diagnose and take action on problems at division level.
2. Objectives	Personal and subjective.	Profits and meeting functionally oriented budgets and performance targets.	ROI, profits, earnings per share.
3. Strategy	Implicit and personal; exploitation of immediate opportunities seen by owner-manager.	Functionally oriented moves restricted to "one product" scope; exploitation of one basic product or service field.	Growth and product diversification; exploitation of general business opportunities.
4. Organization: Major characteristic of structure	One unit, "one-man show."	One-unit, functionally specialized group.	Multiunit general staff office and decentralized operating divisions.

5. (a) Measurement and control	Personal, subjective control based on simple accounting system and daily communication and observation.	Control grows beyond one man; assessment of functional operations necessary; structured control systems evolve.	Complex formal system geared to comparative assessment of performance measures, indicating problems and opportunities and assessing management ability of division managers.
5. (b) Key performance indicators	Personal criteria, relationships with owner, operating efficiency, ability to solve operating problems.	Functional and internal criteria such as sales, performance compared to budget, size of empire, status in group, personal relationships, etc.	More impersonal application of comparisons such as profits, ROI, P/E ratio, sales, market share, productivity, product leadership, personnel development, employee attitudes, public responsibility.
6. Reward-punishment system	Informal, personal, subjective; used to maintain control and divide small pool of resources to provide personal incentives for key performers.	More structured; usually based to a greater extent on agreed policies as opposed to personal opinion and relationships.	Allotment by "due process" of a wide variety of different rewards and punishments on a formal and systematic basis. Company-wide policies usually apply to many different classes of managers and workers with few major exceptions for individual cases.

SOURCE: D. H. Thain, "Stages of Corporate Development," *Business Quarterly* (Winter 1969), p. 37. Copyright © 1969 by *The Business Quarterly*. Reprinted by permission.

Table 8.3   GENERAL EMPHASIS IN BUSINESS FUNCTIONS IN STAGE I, II AND III COMPANIES

FUNCTION	STAGE I	STAGE II	STAGE III
Major emphasis	Usually an operating orientation as opposed to product or functional emphasis.	Functional orientation.	Investment-trusteeship orientation in president's office, functional orientation in staff, and product orientation in line.
Marketing	Major marketing problem is generating sales, usually only one or small number of employees involved.	Specialization develops in advertising, sales, promotion, marketing research, etc.	Marketing functions become well developed and extremely complex with specialization in a wide variety of marketing functions by product line and geographical area.
Production	Usually a simple, efficient factory operation geared to turn out maximum production with minimum investment.	Production operations become more specialized; production management improves with attendant increases in overhead.	Complex production function and product specialization usually accompanied by extensive engineering, research and development studies, and careful consideration of vertical integration and make or buy problems.

Measurement and control	Simple accounting system usually supervised by outside accountant.	Accounting system becomes more complex with emphasis on cost accounting and simple statistical techniques; control system is adapted to functional decisions and problems.	Complex accounting, control and mathematical decision-making tools supervised by functional specialists and emphasizing product profitability and capital investment decisions.
Finance	Almost nonexistent, except to work with banker as necessary.	More sophisticated forecasting and cash budgeting techniques used for purpose of planning capital needs and reducing cost of capital.	Complex problems of portfolio management aimed at increasing return on invested capital in all divisions and overall.
Personnel	Handled on a personal basis by owner-manager.	Additional function specialization: evolution of formal policies for hiring, firing, training, and promoting.	Development of considerable sophistication both in special head office staff department and in division line operating departments in regard to hiring and training personnel necessary to perpetuate the company complex "manpower planning" approach often utilized.

SOURCE: D. H. Thain, "Stages of Corporate Development," *Business Quarterly* (Winter 1969), p. 37. Copyright © 1969 by *The Business Quarterly.* Reprinted by permission.

In his study, Chandler noted that the empire builder was rarely the person who created the new structure to fit the new strategy, and that, as a result, the transition from one stage to another is often a painful one. This was true of both General Motors under the management of William Durant and Ford Motor Company under its founder Henry Ford. Thain, in Table 8.4, summarizes the internal and external blocks to movement from one stage to another.

Although it has been suggested that an additional phase in a corporation's development is the multinational or "global" stage,[18] this could be viewed as just a variation of the Stage III, multidivisional corporation. A truly multinational or global corporation usually has decentralized investment centers based on geography rather than on product line or strategic business unit. (Refer to Chapter 10 for additional information on multinational corporations.)

Organizational life cycle. A more recent approach to better understanding the development of corporations is that of the organizational "life cycle."[19] Instead of considering stages in terms of structure, this approach places the primary emphasis on the dominant issue facing the corporation. The specific organizational structure, therefore, becomes a secondary concern. These stages are *Birth* (Stage I), *Vertical Growth* (Stage II), *Horizontal Growth and Consolidation* (Stage III), *Decline* (Stage IV), and *Death* (Stage V). The impact of these stages on corporate structure and strategy is summarized in Table 8.5.

Some of the characteristics of a *Stage IV* corporation in decline are as follows:

1. Most or all of the product lines are at the mature or declining stage of their product life cycle.

2. Sales are declining or stagnant, especially if expressed in constant dollars.

3. Distributors are cutting back on carrying or promoting the products.

4. The corporation's niche in the market place has been lost.

5. Some or all of the divisional operations are less profitable, some even sustaining losses.

6. Emphasis is on cost cutting and tightening the internal controls over all operations. There is pressure to reduce inventories and collect accounts receivable.

7. Divisional activities—such as purchasing or advertising—are recentralized for economies of scale.

8. Serious cash flow problems arise. The quick ratio is at a dangerous low. The corporation may have only two or three days of cash on hand with annual sales of $30,000,000. The situation can deteriorate to one of holding off creditors to avoid bankruptcy.

Table 8.4 BLOCKS TO DEVELOPMENT

a) Internal Blocks

STAGE I TO II	STAGE II TO III
Lack of ambition and drive. Personal reasons of owner-manager for avoiding change in status quo. Lack of operating efficiency. Lack of quantity and quality of operating personnel. Lack of resources such as borrowing power, plant and equipment, salesmen, etc. Product problems and weaknesses. Lack of planning and organizational ability.	Unwillingness to take the risks involved. Management resistance to change for a variety of reasons including old age, aversion to risk taking, desire to protect personal empires, etc. Personal reasons among managers for defending the status quo. Lack of control system related to appraisal of investment of decentralized operations. Lack of budgetary control ability. Organizational inflexibility. Lack of management vision to see opportunities for expansion. Lack of management development, i.e., not enough managers to handle expansion. Management turnover and loss of promising young managers. Lack of ability to formulate and implement strategy that makes company relevant to changing conditions. Refusal to delegate power and authority for diversification.

b) External Blocks

STAGE I TO II	STAGE II TO III
Unfavorable economic conditions. Lack of market growth. Tight money or lack of an underwriter who will assist the company "to go public." Labor shortages in quality and quantity. Technological obsolescence of product.	Unfavorable economic, political, technological, and social conditions and/or trends. Lack of access to financial or management resources. Overly conservative accountants, lawyers, investment bankers, etc. Lack of domestic markets necessary to support large diversified corporation. "The conservative mentality," e.g., cultural contentment with the status quo and lack of desire to grow and develop.

SOURCE: D. H. Thain, "Stages of Corporate Development," *Business Quarterly* (Winter 1969), pp. 43–44. Copyright © by *The Business Quarterly*. Reprinted by permission.

9. Headquarters staff is reduced, and the overall management structure is streamlined. The hiring of both management and employees stops.

10. Pay raises are frozen; pay reduction may be initiated.

11. Bonuses for executives are eliminated.

12. The main issue becomes survival.

In the early 1980s, corporations finding themselves in Stage IV with many of these characteristics were Chrysler and AM International (previously known as the Addressograph-Multigraph Corporation).

Unless a corporation is able to resolve the critical issues in Stage IV, it is likely to move into *Stage V*, corporate death. The corporation is forced into bankruptcy. In 1979, 29,500 corporations filed for bankruptcy.[20] As in the cases of Rolls Royce and Penn Central, however, the corporation may rise like a phoenix from its own ashes and live again. The company can be reorganized or liquidated, depending upon the individual circumstances. In some liquidations, the corporation's name is purchased, and the purchasing corporation establishes a new subsidiary with that name. Table 8.6 lists what happened to five bankrupt corporations.

It is interesting to note that Penn Central is no longer a railroad. In 1979, it acquired Marathon Manufacturing Co., which makes oil drilling rigs. In 1981, it purchased GK Technologies, Inc., an electronics company, and Colt Industries, Inc. Richard Dicker, Penn Central's chairman and CEO stated that these acquisitions were part of a "strategic plan" to establish the corporation as "a major manufacturer and supplier of capital goods, serving the nation's vital industries."[21]

It is important to realize that not all corporations will move through these five stages in order. Some corporations, for example, may never move past Stage II. Others, like General Motors, may go directly from Stage I to Stage III. A large number will go from Stage I into Stages IV and V. Ford, for example, was unable to move from Stage I into Stage II as long as Henry Ford, I was in command. Its inability to realign itself no doubt contributed to its movement into Stage IV just before World War II. After the war, Henry Ford II's turnaround strategy successfully restructured the corporation as a Stage II firm.

Staffing

The implementation of new strategy and policies often calls for a different utilization of personnel. If growth strategies are to be implemented, new people need to be hired and trained. Experienced people with the necessary skills need to be found for promotion into newly created managerial positions. For example, if a firm has decided to integrate forward by opening its own retail outlets, one key concern is the ability of the corporation to find, hire, and train store managers. If a corporation adopts a retrenchment strategy, however, a large number of people may need

Table 8.5 CORPORATE LIFE CYCLE

STAGE I	STAGE II	STAGE III	STAGE IV	STAGE V
Birth	Vertical growth.	Horizontal growth and consolidation	Decline.	Death.
Entrepreneur domination	Functional management emphasized.	Decentralization into profit centers/investment centers.	Structural surgery.	Dismemberment of structure.
Growth strategies	Growth or stability strategies.	Growth or stability strategies.	Retrenchment strategies.	Liquidation strategies.

Table 8.6 THE INS AND OUTS OF FIVE LARGE BANKRUPTCIES

ORIGINAL COMPANY (Reorganization Filing Date)	Total Liabilities in Millions	Security of Bankrupt Company	Prebankruptcy Market Value of 1 Bond or 100 Shares*	NEW COMPANY (Date Reorganization Completed)	Securities in New Company or Cash Received in Reorganization or Liquidation	Value (Based on Recent Market)
Penn Central Transportation Co. (June 1970)	$3,600	New York Central—6% bonds due 1980.	$720	Penn Central Corp. (October 1978)	.275 Series A and 164 Series B mortgage bonds + 21.98 shares B preferred + 9.91 shares common + $147	$798
Penn Central Co.—100% owner of P.C.T.C. (July 1976)	$125	Common stock.	$150		4 shares common.	$83
W. T. Grant Co. (October 1975)	$1,031	4¾% sinking-fund debentures due 1987.	$360	Company is in liquidation.	$1,000.	$1,000
		Common stock.	$338		Probably none.	—

Company		Security				
Equity Funding Corp. of America (April 1973)	$594	9½% debentures due 1990.	$1,048	Orion Capital Corp. (March 1976)	71.2 shares common.	$703
		Common stock.	$2,538		28.7 shares common.	$284
Interstate Stores Inc. (May 1974)	$208	4% convertible subordinated debentures due 1992.	$220	Toys R Us Inc. (April 1978)	117 shares common.	$1,931
		Common stock.	$163		66.7 shares common.	$1,101
King Resources Co. (August 1971)	$117	5½% convertible subordinated debentures in 1988.	$90	Phoenix Resources Co. (January 1978)	55.5 shares B common + $2.83	$1,182
		Common stock.	$181		1 share B common + $2.13	$23

*One month before bankruptcy filing, except for stock of Equity Funding and King Resources. The price on March 16, 1973, was used for determining stock purchasers' participation in the Equity Funding reorganization. Purchasers who bought King Resources stock after January 29, 1971, the date used in these calculations, got nothing from that reorganization.

source: M. Greenebaum, "Profiting from Investment in Corporate Failures," *Fortune*, May 7, 1979, p. 317. Adapted from material originally appearing in *Fortune* Magazine (Copyright © 1979 Time, Inc.) by permission.

to be laid off or fired; and top management, as well as the divisional managers, need to specify criteria used to make these personnel decisions. Should employees be fired on the basis of low seniority or on the basis of poor performance? Sometimes corporations find it easier to close an entire division in order to avoid choosing which individuals to fire. The University of Michigan followed this approach in 1981 when it cut back expenses by dropping its entire Geography Department.

Some authorities have suggested that the types of general managers needed to effectively implement a new divisional or SBU strategy varies depending upon the strategic direction of the division.[22] Depending on the situation of a specific division as determined by the GE Business Screen Matrix (Fig. 6.3), the "best" or most appropriate division manager may need to have a specific mix of skills and experiences. Some of these "types" are depicted in Fig. 8.3.

There are a number of ways to ensure a continuous development of people for important managerial positions. One approach is to establish a sound *performance appraisal system* to identify good performers with

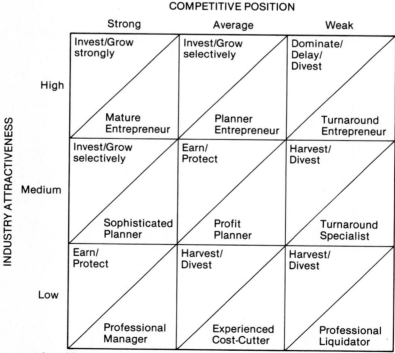

SOURCE: Adapted from C. W. Hofer and M. J. Davoust, *Successful Strategic Management,* (Chicago, Ill.: Kearney, 1977), pp. 45 and 82.

Figure 8.3 *The types of general managers needed to strategically manage different types of businesses.*

managerial potential. People need to be rewarded through pay increases and promotions on the basis of performance rather than on personality traits or ingratiating behavior. Sloan reports that the heavy emphasis in General Motors on the rate of return as a standard of performance was a key reason for GM's early success: "It provided executives with a quantitative basis for sound decision making, and thereby laid the foundation for what was to be one of General Motors' most important characteristics, namely, its effort to achieve open-minded communication and objective consideration of facts."[23]

A number of large organizations have started to use *assessment centers* to evaluate a person's suitability for a management position. Popularized by AT&T in the mid-1950s, corporations such as Standard Oil of Ohio and GE now use them.[24] Each specifically tailored to its corporation, these assessment centers are unique in that they use special interviews, management games, in-basket exercises, leaderless group discussions, case analyses, decision making exercises, and oral presentations to assess the potential of employees for higher-level positions. People are promoted into specific positions based on their performance in the assessment center. Many assessment centers have proved to be highly predictive of subsequent managerial performance.[25]

Directing

To effectively implement a new strategy, appropriate authority and responsibility must be delegated to the operational managers. People should be motivated to act in desired ways. Further, the actions must be coordinated to result in effective performance. Managers should be stimulated to find creative solutions to implementation problems without getting bogged down in conflict. When the proper people have been placed in the proper positions, a corporation needs a system to direct them toward the proper implementation of corporate, business, and functional strategies.

Management by objectives. One organization-wide approach to help assure purposeful action toward desired objectives is management by objectives (MBO). MBO serves as a link between organizational objectives and the behavior of individuals. Since it is a system that links plans with performance, it is a powerful implementation technique.

Although there is some disagreement about the purpose of MBO, most authorities agree that this approach involves (1) establishing and communicating organizational objectives, (2) setting individual objectives that help implement organizational ones, and (3) periodically reviewing performance as it relates to the objectives.[26] MBO provides an opportunity to connect the objectives of people at each level to those at the next higher level: "If carried out logically and ideally, the goals at each level would be contributing most directly toward overall organizational objectives . . . . MBO provides a potential method of integrating the physical, financial, and human resource plans of the organization to the goals that an individual is expected to achieve."[27] MBO, therefore, acts to tie together corporate, business, and functional objectives as well as the strategies developed to achieve them. The MBO process is depicted in Fig. 8.4.

Research on corporate MBO programs is mixed, but tends to support the belief that MBO should result in higher levels of performance than other approaches that do not include performance goals, relevant feedback, and joint supervisor/subordinate goal setting.[28] Galbraith and Nathanson point out that the existence of an MBO program at Dow-Corning permits its matrix structure (as discussed in Chapter 5) to function effectively: "Because people work against goals and problems, rather than against each other, they have less need for hierarchy and tie-breaking."[29] At Dow-Corning, the agreed-upon objectives are used to help reach consensus and thus reduce the potential for the conflict inherent in a matrix-style organization.

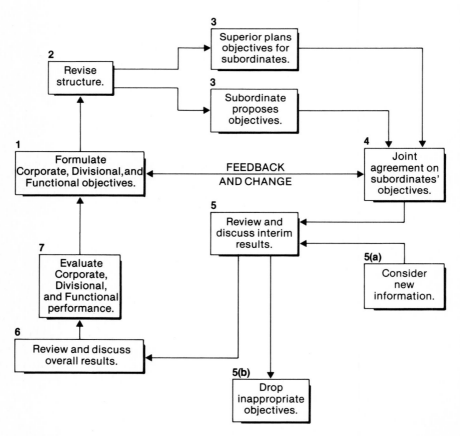

Figure 8.4   *The process of management by objectives.*

Incentive management. To ensure that there is a congruence between the needs of the corporation as a whole and the needs of the employees as individuals, an incentive system that rewards desired performance should be developed. Research confirms the conventional wisdom that when pay is tied to performance, it motivates higher productivity, strongly affecting both absenteeism and work quality.[30] Corporations have, therefore, developed various types of incentives for executives that range from stock options to cash bonuses. All these incentive plans should be linked in some way to corporate and divisional strategy.[31] Typical problems with reward systems are discussed in Chapter 9.

8.4 SUMMARY AND CONCLUSION

This chapter explains the implementation of strategy in terms of (1) *who* the operational managers are who must carry out strategic plans, (2) *what* they must do in order to implement strategy, and (3) *how* they should go about their activities. Vice-presidents of functional areas and directors of divisions or SBUs work with their subordinates to put together large-scale implementation plans. These plans include *programs*, *budgets*, and *procedures* and become more detailed as they move down the corporate "chain of command."

Strategy is implemented by management through planning, organizing, staffing, and directing activities.

Planning results in fairly detailed programs, budgets, and procedures.

Organizing deals with the design of an appropriate structure for the corporation. Research generally supports Chandler's proposal that changes in corporate strategy tend to lead to changes in organizational structure. Not only should a firm work to make its structure congruent with its strategy, it should also be aware that there is an organizational life cycle composed of stages of corporate development through which a corporation is likely to move.

Staffing focuses on finding and developing appropriate people for key positions. Without capable and committed middle managers, strategy can never be implemented satisfactorily. To this end, performance appraisal systems and assessment centers are used by a number of large corporations.

Directing deals with organization-wide approaches that direct operational managers and employees to effect the implementation of corporate, business, and functional strategies. One such approach is management by objectives (MBO), which is a link between organizational objectives and the behavior of operational managers. Its ability to tie planning with performance makes it a powerful implementation technique. The proper use of financial incentives, when integrated with a goal-centered approach such as MBO, is another method of directing effort toward achieving desired results.

DISCUSSION QUESTIONS

1. Japanese corporations typically involve many more organizational levels and people in the development of implementation plans than do U.S. corporations. Is this appropriate? Why or why not?

2. To what extent should top management be involved in strategy implementation?

3. Does structure follow strategy or does strategy follow structure? Why?

4. To what extent do you think top management in corporations operating in high-technology industries should be technically trained and educated?

5. Should corporations select a certain type of person to be a general manager of a division depending on the strategic situation of that particular division? Why or why not?

NOTES

1. A. D. Chandler, *Strategy and Structure* (Cambridge, Mass.: MIT Press, 1962), p. 14.

2. A. P. Sloan, Jr., *My Years With General Motors* (Garden City, N.Y.: Doubleday, Anchor Books, 1972).

3. J. R. Galbraith and D. A. Nathanson, *Strategy Implementation: The Role of Structure and Process* (St. Paul, Minn.: West Publishing Co., 1978), p. 47.

   P. H. Grinyer and M. Yasai-Ardekani, "Strategy, Structure, Size, and Bureaucracy," *Academy of Management Journal* (September 1981), pp. 471–486.

   P. Lorange, *Implementation of Strategic Planning* (Englewood Cliffs, N.J.: Prentice-Hall, 1982), p. 109.

4. Galbraith and Nathanson, p. 139.

5. D. R. Dalton, W. D. Todor, M. J. Spendolini, G. J. Fielding, and L. W. Porter, "Organization Structure and Performance: A Critical Review," *Academy of Management Review* (January 1980), pp. 49–64.

6. T. Burns and G. M. Stalker, *The Management of Innovation* (London: Tavistok Publications, 1961).

7. P. R. Lawrence and J. W. Lorsch, *Organization and Environment* (Homewood, Ill.: Richard D. Irwin, Inc., 1967), p. 138.

8. William K. Hall, "SBUs: Hot New Topic in the Management of Diversification," *Business Horizons* (February 1978), p. 19.

9. "Evolving the GE Management System," *General Electric Monogram* (November–December 1977), p. 4.

10. Hall, pp. 19 and 25.

11. Hall, p. 25.

12. P. G. W. Keen, "Communications in the 21st Century: Telecommunications and Business Policy," *Organizational Dynamics* (Autumn 1981), pp. 54–67.

13. A. L. Frohman, "Technology As a Competitive Weapon," *Harvard Business Review* (January–February 1982), p. 97.

14. A. L. Frohman, p. 97.

15. D. H. Thain, "Stages of Corporate Development," *The Business Quarterly* (Winter 1969), pp. 32–45.

    B. R. Scott, "Stages of Corporate Development" (Boston: Intercollegiate Case Clearing House, no. 9-371-294, 1971); and "The Industrial State: Old Myths and New Realities," *Harvard Business Review* (March–April 1973).

    R. V. Tuason, "Corporate Life Cycle and the Evaluation of Corporate Strategy," *Proceedings, The Academy of Management* (August 1973), pp. 35–40.

16. Thain, p. 35.

17. Thain, p. 39.

18. Galbraith and Nathanson, p. 118.

19. D. A. Tansik, R. B. Chase, and N. J. Aquilano, *Management: A Life Cycle Approach* (Homewood, Ill.: Richard D. Irwin, Inc., 1980).

    J. R. Kimberly, R. H. Miles, and Associates, *The Organizational Life Cycle* (San Francisco: Jossey-Bass, 1980).

20. "The Economic Case against Federal Bailouts," *Business Week* (March 24, 1980), p. 105.

21. "Penn Central Signs Colt Merger Accord, Says It's Discussing Sale of Some Units," *Wall Street Journal* (August 31, 1981), p. 8.

22. C. W. Hofer, E. A. Murray, Jr., R. Charam, and R. A. Pitts, *Strategic Management: A Casebook in Business Policy and Planning* (St. Paul, Minn.: West Publishing Co., 1980), p. 19.

23. Sloan, p. 163.

24. J. B. Miner and M. G. Miner, *Personnel and Industrial Relations*, 3rd ed. (New York: Macmillan, 1977), pp. 194–196.

25. Miner and Miner, p. 196.

26. S. J. Carroll, Jr. and H. L. Tosi, Jr., *Management by Objectives* (New York: Macmillan, 1973), p. 3.

27. M. D. Richards, *Organizational Goal Structures.* (St. Paul, Minn.: West Publishing Co., 1978), p. 128.

28. Carroll and Tosi, p. 16.

29. Galbraith and Nathanson, p. 99.

30. E. E. Lawler III, *Pay and Organizational Effectiveness* (New York: MacGraw-Hill, 1971).

    E. A. Locke, "How to Motivate Employees" (Paper presented at the NATO conference on changes in the nature and quality of working life, Thessaloniki, Greece, August 19–24, 1979.) Cited in E. E. Lawler III, *Pay and Organizational Development* (Reading, Mass.: Addison-Wesley, 1981), p. 3.

31. M. S. Salter, "Tailor Incentive Compensation to Strategy," *Harvard Business Review* (March–April 1973), pp. 94–102.

STRATEGIC MANAGEMENT MODEL

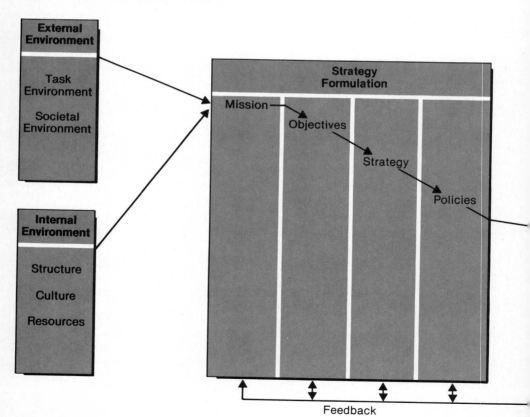

EVALUATION
AND CONTROL

CHAPTER 9

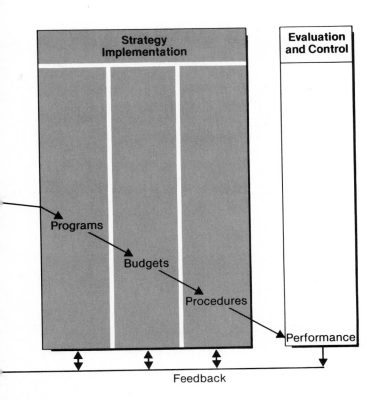

The last part of the strategic management model is the evaluation of performance and the control of work activities. This process may be viewed as a five-step feedback model as depicted in Fig. 9.1.

1. *Determine what to measure.* Top managers as well as operational managers need to specify what implementation processes and results will be monitored and evaluated. The processes and results must be capable of being measured in a reasonably objective and consistent manner. The focus should be on the most significant elements in a process—the ones that account for the highest proportion of expense or the greatest number of problems.

2. *Establish standards of performance.* Standards used to measure performance are detailed expressions of strategic objectives. They are *measures* of what are acceptable performance results. Each standard usually includes a *tolerance range* within which certain deviations will be accepted as satisfactory. Standards can be set not only for final output, but for intermediate stages of production output.

3. *Measure actual performance.* Measurements must be made at predetermined times.

4. *Compare actual performance with the standard.* If actual performance results are within the desired tolerance range, the measurement process stops here.

5. *Take corrective action.* If actual results fall outside the desired tolerance range, action must be taken to correct the deviation. The following must be determined:

   a) Is the deviation only a chance fluctuation?

   b) Are the processes being carried out incorrectly?

   c) Are the processes appropriate to the achievement of the desired standard?

Action must be taken that will not only correct the deviation, but also prevent its happening again.

The strategic management model shows that evaluation and control information is fed back and assimilated into the entire management process. This information consists of performance data and activity reports (gathered in step 3 of Fig. 9.1). If undesired performance is the result of an inappropriate *use* of the strategic management processes, operational managers must know about it in order to correct employee activity. Top management need not be involved. If, however, undesired performance results from the processes themselves, top managers, as well as operational managers, must know about it in order to develop new implementation programs or procedures.

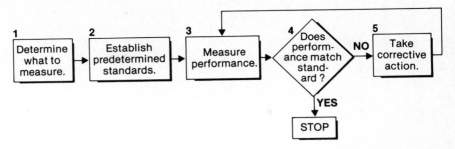

Figure 9.1 *Evaluation and control process.*

9.1 MEASURING PERFORMANCE

The kind of measures used will depend on the organizational unit to be measured, as well as on the objectives to be achieved. Certain measures, such as return on investment, are very appropriate for evaluating the ability of a corporation or division to achieve a profitability objective. These measures, however, are inadequate for evaluating other objectives a corporation may want to achieve: social responsibility or employee development, for instance. Different measures are required for different objectives. Even though profitability is the major objective for a corporation, using return on investment alone may be insufficient as a control device. ROI, for example, can only be computed *after* profits are totaled for a period. It tells what happened–not what *is* happening or what *will* happen. A firm, therefore, needs to develop measures that predict likely profitability. These are referred to as "steering" or "feedforward" controls because they measure variables that influence profitability.

Measures of Corporate Performance

The most commonly used measure of corporate performance (in terms of profits) is return on investment. As discussed in Chapter 2, it is simply the result of dividing net income before taxes by total assets. Other popular measures are return on equity and earnings per share. Although there are a number of advantages to using ROI, there are also a number of distinct limitations. Some of these are detailed in Table 9.1.

Value added measures. Assuming that any one measure is bound to have some shortcomings, Hofer recommends the use of three new measures to evaluate a corporation's performance results (see Table 9.2). These measures are based on *value added* and are attempts to measure

**Table 9.1   ADVANTAGES AND LIMITATIONS OF ROI AS A
MEASURE OF CORPORATE PERFORMANCE**

ADVANTAGES

1. ROI is a single comprehensive figure influenced by everything that happens.
2. It measures how well the division manager uses the property of the company to generate profits. It is also a good way to check on the accuracy of capital investment proposals.
3. It is a common denominator that can be compared with many entities.
4. It provides an incentive to use existing assets efficiently.
5. It provides an incentive to acquire new assets only when doing so would increase the return.

LIMITATIONS

1. ROI is very sensitive to depreciation policy. Depreciation write-off variances between divisions affect ROI performance. Accelerated depreciation techniques reduce ROI, conflicting with capital budgeting discounted cash-flow analysis.
2. ROI is sensitive to book value. Older plants with more depreciated assets have relatively lower investment bases than newer plants (note also the effect of inflation), thus increasing ROI. Note that asset investment may be held down or assets disposed of in order to increase ROI performance.
3. In many firms that use ROI, one division sells to another. As a result, transfer pricing must occur. Expenses incurred affect profit. Since, in theory, the transfer price should be based on the total impact on firm profit, some investment center managers are bound to suffer. Equitable transfer prices are difficult to determine.
4. If one division operates in an industry that has favorable conditions and another division operates in an industry that has unfavorable conditions, the former division will automatically "look" better than the other.
5. The time span of concern here is short range. The performance of division managers should be measured in the long run. This is top management's time-span capacity.
6. The business cycle strongly affects ROI performance, often despite managerial performance.

SOURCE: J. M. Higgins, *Organizational Policy and Strategic Management: Text and Cases*, (Hinsdale, Ill.: The Dryden Press, 1979), p. 141. Copyright © 1979 by the Dryden Press, a division of Holt, Rinehart and Winston, Publishers. Reprinted by permission of Holt, Rinehart and Winston, CBS College Publishing.

directly the contribution a corporation makes to society. Value added is the difference between dollar sales and the cost of raw materials and purchased parts. Return on value added (ROVA) is a second measure, one that divides net profits before tax by value added and converts the quotient to a percentage. Preliminary studies by Hofer suggest that ROVA tends to stabilize in the range of 12% to 18% for most industries in the maturity or saturation phases of market evolution.[1]

Evaluation of top management. Through its strategy, audit, and compensation committees, a board of directors closely evaluates the job per-

Table 9.2 THREE NEW MEASURES OF CORPORATE PERFORMANCE

PERFORMANCE CHARACTERISTIC	SOME TRADITIONAL MEASURES	PROPOSED NEW MEASURES
Growth	Dollar sales, unit sales, dollar assets.	Value added*
Efficiency	Gross margin, net profits, net profits/dollar sales.	ROVA†
Asset utilization	ROI, return on equity, earnings per share.	ROVA/ROI

*Value added = Dollar sales − Cost of raw materials and purchased parts.

†ROVA: Return on value added = $\dfrac{\text{Net profits before tax}}{\text{Value}} \times 100\%$.

SOURCE: As reported in W. G. Glueck, *Business Policy and Strategic Management*, 3rd ed. (New York: McGraw-Hill, 1980), p. 355. From C. W. Hofer, "ROVA: A New Measure for Assessing Organizational Effectiveness," Graduate School of Business, New York University, 1979. Copyright © C. W. Hofer, 1979. Reprinted by permission.

formance of the CEO and the top management team. It is, of course, primarily concerned with overall profitability as measured by return on investment, return on assets, and return on equity. The absence of short-run profitability is certainly a factor contributing to the firing of any CEO.[2] The board will also, however, be concerned with other factors. For example, McSweeney recommends the incorporation of a number of areas of concern on a scorecard for use by the board. Figure 9.2 is one example of such a scorecard.

As shown in Fig. 9.2, the board should evaluate top management not only on return, but also on factors relating to its strategic management practices. Has the top management team set reasonable long-run as well as short-run objectives? Has it formulated innovative strategies? Has it worked closely with operational managers to develop realistic implementation plans, schedules, and budgets? Has it developed and used appropriate measures of corporate and divisional performance for feedback and control? Has it provided the board with appropriate feedback on corporate performance in advance of key decision points? These and other questions should be raised by a board of directors as they evaluate the performance of top management.

The specific items that are used by a board to evalute its top management should be derived from the objectives agreed to earlier by both the board and top management. If better relations with the local community and improved safety practices in work areas were selected as objectives for the year (or for five years), these items should be included in the evaluation. In addition, other factors should be included that tend to predict profitability. The PIMS study, for example, found certain factors to be related to corporate profitability. Some of the most important ones were market share, product quality, marketing expenditures, R&D ex-

General scoreboard	Good	Fair	Poor
Return on stockholders' equity			
Return on sales			
Management of stockholders' assets			
Development of sound organizational structure			
Development of successors			
Development of proprietary products			
Development of organization morale			
Development of corporate image			
Development of growth potential			
Percentage of industry by segments			
Divestments			
Acquisitions			
Application of research & development			
Application of engineering & technology			
International			

SOURCE: E. McSweeney, "A Scorecard For Rating Management," *Business Week* (June 8, 1974), p. 15. Reprinted from the June 8, 1974 issue of *Business Week* by special permission. Copyright © 1974 by McGraw-Hill, Inc., New York. All rights reserved.

Figure 9.2 *Scorecard to rate top management.*

penditures, investment intensity (total investment over sales), and corporate diversity. In particular, those corporations with both high market share and superior quality were found in the study to average a 28.3% ROI. The third most important factor after market share and quality was investment intensity. The higher the ratio of investment to sales, the lower the ROI.[3]

Key performance areas. In order for top management to establish effective control systems for the entire corporation, it must identify "key performance areas." These areas must reflect important corporate objectives. According to Stoner, "Key performance or key result areas are those aspects of the unit or organization that *have* to function effectively in order for the entire unit or organization to succeed".[4] The broad controls that top management establishes for these key areas help to define the more detailed control systems and performance standards for lower-level managers. GE developed eight key performance areas and established standards for them. These areas are as follows:

1. *Profitability.* GE chose to use total dollar profits minus a charge for capital investment.

2. *Market position.* Market share, that is, the percent of available business for each product or service.

3. *Productivity.* Two measures were used—payroll dollar cost and the depreciation dollar costs of goods produced. These enabled GE to assess the efficiency with which labor and equipment were being used.

4. *Product leadership.* In each of GE's businesses, members of the engineering, manufacturing, marketing, and finance departments annually evaluated the costs, quality, and market position of each existing and each planned product.

5. *Personnel development.* Various reports were compiled to evaluate the manner in which GE was providing for present and future personnel needs.

6. *Employee attitudes.* Attitudes of employees toward the company were measured directly by regular attitude surveys, as well as indirectly by absenteeism and turnover.

7. *Public responsibility.* Indicators were developed to assess how well GE was carrying out its responsibilities to its employees, suppliers, and local communities.

8. *Balance between short-range and long-range goals.* An in-depth study of the interrelationships between key performance areas was carried out to ensure that immediate goals were not being attained at the expense of future profits and stability.[5]

Measures of Divisional and Functional Unit Performance

Corporations use a variety of techniques to evaluate and control performance in divisions, SBUs, and functional units. If a corporation is composed of SBUs or divisions, it will use many of the same performance measures (ROI, for instance) that it uses to assess overall corporation performance. To the extent that it can isolate specific functional units, such as R&D, the corporation may develop responsibility centers (cost centers or expense centers). A sophisticated corporation with an active board of directors will also use strategic audits to force feedback and evaluation on all corporate activities.

Evaluating a division or SBU. At Norton Company, each SBU is evaluated in depth every two years. This evaluation is conducted by the Strategy Guidance Committee, composed of the CEO, the financial vice-president, eight vice-presidents in charge of operations, the controller, assistant controller, vice-president for corporate development, and an assistant vice-president. At the same time that the line manager in charge of an SBU comes before the committee with a detailed strategy for each major segment of the unit's operations, the committee is evaluating the unit's performance according to past objectives, and arriving at its strategic position within the corporation and, therefore, its potential.

> The Strategy Guidance Committee looks at a strategic business unit from many viewpoints—return on net assets, return on sales, asset turnover, market share strategy. The committee might test sales growth rate against market growth rate against market share strategy. The committee also looks at competition, relative strengths and weaknesses, and cash generation plotted against market share strategy. It also places the unit on a balloon chart or growth/market share matrix for the entire company, to see how this unit fits in with all the others.[6]

The Strategy Guidance Committee looks at the SBU from all angles and asks a number of penetrating questions. Some of these questions are listed below.

EVALUATION OF A STRATEGIC BUSINESS UNIT AT NORTON COMPANY

- ☐ How does this unit contribute to the overall scheme of things?
- ☐ Does it help to balance the total?
- ☐ Does it increase or decrease the cyclical nature of the company?
- ☐ How does it relate to other Norton technologies, processes, or distribution systems?
- ☐ How successfully does it compete?
- ☐ How is it regarded by its customers and by its competitors?
- ☐ Does it hurt or improve the company's image with the investment community?
- ☐ What are its mission and mode of operation in terms of build, maintain, or harvest?
- ☐ Is its current strategy appropriate?
- ☐ Can we win and, if so, how?
- ☐ If it has changed its strategy or performance since the last review, why has it changed?
- ☐ What does our analysis suggest about the unit's profitability in comparison with similar businesses?

SOURCE: D. R. Melville, "Top Management's Role in Strategic Planning," *The Journal of Business Strategy*, vol. 1, no. 4, (Spring 1981), p. 63. Reprinted by permission from the *Journal of Business Strategy*. Copyright © 1981 by Warren, Gorham & Lamont Inc., Boston. All rights reserved.

Responsibility Centers. Control systems can be established to monitor functions, projects, or divisions. Budgets are typically used to control the financial indicators of performance. Responsibility centers are also used to isolate a unit so that it can be evaluated separately from the rest of the corporation. A responsibility center is headed by a manager responsible for the center's performance. It uses resources (measured in terms of costs) to produce a service or a product (measured in terms of volume or revenues). There are five major types of responsibility centers. They are determined by the way these resources and services or products are measured by the corporation's control system:[7]

1. *Standard cost centers.* Primarily used in manufacturing facilities, standard (or expected) costs are computed for each operation on the basis of historical data. To evaluate the center's performance, its total standard costs are multiplied by the units produced to give the expected cost of production, which is then compared to the actual cost of production.

2. *Revenue centers.* Production, usually in terms of unit or dollar sales, is measured without consideration of resource costs (e.g., salaries). The center is thus judged in terms of effectiveness rather than efficiency. The effectiveness of a sales region, for example, is determined by its actual sales compared to its projected or previous year's sales. Profits are not considered because sales departments have very limited influence over the cost of the products they sell.

3. *Expense centers.* Resources are measured in dollars without consideration of service or product costs. Thus budgets will have been prepared for "engineered" expenses (those costs that can be calculated) and for "discretionary" expenses. Typical expense centers are administrative, service, and research departments. They cost an organization money, but they only indirectly contribute to revenues.

4. *Profit centers.* Performance is measured in terms of the difference between revenues (which measure production) and expenditures (which measure resources). A profit center is typically established whenever an organizational unit has control over both its resources and its products or services. By having such centers, a corporation can be organized into divisions of separate product lines. The manager of each division is given autonomy to the extent that she or he is able to keep profits at a satisfactory (or better) level. Some organizational units that are not usually thought of as potentially autonomous can, for the purpose of profit-center evaluations, be made so. A manufacturing department, for example, may be converted from a standard cost center (or expense center) into a profit center by allowing it to charge a "transfer price" for each product it "sells" to

the sales department. The difference between the manufacturing cost per unit and the agreed-upon transfer price is the unit's "profit."

5. *Investment Centers.* As with profit centers, investment center performance is measured in terms of the difference between its resources and its services or products. Since most divisions in large manufacturing corporations use huge assets, such as plants and equipment, to make their products, evaluating their performance on the basis of profits alone ignores the size of their assets. For example, two divisions in a corporation make identical profits, but one division owns a $3 million plant, whereas the other owns a $1 million plant. Both make the same profits, but one is obviously more efficient: The smaller plant provides the stockholders with a better return on their investment.

The most widely used measure of investment center performance is ROI. Another measure, called residual income, is found by subtracting an interest charge from the net income. This interest charge could be based on the interest the corporation is actually paying to lenders for the assets being used. It could also be based on the amount of income that could have been earned if the assets had been invested somewhere else.

Sloan reports that the concept of rate of return on investments was crucial to General Motors' exercise of its permanent control of the whole corporation in a way consistent with its decentralized organization.[8] Donaldson Brown, who came to GM from DuPont in 1921, defined return on investment as a function of the profit margin and the rate of turnover of invested capital. Multiplying the profit margin by the investment turnover equals the percent of return on investment. Management can, therefore, increase the return on investment by increasing the rate of capital turnover in relation to sales (that is, increase volume) as well as by increasing profit margins (increase revenue and/or cut costs and expenses).[9]

Strategic Audits. Audits of corporate activities are used by various consulting firms as a way to measure performance, and are increasingly suggested for use by boards of directors as well as by others in managerial positions. Management audits have been developed to evaluate activities such as corporate social responsibility, functional areas such as the marketing department, divisions such as the international division, as well as to evaluate the corporation itself in a strategic audit (see Chapter 2). The strategic audit approach is likely to be increasingly used by corporations that become concerned with closely monitoring those activities that affect overall corporate effectiveness and efficiency.

9.2 PROBLEMS IN MEASURING PERFORMANCE

The measurement of performance is a crucial part of evaluation and control. Without objective measurements, it would be extremely difficult to make operational, let alone strategic decisions. Nevertheless, the monitoring and measurement of performance can cause side effects that to overall corporate performance are dysfunctional. Among the most frequent negative side effects are a *short-term orientation* and *goal displacement.*

Short-Term Orientation

Hodgetts and Wortman state that in many situations top executives do not analyze *either* the long-term implications of present operations on the strategy they have adopted *or* the operational impact of a strategy on the corporate mission. They report that long-run evaluations are *not* conducted because executives (1) may not realize their importance, (2) may feel that short-run considerations are more important than long-run considerations, (3) may not be personally evaluated on a long-term basis, or (4) may not have the time to make a long-run analysis.[10] There is no real justification for the first and last "reasons." If executives realize the importance of long-run evaluations, they make the time needed to conduct them. The short-term nature of most incentive and promotion plans, however, provide a rationale for the second and third reasons.

In Table 9.1, Higgins has shown that one of the limitations of ROI as a performance measure is its short-term nature. If the performance of corporation and division managers is evaluted primarily on the basis of a yearly ROI, the managers tend to focus their effort on those factors that have positive short-term effects. Of 174 corporations surveyed by Hewitt Associates, 79% rewarded executives for short-term performance (typically an annual bonus linked to pretax profit). In contrast, only 42% of the same firms offered long-term (more than one year) incentive plans. Pearl Meyer, executive consultant for Handy Associates, states, "... of the top 250 corporations, perhaps 10% to 15% have true long-run incentive plans, running from a minimum of seven to ten years to the entire length of an executive's career."[11]

As a result of this typical emphasis upon short-run performance, executives tend to find ways to improve their short-term reports. One way is to cut back on advertising and research. Another is to neglect maintenance or to make mergers that do more for this year's earnings than for the division's or corporation's future profits. Expensive retooling and plant modernization can be delayed as long as a manager can hide figures on production defects and absenteeism. Divisional or functional managers may be encouraged to "fudge" figures by top managers anxious to look good to the board. The system perpetuates itself until disaster strikes.

A more insidious danger resulting from heavy emphasis on short-term performance measures is their effect on top-level strategic decisions. Hayes and Abernathy contend that such control measures have helped cause a decline in technological innovations: "Conditioned by a market-driven strategy and held closely to account by a 'results now' ROI-oriented control system, American managers have increasingly refused to take the chance on innovative product/market development."[12] Even the highly-touted PIMS research (discussed in Chapters 6 and 7), has contributed to this short-run tendency by focusing on only those variables that affect ROI as a measure of corporate performance. For example, PIMS research has concluded that "increased investment almost invariably reduced ROI and cash flow in the short run. . ."[13]

Goal Displacement

The very monitoring and measuring of performance (if not carefully done) can actually result in a decline in overall corporate performance. A dysfunctional side effect known as "goal displacement" can occur. It is the confusion of means with ends. Goal displacement occurs when activities originally intended to help attain corporate objectives become ends in themselves—or are adapted to meet ends other than those for which they were intended.[14] Two types of goal displacement are *behavior substitution* and *suboptimization*.

Behavior substitution. Not all activities or aspects of performance can be easily quantified and measured. It may be very difficult to set standards for such desired activities as cooperation or initiative. As a result, managers of divisions or functional units tend to focus more of their attention on those behaviors that are measurable (and, therefore, easy to monitor and measure) than on those that are not. They ignore behaviors that are either unmeasurable or difficult to measure. A U.S. Navy quip sums up this problem: "What you inspect is what you get." If a person inspects the top of lockers for dust, but fails to check under the beds, soon the lockers will sparkle, but the dust under the beds will pile up!

The most frequently mentioned problem with management by objectives (MBO) is that the measurement process partially distorts the realities of the job. Objectives are made for areas where the measurement of accomplishments is relatively easy, such as with ROI, increased sales, or reduced cost. But these may not always be the most important areas. This problem becomes crucial in professional, service, or staff activities where the quantitative measurements are difficult. If, for example, a manager is achieving all of the quantifiable objectives, but in so doing, alienates the work force, the result may be a long-term drop in performance. If promotions are strictly based on measurable performance results, this manager may very likely be promoted or transferred before the negative employee attitudes result in complaints to the personnel office, strikes, or sabotage. The law governing the effect of measurement on behavior seems to be: *Quantifiable measures drive out nonquantifiable measures.*

Suboptimization. The emphasis in large corporations to develop separate responsibility centers can create some problems for the corporation as a whole. To the extent that a division or functional unit views itself as a separate entity, it may refuse to cooperate with other units or divisions in the same corporation if cooperation may in some way negatively affect its performance evaluation. The competition between divisions to achieve a high ROI can result in a refusal to share new technology or work process improvements. One division's attempt to optimize the accomplishment of its goals can cause other divisions to fall behind and thus negatively effect overall corporate performance. One common example of this type of suboptimization occurs when a marketing department approves an early shipment date to a customer as a means of getting an order, and forces the manufacturing department into overtime production for this one order. Production costs are raised, which reduces the manufacturing department's overall efficiency. The end result may be that, although marketing achieves its sales goal, the corporation fails to achieve its expected profitability.

9.3 GUIDELINES FOR PROPER CONTROL

In designing a control system, top management should remember that controls follow strategy.[15] Unless controls are a means to ensure the use of the proper strategy to achieve objectives, there is a strong likelihood that dysfunctional side effects will completely undermine the implementation of the objectives. The following guidelines are recommended:

1. Control should involve only the minimum amount of information needed to give a reliable picture of events. Too many controls create confusion.

2. Controls should monitor only meaningful activities and results, regardless of measurement difficulty. If cooperation between divisions is important to corporate performance, some form of qualitative or quantitative measure should be established in order to monitor cooperation.

3. Controls should be timely so that corrective action can be taken before it is too late. *Steering controls*, controls that monitor or measure the factors influencing performance, should be stressed in order to give advance notice of problems.

4. Long-term as well as short-term controls should be used. If only short-term measures are emphasized, a short-term managerial orientation is likely.

5. Controls should aim at pinpointing exceptions. Only those activities or results falling outside a predetermined tolerance range should call for action.

6. Emphasize the reward of meeting or exceeding standards rather than punishment for failing to meet standards. Heavy punishment of failure will typically result in goal displacement. Managers will "fudge" reports and lobby for lower standards.

Boards of directors need to take the initiative in developing long-term controls and corresponding incentive plans. According to Andrews, "The best criterion for appraising the quality of management performance, in the absence of personal failures or unexpected breakdowns, is management's success over time in executing a demanding and approved strategy that is continually tested against opportunity and need."[16]

The following are three approaches to better match rewards and the accomplishing of strategic objectives: (1) the *weighted-factor method*, (2) the *long-term evaluation method*, and (3) the *strategic funds deferral method*.

1. *Weighted-factor method.* Particularly appropriate for measuring and rewarding the performance of top SBU managers and group-level executives, when performance factors and their importance vary from one SBU to another. In one corporation we might find the following variations: the performance of high-growth SBUs measured in terms of market share, sales growth, designated future payoff, and progress on several future-oriented strategic projects; the performance of low-growth SBUs, in contrast, measured in terms of ROA and cash generation; and the performance of medium-growth SBUs measured for a combination of these factors.

2. *Long-term evaluation method.* This approach compensates managers for achieving objectives set over a multi-year period. An executive is promised some company stock or "performance units" (convertible into dollars) on the basis of long-term performance. An executive committee, for example, might set a particular objective in terms of growth in earnings per share during a five-year period. The giving of awards would be contingent on the corporation's meeting that objective within the designated time limit. Any executive leaving the corporation before the objective is met receives nothing.

3. *Strategic funds deferral method.* This method encourages executives to look at developmental expenses as different from expenses required to sustain current operations. The accounting statement for a corporate unit enters strategic funds as a separate entry below the current ROA. It is therefore possible to distinguish between those expense dollars consumed in the generation of current revenues and those invested in the future of the business.[17]

These incentive plans will probably gain increasing acceptance with U.S. business corporations in the near future. According to Stonich, "The most effective way to use a reward system to encourage future-oriented behavior is to combine the weighted-factor, long-term evaluation, and strategic funds deferral methods."[18]

9.4 SUMMARY AND CONCLUSION

The evaluation and control of performance is a five-step process: (1) determine what to measure, (2) establish standards for performance, (3) measure actual performance, (4) compare actual performance with the standard, and (5) take corrective action. Information coming from this process is fed back into the strategic management system so that both strategic and operational managers can correct performance deviations.

Although the most commonly used measures of corporate performance are the various return ratios, measures based on a value-added approach may be of some use. A number of corporations also monitor key factors related to ROI that may have predictive value. If a corporation has objectives other than profitability, it may wish to follow GE's example by establishing "key performance areas" for special attention.

Divisions, SBUs, and functional units are often broken down into responsibility centers to aid control. Such areas are often categorized as standard cost centers, revenue centers, expense centers, profit centers, and investment centers. Audits are becoming increasingly popular as a method to evaluate activities throughout the corporation.

The monitoring and measurement of performance can result in dysfunctional side effects that negatively affect overall corporate performance. Among the likely side effects are a short-term orientation and goal displacement. These problems can be reduced if top management remembers that controls should follow strategy. There should be as few controls as possible, and only meaningful activities and results should be monitored. Controls should be timely to both long-term as well as short-term orientations. They should pinpoint exceptions, but should be used more to reward than to punish individuals. Incentive plans should be based upon long-term as well as short-term results.

A proper evaluation and control system should act to complete the loop shown in the strategic management model. It should feed back information important not only to the implementation of strategy, but also to the initial formulation of strategy. In terms of the strategic decision-making process depicted in Fig. 6.1, the data coming from evaluation and control are the basis for step 1—evaluating current performance results. Because of this feedback effect, evaluation and control is the beginning as well as the end of the strategic management process.

DISCUSSION QUESTIONS

1. Is Fig. 9.1 a realistic model of the control process? Why or why not?
2. Are Hofer's value-added measures an improvement over traditional performance measures? Why or why not?
3. What are the values to a corporation of establishing "key performance areas"?
4. Why are goal displacement and short-run orientation likely side effects of the monitoring of performance? What can a corporation do to avoid them?
5. Is the evaluation and control process appropriate for a corporation that emphasizes creativity? Are control and creativity compatible? Explain.

NOTES

1. C. W. Hofer and D. Schendel, *Strategy Formulation: Analytical Concepts* (St. Paul, Minn.: West Publishing Co., 1978), p. 130.
2. L. R. Jauch, T. N. Martin, and R. N. Osborn, "Top Management under Fire," *Journal of Business Strategy* (Spring 1981), p. 39.
3. S. Schoeffler, R. D. Buzzell, and D. F. Heany, "Impact of Strategic Planning on Profit Performance," *Harvard Business Review* (March–April 1974), pp. 140–144.
4. J. A. F. Stoner, *Management*, 2nd ed. (Englewood Cliffs, N.J.: Prentice-Hall, 1982), pp. 603–604.
5. J. A. F. Stoner, *Management*, 1st ed. (Englewood Cliffs, N.J.: Prentice Hall, 1978), pp. 583–586.
6. D. R. Melville, "Top Management's Role in Strategic Planning," *Journal of Business Strategy* (Spring 1981), p. 63.
7. This discussion is based on R. N. Anthony, J. Dearden, and R. F. Vancil, *Management Control Systems* (Homewood, Ill.: Richard D. Irwin, Inc., 1972), pp. 200–203.
8. A. P. Sloan, Jr., *My Years with General Motors* (Garden City, N.Y.: Doubleday, Anchor Books, 1972), p. 159.
9. Sloan, p. 161.

10. R. M. Hodgetts and M. S. Wortman, *Administrative Policy*, 2nd ed. (New York: John Wiley & Sons, 1980), p. 128.

11. J. B. Quinn, "Why Executives Think Short," *Newsweek* (July 13, 1981), p. 11c.

12. R. H. Hayes and W. J. Abernathy, "Managing Our Way to Economic Decline," *Harvard Business Review* (July–August 1980), p. 72.

13. C. P. Zeithaml, C. R. Anderson, and F. T. Paine, "An Empirical Re-examination of Selected PIMS Findings," *Proceedings, Academy of Management* (August, 1981), p. 14.

14. H. R. Bobbitt, Jr., R. H. Breinholt, R. H. Doktor, and J. P. McNaul, *Organizational Behavior*, 2nd ed. (Englewood Cliffs, N.J.: Prentice-Hall, 1978), p. 99.

15. A. A. Thompson, Jr. and A. J. Strickland, III, *Strategy and Policy* (Plano, Tex.: Business Publications, 1981), p. 190.

16. K. R. Andrews, "Directors' Responsibility for Corporate Strategy," *Harvard Business Review* (November–December, 1980), p. 32.

17. P. J. Stonich, "Using Rewards in Implementing Strategy," *Strategic Management Journal*, vol. 2, no. 3 (1981), pp. 345–352.

18. Stonich, p. 351.

OTHER STRATEGIC CONCERNS

PART V

STRATEGIC MANAGEMENT MODEL

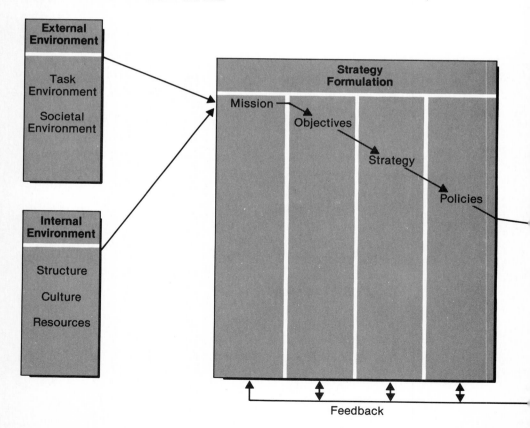

STRATEGIC MANAGEMENT OF MULTINATIONAL CORPORATIONS

CHAPTER 10

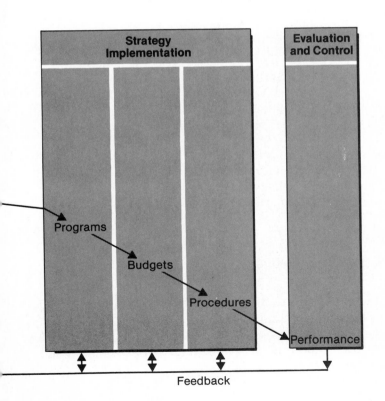

During much of its history, the United States was virtually self-sufficient. The distance between North America and Europe during the 1700s and 1800s helped force the country to develop its own industries if it was to expand and develop. As late as the 1960s, combined exports and imports of merchandise represented only 7% to 8% of the U.S. gross national product—the lowest of any major industrialized nation.[1] A large domestic market, plus a bountiful supply of natural resources and labor enabled major corporations to grow and become successful with only a casual interest in "foreign" markets. High tariff laws served to keep the business interests of other countries out of the United States while the infant domestic companies matured.

Since World War II, however, international trade has increased dramatically. In the past quarter century, the volume of goods traded between nations has climbed from less than $100 billion (in 1975 dollars) to more than $1 trillion.[2] The United States became much more concerned about international trade. From 1966 to 1975, U.S. exports of manufactured products and other nonagricultural goods expanded 266% from $23.4 billion to $85.6 billion. During this same period, sales by majority-owned affiliates of U.S. corporations doing business in other countries increased 370% from $97.8 billion to $458.3 billion.[3] By the 1980s, international considerations had become crucial to the strategic decisions of any large U.S. business corporation.

10.1 THE COMING GLOBAL VILLAGE

In 1965, Marshall McLuhan suggested that advances in communications and transportation technologies were drawing the people of the world closer together. As the time necessary for people and messages to travel from one continent to another was decreasing, the world was on its way to becoming a "global village" of interdependent people.[4] People in all countries were finding themselves becoming increasingly affected by huge multinational corporations (MNCs).

Going International

Three basic reasons can be listed for business corporations expanding their operations internationally:

1. Increased sales and profits can be earned by expanding market outlets and by exploiting growth opportunities. Foreign sales could thus absorb extra capacity and reduce unit costs. They could also spread economic risks over a wider number of markets. For example, while Ford's U.S. market share dropped below 25% in 1980, Ford of Britain's had risen to 32%, up six percentage points in four years.[5]

2. Competitive advantages can be gained by seeking low-cost production facilities in locations close to raw materials and/or cheap labor. Wider channels of distribution and access to new technology can be achieved through joint ventures. Both General Electric and Société Nationale d' Étude et de Construction de Moteurs d'Aviation (SNECMA), the French engine maker, benefited from their joint venture in forming CFM International to produce and sell jet engines to airlines.[6]

3. Raw material resources can be secured by engaging in the worldwide exploration for, and the processing, transportation, and marketing of raw materials. For years, the major rubber companies have owned rubber plantations in Southeast Asia. Oil companies have, of course, gone international for the same reason.

There are a number of *disadvantages*, however, in international expansion. For one thing, the strategic management process is far more complex for a multinational than for a domestic firm. Dymsza lists six limitations to international expansion.[7]

First, the multinational company faces a multiplicity of political, economic, legal, social, and cultural environments as well as a differential rate of change in them.

Second, there are complex interactions between a multinational firm and the multiplicity of their national environments because of national sovereignties, widely disparate economic and social conditions, as well as other factors.

Third, geographical distance, cultural and national differences, variations in business practices, and other differences make communications difficult between the parent corporation and its subsidiaries.

Fourth, the degree of significant economic, marketing, and other information required for planning varies a great deal among countries in availability, depth, and reliability. Furthermore, in any given host country, modern techniques for analyzing and developing data may not be highly developed. For example, an international corporation may find it difficult and expensive to conduct the effective market research essential for business planning.

Fifth, analysis of present and future competition may be more difficult to undertake in a number of countries because of differences in industrial structure and business practices.

Sixth, the multinational company is confronted not only with different national environments but also with regional organizations such as the European Economic Community, the European Trade Area, and the Latin American Free Trade Area, all of which are achieving various degrees of economic integration. The United Nations and specialized international organizations such as the International Bank for Reconstruction and Development, the International Finance Corporation, and the General Agreement of Tariffs and Trade (GATT) may also affect its future opportunities.

Becoming International

Perhaps the best reason for taking an international viewpoint in strategic management is the increasing rate of international investment and the marketing of imports in the United States. As depicted in Fig. 10.1, investments by foreign-based corporations in U.S. firms and properties have increased from slightly under $5 billion in 1954 to $43 billion in 1979. In 1982, according to Arthur D. Little, Inc., these investments should be $50 billion and still rising.[8] As in the case of American Motors and Renault, foreign investment may be the outright purchase of a domestic corporation's stock. Seagram, the Canadian distiller, made a valiant attempt in 1981 to outbid DuPont and Mobil Oil for control of Conoco, Inc. More often, however, investment takes the form of building or purchasing plants and facilities. As the 1980s began, Japanese firms such as Mitsubishi, Nissan, Honda, Daiwa House, and Zen-Noh Grain Corp. were building production facilities in the United States to manufacture automobiles, jet airplanes, television sets, houses, and grain elevators.[9] In 1976, Volkswagen purchased from Chrysler a recently built assembly plant near New Stanton, Pennsylvania to produce its new Rabbit model. In 1981, Bridgestone Tire and Rubber Co. of Japan was considering the purchase of the Nashville plant of Firestone Tire and Rubber.[10]

The Multinational Corporation

The multinational corporation is a very special type of international firm. Any U.S. company can call itself "international" if it has a small branch office in Juarez or Toronto. An international company engages in any

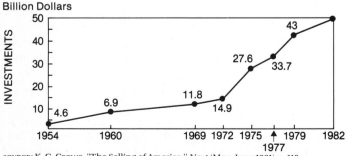

SOURCE: K. C. Crowe, "The Selling of America," *Next* (May–June 1981), p. 112. Reprinted by permission of *Next* Magazine, Medical Economics Co., Oradell, N.J.

Figure 10.1   *Foreign investment in the United States.*

combination of activities from exporting/importing to full-scale manu-facturing in foreign countries. The multinational corporation, in contrast, is a highly developed international company with a deep worldwide involvement, plus a global perspective in its management and decision making.[11] A more specific definition of an MNC is suggested by Dymsza:[12]

1. Although a multinational corporation may not do business in every region of the world, its decision makers consider opportunities throughout the world.

2. A considerable portion of its assets are invested internationally. One authority suggests that a firm becomes global when 20% of its assets are in other countries. Another suggests that the point is reached when operations in other nations account for at least 35% of the corporation's total sales and profits.

3. The corporation engages in international production and operates plants in a number of countries. These plants may range from assembly to fully integrated facilities.

4. Managerial decision making is based on a world-wide perspective. The international business is no longer a sideline or segregated activity. International operations are integrated into the corporation's overall business.

10.2 STRATEGY FORMULATION

As described in Chapter 1, the strategic management process includes strategy formulation, implementation, and evaluation and control. In order to formulate strategy, the top management of a multinational corporation must scan both the external environment for opportunities and threats, and the internal environment for strengths and weaknesses.

Scanning the External Environment

The dominant issue in the strategic management process of a multinational corporation is the external environment. The type of relationship an MNC can have with each factor in its task environment varies from one country to another and from one region to another. Societal environments vary so widely around the world that a corporation's internal environment and strategic management process must be very flexible. Cultural trends in West Germany, for example, have resulted in the inclusion of worker representatives in corporate strategic planning. Differences in the socio-cultural, economic, political-legal, and technological aspects of societal environments among countries strongly affects how an MNC conducts its marketing, financial, manufacturing, and other functional activities.

Socio-cultural. Different socio-cultural norms and values among nations will have important affects on MNC activities. For example, some cultures accept bribery and payoffs as a fact of life, whereas others punish them heavily. Most countries differentiate between "lubrication" or "grease" payments made to minor officials to expedite the execution of their duties and large-scale "whitemail" bribes intended to allow either a violation of the law or an illegal contribution designed to influence government policy. In some countries grease payments may be viewed by its citizens as an entitlement—necessary income to supplement low public salaries.[13] Since the dividing line between these two forms of extra payment is indistinct, an MNC must carefully monitor each country's norms to ensure its actions are in line with local practice. Ethics tend to become pragmatically bound to situations, and the top managers of MNCs may find themselves open to charges of being amoral.

In less developed countries (LDCs), most of the working population may be illiterate. As a result, there will likely be a shortage of skilled labor and supervisors. Manufacturing facilities have to be designed that mesh with the technical sophistication of the work force. If U.S. managers are used, they must be aware of the wide variance in working practices around the world, and totally familiar with those in the country where they are stationed. For example, it is common in Europe for employees to get added compensation according to the number of their family members or because of unpleasant working conditions. Finnish paper mill workers get a "sauna premium" for missing baths when they are asked to work on Sunday. Fiji Island miners receive a daily half-hour "sex break" to fulfill marital obligations.[14] Other examples abound.

Differences in language and social norms will heavily affect the marketing mix for a particular country. Product presentation, packaging, distribution channels, pricing, and advertising must be attuned to each culture. Examples are the many U.S. products and advertising approaches that were transferred to foreign countries without any adjustment. The chairman of the board of the Ogilvy and Mather advertising agency in England was quoted as saying, "It is probably safe to say that 90% of the commercially successful new products or services in Europe were first developed in the United States. So were 90% of the failures."[15] For example, western cosmetic firms such as Max Factor, Revlon, and Avon have had little success in selling their usual products in Japan. Some of the cultural factors affecting their sales were that in Japan perfume is hardly used, suntans are considered ugly, and bath oil is impractical in communal baths.[16]

Even if a product is desired by the public, literal translation of product names and slogans can ruin sales. For example, Pepsi Cola's "come alive" jingle was translated into German as "come alive out of the grave."[17] When General Motors introduced its Nova model into Latin America, it believed the name would translate well. Nova means star in Spanish.

Nevertheless, people began to pronounce it "no va," which in Spanish means "it does not go."[18]

Economic. The type of economic system in a country can strongly affect the kind of relationship an MNC can establish with a host country. The managers of an MNC based in a free market capitalistic country may have difficulty understanding the regulations affecting trade with a centrally planned socialistic country. Licensing, acquisition, and joint ventures may be severely restricted by such a host country. In addition, in most countries inflation and currency exchange rates create further difficulties for an MNC. An MNC's financial policy in an economy subject to rapid inflation must be altered to protect the firm against inflationary losses. Cash balances must be minimized. Credit terms must be restricted. Prices must be constantly watched. In addition, balance of payments problems in a host country may lead to currency devaluation, as occurred in Mexico in 1980 and 1982. Such devaluation leads to an MNC's taking large losses in terms of the assets and profits of its subsidiary in the devaluating country. In addition, a socialistic country may control the prices of the products sold by the MNC in that country, but may increase the price of the raw materials it sells to the MNC. This results in a severe profit squeeze as the host government attempts to pass the burden of inflation to "rich" multinational corporations.

Political-Legal. The system of laws and public policies governing business formation, acquisitions, and competitive activities acts to constrain the strategic options open to a multinational company. It is likely that a particular country will specify guidelines for hiring, firing, and promoting people, as well as giving employment ratios of "foreigners" to its citizens and restricting management prerogatives regarding unions. In addition, there are likely to be government policies dealing with ownership, licensing, repatriation of profits (profits leaving the host country for the MNC's home country), royalties, importing, and purchasing. Beyond these, there are likely to be both some sentiment for keeping out foreign goods by erecting tariff barriers, and some strong negative feeling about foreign control by an MNC of the host country's assets.

Many examples exist of countries expropriating and nationalizing foreign as well as domestic holdings. A recent example is that of France under socialist leader François Mitterand. In July 1981, the French government ordered immediate negotiations to discuss the purchase of three large firms: Honeywell Bull Computers (47% U.S. owned), ITT-France (99% U.S. owned), and Rouseel-Uclaf Drugs (57% West German owned).[19] Another example is that of Canada's recent legislation requiring U.S. energy companies operating in Canada to sell the majority of their stock to Canadian owners. The goal was to raise domestic ownership of Canada's petroleum industry from 28% in 1981 to 50% by 1990.[20]

Similar nationalistic tendencies periodically occur in the United States. Michael Butler, Seagram's Washington lobbiest, heard during the negotiations to buy Conoco that Secretary of the Interior James Watt was planning to testify before a House subcommittee that Seagram should not be allowed to bid for Conoco because of the Minerals Leasing Act. This act specifies that a foreign company should not be allowed to buy U.S. natural resources unless it has a reciprocal arrangement with U.S. companies. Given Canada's goal of nationalizing U.S. energy companies, reciprocity appeared to be in doubt.[21] Another example was the pressure placed on Japan by the U.S. government to put a voluntary limit on its automobile exports to the United States during 1981 and 1982. Japan acquiesced voluntarily to this demand in order to avoid restrictive quotas being legislated by the U.S. Congress.[22]

In order to introduce some stability into international trade, a number of countries have formed alliances and negotiated mutual cooperation agreements. One such agreement was the General Agreement on Tariffs and Trade (GATT) established in 1948 by twenty-three countries. This agreement was formed to create a relatively free system of trading, primarily through the reduction of tariffs. It provided a forum for negotiating mutual reduction of trade restrictions. Since 1948, most nations in the "free" world have become parties to GATT. According to Daniels, Ogram, and Radebaugh, "Through the most-favored-nation provision of GATT, countries have agreed to apply the same trade regulations to nearly all countries in the world. This greatly simplifies the negotiation process and allows exporters from almost any nation to have the same access, in terms of restrictions, to the market in any participating country."[23] An example of a political/trade alliance is the European Economic Community (Common Market), which agreed not only to reduce duties and other trade restrictions among member countries, but also to have a common tariff against nonmember countries. This provision was a major factor in encouraging firms from nonmember countries, such as the United States, to locate some manufacturing and marketing facilities inside the EEC to avoid tariffs.[24]

Technological. As mentioned in Chapter 4, the question of technology "transfer" has become an important issue in international dealings. Most less developed countries welcome multinational corporations into their nation as conduits of advanced technology and management expertise. They realize that not only will local labor be hired to work for the firm, but that the MNC will have to educate the work force to deal with advanced methods and techniques. As the largest donor country for foreign licensing and investment, however, the United States has been criticized by organized labor for allowing foreign products to displace what would have been U.S. exports. They cite many examples of highly advanced technology being sold abroad by U.S. firms. Examples are hardware for antimissle systems assembled by Lockheed in Hong Kong, the licensing to Japan by McDonnell Douglas of its rocket technology for launching satellites, and the licensing to Taiwan by Northrup of F-5E fighter production.[25]

Political-legal considerations become important when aerospace firms, with their heavy dependence on government contracts, want to transfer technology developed for military purposes into profitable commercial products sold internationally. General Electric, for example, had a great deal of difficulty forming a joint venture with the French national engine firm SNECMA in the early 1970s. The venture involved the sharing of jet engines developed specifically for the prototype of the B-1 bomber. Although the U.S. Federal Government refused, for political reasons, to put the B-1 bomber into production, it did not like the idea of GE's selling such advanced technology to another country.[26] In the 1980s, the federal government has similar fears of semiconductor technology being sold to countries behind the "iron curtain."

Another technological issue raised in international trade is the determination of the appropriate technology to use in production plants located in host countries. For example, labor-saving devices (robots, for instance) that are economically justifiable in highly developed countries where wage rates are high, may be more costly than labor-intensive types of production in less developed countries with high unemployment and low wage rates. The knowledge of technology may be so low in a country that the MNC may be tempted to employ very few local people and automate the plant as much as possible to gain operating leverage. The host country's government, however, faced with massive unemployment, may strongly desire a labor intensive plant. The basic question an MNC may face is whether the benefits to be gained by modifying technologies for the unique conditions of each country are worth the costs that must be incurred.[27]

Assessing International Opportunities and Risks

In searching for an advantageous market or manufacturing location, a multinational corporation must gather and evaluate data on strategic factors in a large number of countries and regions. Some firms, such as American Can Company, develop an elaborate computerized system to rank investment risks. Smaller companies may hire outside consultants like Chicago's Associated Consultants International or Boston's Arthur D. Little, Inc. to provide political risk assessments.

Regardless of the source of data, a firm must develop its own method of assessing risk. It must decide upon the most important factors from its point of view and assign weights to each. An example of such a rating method is depicted in Table 10.1.

Table 10.1 EXAMPLE OF WEIGHTED RATING OF INVESTMENT CLIMATE

FACTORS LISTED IN ORDER OF IMPORTANCE	COUNTRY A			COUNTRY B		
	(1) Assigned Weights Considering Importance of Adverse Developments	(2) Rating of Factor from 0 (Completely Unfavorable) to 100 (Completely Favorable)	(3) Weighted Rating (Column 1 × Column 2)	(1) Assigned Weights Considering Importance of Adverse Developments	(2) Rating of Factor from 0 (Completely Unfavorable) to 100 (Completely Favorable)	(3) Weighted Rating (Column 1 × Column 2)
1. Possibility of expropriation.	10	90	900	10	55	550
2. Possibility of damage to property from rebellion or war.	9	80	720	9	50	450
3. Remission of earnings.	8	70	560	8	50	400
4. Governmental restrictions of foreign business compared to domestic-owned enterprise.	8	70	560	8	60	480
5. Availability of local capital at reasonable cost.	7	50	350	7	90	630
6. Political stability.	7	80	560	7	50	350
7. Repatriation of capital.	7	80	560	7	60	420
8. Currency stability.	6	70	420	6	30	180
9. Price stability.	5	40	200	5	30	150
10. Taxes on business (including any discriminatory provisions).	4	80	320	4	90	360
11. Problems of dealing with labor unions.	3	70	210	3	80	240
12. Government investment incentives.	2	0	0	2	90	180
TOTAL WEIGHTED RATING OF INVESTMENT CLIMATE			5,360			4,390

SOURCE: W. A. Dymsza, *Multinational Business Strategy* (New York: McGraw-Hill, 1972), p. 90. Copyright © 1972 by McGraw-Hill, Inc. Reprinted by permission.

Even with such a rating method, without an in-depth understanding of the country under consideration, it is very difficult to assess the probability of expropriation or currency stability. Some research, however, indicates that there is a correlation between the frustration level of a country's population and expropriation.[28]

Scanning the Internal Environment

Any corporation desiring to move into the international arena will also need to assess its own strengths and weaknesses. Chang and Campo-Flores suggest that a corporation's chances for success are enhanced if it has or can develop the following capabilities:

1. *Technological lead.* An innovative approach or a new product or a new process gives one a short-term monopoly position.

2. *A strong trade name.* Snob appeal of a well-known product can permit a higher profit margin to cover initial entry costs.

3. *Advantage of scale.* A large corporation has the advantage of low unit costs and a financial base strong enough to weather setbacks.

4. *A scanning capability.* An ability to search successfully and efficiently for opportunities will take on greater importance in international dealings.

5. *An outstanding product or service.* A solid product or service is more likely to have staying power in international competition.

6. *An outstanding international executive.* The presence of an executive who understands international situations and is able to develop a core of local executives who can work well with the home office is likely to result in the building of a strong and long-lasting international organization.[29]

Evaluating the Mission

Once a corporation has decided to become multinational in orientation, the first step is to restate the corporate mission. An example of such a mission statement is that of General Electric Company:

> To carry on a diversified, growing, and profitable world-wide manufacturing business in electrical apparatus, appliances, and supplies, and in related materials, products, systems, and services for industry, commerce, agriculture, government, the community, and the home.[30]

Setting Objectives

Upon completing an assessment of its external and internal environments, a multinational corporation can determine specific objectives for foreign affiliates, corporate divisions, and the entire firm. Dymsza states that a multinational corporation usually starts with profitability goals in terms of amounts: return on investment, assets, or sales; rate of growth per year; or growth in earnings per share by major unit. It then sets specific marketing, production, logistics, technology, personnel, acquisition, and other goals for a given period. These goals provide the basis for determining strategies.[31]

Developing International Strategies

A multinational corporation can pick from a number of strategic options the ways to enter a foreign market or to establish manufacturing facilities in another country. An experienced firm with a global orientation will usually select a strategy based on specific product strengths and on host country attractiveness.

Export operations. A good way to minimize risk and to experiment with a specific product, exporting can be conducted in a number of ways. An MNC could choose to handle all critical functions itself, or it could contract these functions to an export management company. To operate in a country such as Japan, which has a series of complex regulations, an MNC could use the services of an agent or distributor.

Licensing. Under a licensing agreement, the licensing firm grants rights to a firm in the host country to produce and/or sell a product. The licensee pays compensation to the licensing firm in return for technical expertise. This is an especially useful strategy if the trademark or brand name is well known, but the MNC does not have sufficient funds to enter the country directly. It also becomes an important strategy if the country makes entry via investment either difficult or impossible. Examples are Japan and Eastern European countries. There is always the danger, however, that the licensee may develop its competence to the point that it becomes a competitor to the licensing firm.

Franchising. Franchising is a form of licensing in which a firm, in addition to granting the use of some asset to a franchisee, will supply on a continuing basis some ingredient important to the end product. The ingredient may be either a service or a component of the product. Holiday Inn, McDonald's, Wimpy's, and Wienerwald are examples of successful international franchisers.

Joint ventures. Joint ventures are very popular with MNCs. The corporation engages in international ownership at a much lower risk. A joint venture may be an association between an MNC and a firm in the host country, or a government agency. A quick method of obtaining local management, it also reduces the risks of expropriation and harassment by host country officials. When more than two organizations participate in a joint venture, it is sometimes referred to as a *consortium*. For example, Australia Aluminum is owned by two U.S. companies, two Japanese companies, one Dutch company, and one German company.[32] Disadvantages of joint ventures include loss of control, lower profits, possible conflicts with local managers, and the transfer of technological advantage to the local partner.

Acquisitions. If an MNC wishes total control of its operations, it may want to start a business from scratch or to acquire a firm already established in the host country. An acquisition has merits because assets can be bought in their entirety rather than on a piece-meal basis. Synergistic benefits may result if the MNC acquires a firm with strong complementary product lines and a good distribution network. In some countries, however, acquisitions may be difficult to arrange due to a lack of available information about potential candidates. Government restrictions on ownership, such as Canada's requirement that all energy corporations in Canada be controlled by Canadians, may also discourage acquisitions. It may be possible, however, to have control of a foreign enterprise even though the MNC cannot attain more than 50% of the ownership. One way is to maintain control over some asset required by the foreign firm. Another device is to separate equity into voting and nonvoting stock so that the minority MNC investor has a majority of the voting stock.[33]

Management contracts. A large multinational corporation is likely to have a large amount of management talent at its disposal. Management contracts offer a means through which an MNC may use part of its personnel to assist a firm in a host country for a specified fee and period of time. Such arrangements are common when a host government expropriates part or all of an MNC's holdings in its country. This allows the MNC to continue to earn some income from its investment and keep the operations going until local management is trained. Management contracts are also used by a number of less developed countries that have the capital but neither the labor nor the managerial skills required to utilize available technology.

Turn-key operations. These operations are typically contracts for the construction of operating facilities in exchange for a fee. The facilities are transferred to the host country or firm when they are complete. The customer is usually a government agency of, say, an Eastern European or Middle Eastern country that has decreed a given product must be produced locally and under its control. MNCs that perform turn-key operations are frequently industrial equipment manufacturers that supply some of their own equipment for the project and that commonly sell to the host country replacement parts and maintenance services. They thereby create customers as well as future competitors.

Subcontract arrangements. MNCs may find that in times of national fervor in the less developed countries, facilities that mine and process raw materials are prime targets for expropriation. As a result, an MNC may contract with a foreign government or local firm to trade raw materials for certain resources belonging to the MNC. For example, several oil producing countries have made arrangements with oil firms to let the firms take all exploration and development risks in exchange for a share of the sales of the oil produced.[34]

International Product Portfolio

Strategic planning, broadly viewed, seeks to match markets with products and other corporate resources in order to strengthen a firm's competitive position. Since most multinational corporations manufacture and sell a wide range of products, it is necessary, when formulating strategy, to keep track of country attractiveness as well as product strength. Nevertheless, there is a strong tendency for top management in MNCs to plan around either products or markets, but not both.[35]

To aid international strategic planning, Harrell and Keifer have shown how the product portfolio concept developed by the Boston Consulting Group and General Electric can be applied to international markets. As depicted in Fig. 10.2, each axis summarizes a host of data concerning the attractiveness of a particular country and the competitive strength of a particular product.

Country attractiveness is composed of market size, market rate of growth, government regulation, and economic and political factors. *Competitive strength* is composed of market share, product fit, contribution margin, and market support. The two scales form the axes of the matrix in Fig. 10.2. Those countries falling in the upper left generally should receive funding for growth, whereas countries in the lower right are prime for "harvesting," or divesting. Those countries falling on the lower left to upper right diagonal require selective funding strategies.[36] Those falling in the upper right block require additional funding if the product is to contribute in the future to the firm's profits. Joint ventures or divestitures would be most appropriate if cash is limited. Those falling in the center and lower left blocks are probably good candidates for "milking." They can produce strong cash flows in the short run.

10.3 STRATEGY IMPLEMENTATION

To be effective, international strategy must be implemented through the corporation's structure and its management practices. A number of approaches are possible, but some are more popular than others.

COMPETITIVE STRENGTHS

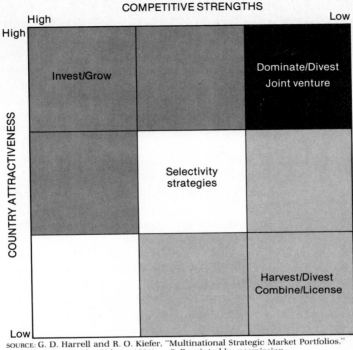

SOURCE: G. D. Harrell and R. O. Kiefer, "Multinational Strategic Market Portfolios," *MSU Business Topics* (Winter 1981), p. 7. Reprinted by permission.

Figure 10.2 *Matrix for plottting products.*

Organization Structure

Rarely, if ever, do multinational corporations suddenly appear as full-blown world-wide organizations. They tend to go through three common evolutionary stages both in their relationships with widely dispersed geographic markets and in the manner in which they structure their operations and programs.

Stage 1: Initial entry. The "parent" corporation is attracted to a particular market in another country and seeks to test the potential of its products in this market with minimal risk. The firm thus introduces a number of product lines into the market through home-based export programs, licensing agreements, joint ventures, and/or through local commercial offices. The product divisions at headquarters continue to be responsible for all functional activities.

Stage 2: Early development. Sucess in Stage 1 leads the parent corporation to believe that a stronger presence and broader product lines are needed if it is to fully exploit its advantage in the host country. The parent company establishes a local operating division or company in the host country, such as Ford of Britain, to better serve the market. The product line is expanded. Local manufacturing capacity is established. Managerial functions (product development, finance, marketing, etc.) are organized locally. As time goes by, other related businesses are acquired by the parent company to broaden the base of the local operating division. As the subsidary in the host country successfully develops a strong regional presence, it achieves greater autonomy and self-sufficiency.

Stage 3: Maturity. As the parent corporation becomes aware of the success of its subsidiaries in other countries and the skills of its local managers, it consolidates operations under a regional management organization. Greater attention is given to a wider range of investment opportunities, such as mergers and acquisitions. These activities are often initiated by the local managers of the subsidiaries. Although the regional or local company continues to maintain ties with the parent corporation and the product divisions in the home country, it tends to enjoy relative autonomy in terms of local policy-setting and managerial practices. As was the case with the North American Philips Corporation, originally an affiliate of N. V. Philips' Gloeilampenfabrieken, a subsidiary may become a totally separate company with local shareholders and publicly traded stock.[37] Table 10.2 summarizes some of the structural arrangements possible in each stage of MNC development.

Even though most international and multinational corporations move through these stages in their involvement with host countries, any one corporation may be at different stages with different products in different markets. An example of diversity in international operations is Hewlett-Packard. The company began international activity by exporting its products. It used its own staff for exports to Canada and export management companies (export intermediaries operating on a buy-and-sell basis and providing financing for export shipments) for exports to other countries. These exports were then sold in both cases to middlemen abroad. As sales expanded, Hewlett-Packard took over the exporting functions, opened its own sales office in Mexico, purchased a warehousing facility in Switzerland, organized a wholly owned manufacturing subsidiary in West Germany, and entered into a partly owned venture in Japan.[38]

Many mature multinational corporations are structured along the lines of a matrix organization combining *product* and *geography*. Typically, multinational corporations do not organize themselves around business functions, such as marketing or manufacturing, unless they are in an extractive raw-materials industry. Basic functions are thus subsumed under either product or geographic units.[39] Two extremes of the usual matrix are Nestlé and American Cyanamid. Nestlé's structure is

Table 10.2   INTERNATIONAL ACTIVITY AND STRUCTURE

STAGE	ACTIVITIES OF COMPANY	ORGANIZATION RESPONSIBLE FOR INTERNATIONAL ACTIVITIES	EXECUTIVE IN CHARGE
1	Exports directly and indirectly, but trade is minor.	Export department.	Export manager, reporting to domestic marketing executive.
	Exports become more important.	Export division.	Division manager.
2	Company undertakes licensing and invests in production overseas.	International division.	Director of international operations, usually vice-president.
	International investments increase.	Sometimes international headquarters company as wholly owned subsidiary [of domestic parent company].	President, who is vice-president in parent company.
3	International investments substantial and widespread; diversified international business activities.	Global organizational structure by geographic areas, product lines, functions, or some combination. Also worldwide staff support.	No single executive in charge of international business.

SOURCE: Adapted from W. A. Dymsza, *Multinational Business Strategy* (New York: McGraw-Hill, 1972), p. 22. Copyright © 1972 by McGraw-Hill, Inc. Reprinted by permission.

one in which significant power and authority have been decentralized to geographic entities. This structure is similar to that depicted in Fig. 10.3, with each geographic set of operating companies having a similar set of products. In contrast, American Cyanamid has a series of product groups with world-wide responsibilities. To depict this structure, the geographical entities in Fig. 10.3 would have to be replaced by product or strategic business unit names. There does appear to be a trend, however, toward the Nestlé version of the matrix structure in which the geographic unit dominates the product unit.[40]

Management practices

As is true of people from any highly developed society, managers trained in the United States tend to believe that what works well in their society will work well anywhere. Thus, someone well schooled in the virtues of MBO, participative decision making, theory Y practices, job enrichment,

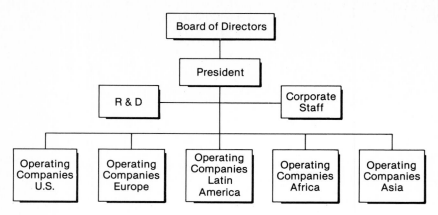

Figure 10.3   *Structure of a mature MNC.*

and management science will have a tendency to transplant these practices without alteration to foreign nations. Unfortunately, just as products often need to be altered to appeal to a new market, so too do most management practices.

In a study of 40 different cultures, Hofstede found that he could explain the success or failure of certain management practices on the basis of four cultural dimensions: power distance, uncertainty avoidance, individualism–collectivism, and masculinity–femininity. He points out that management by objectives (MBO) has been the single most popular management technique "made in U.S.A." It has succeeded in Germany because the idea of replacing the arbitrary authority of the boss with the impersonal authority of mutually agreed-upon objectives fits the small power distance and strong uncertainty avoidance that are dimensions in the German culture. It has failed in France, however, because the French are used to large power distances—to accepting orders from a highly personalized authority such as Charles de Gaulle. This cultural dimension goes counter to key aspects of MBO: small power distance between superior and subordinate and impersonal, objective goal setting.[41]

Because of these differences in culture, managerial style and practices must be tailored to fit the situations in other countries. Most multinational corporations based in the United States, therefore, attempt to fill executive positions in their subsidiaries with well-qualified citizens of the host countries. IBM for example, follows the practice of filling all executive positions with the citizens of the many countries in which it operates.[42] This serves to placate nationalistic governments and to better attune IBM management practices to the host country's culture.

10.4 EVALUATION AND CONTROL

In evaluating the activities of its international operations, the MNC should consider not only return on investment and other financial measures, but also the effect of its activities on the host country.

Financial Measures

The three most widely used techniques for international performance evaluation are return on investment, budget analysis, and historical comparisons. In one study, 95% of the corporate officers interviewed stated that they use the same evaluation techniques for foreign and domestic operations. Rate of return was mentioned as the single most important measure.[43] The use of ROI, however, can cause problems when applied to international operations: "Because of foreign currencies, different rates of inflation, different tax laws, and the use of transfer pricing, both the net income figure and the investment base may be seriously distorted."[44] Consequently, Daniels, Ogram, and Radebaugh recommend that MNC top management emphasize budgets as a means of differentiating between the worth of the subsidiary and the performance of its management.

Since differences among countries magnify the usual problems of comparability, multiple performance indicators should be used. Dymsza suggests that MNCs use management audits for their operations in foreign countries.[45]

MNC/Host Country Relationships

There are four basic relationships an MNC can assume *vis-à-vis* a host country. They range from contributory to undermining.[46]

Contributory. An MNC acts in such a way that it directly augments or contributes to the goals or achievement of a host nation without any negative effect.

Reinforcing. The actions of an MNC stimulate the functioning of a nation or enhance its usefulness so that its value and competence are reinforced.

Frustrating. Actions of an MNC are contrary to the goals of the nation or impede its immediate functioning in ways to which the nation cannot respond effectively so that its government is frustrated.

Undermining. The effect of an MNC is to reduce the basic logic (in terms of norms, values, and philosophy) of a nation so that its functioning is weakened or undermined.

To the extent that an MNC fails to contribute to or reinforce the functioning of a host country, it may find its assets expropriated and its home-country management team asked to leave. A cycle develops for those corporations that go to less-developed countries to locate and extract needed raw materials, but see the host countries only as something to manipulate and use:

> *First*, they are welcomed by the host country as a source of foreign currency, a major employer, a means of upgrading the country's skills, a stimulant to the economy, and a catalyst to attract other investors. *Second*, after a few years pressure increases on the firm to process in addition to only extracting the material. This often leads to a second phase of investment by the company and more benefits to the country. *Third*, the company is now sufficiently dependent to be vulnerable to a request to have local participation in ownership, either through private parties or directly by the host government. *Fourth*, nationalization advances to a takeout stage after more years of evolving relationships, usually involving compensation for assets and some arrangement on management. *Fifth*, recalling the primary reason for the original investment was a source of materials, and recognizing that government owned operations are almost always inefficient, the company is forced to pay increasing prices and turns to alternative sources if they exist.[47]

10.5 SUMMARY AND CONCLUSION

A knowledge of international considerations is becoming extremely important for the proper understanding of the strategic management process in large corporations. Just as U.S. firms are becoming more involved every year with operations and markets in other countries, imports and subsidiaries from other countries are becoming more a part of the American landscape. International corporations have been slowly transforming themselves into multinational corporations (MNCs) with a global orientation and flexible management styles.

The dominant issue in the strategic management process of a multinational corporation is the effect of widely different external environments on internal activities. A firm's top management must therefore be well schooled in the differences among nations in terms of their sociocultural, economic, political-legal, and technological environmental variables. Data search procedures and analytical techniques must be used to assess the many possible investment opportunities and their risks in world business. Assuming that top management feels that the corporation has the requisite internal qualifications to become international, it must determine the appropriate set of strategies for entering and investing in potential host countries. These may vary from simple exportation to the formation with other companies of very complex consortiums. The corporation's product portfolio must be constantly monitored for strengths and weaknesses.

Attention must also be paid to selecting the most appropriate organization structure and management system for a world-wide enterprise. An overall system of control and coordination must be balanced against a host country's need for local flexibility and autonomy. An MNC should use a series of performance indicators so that return on investment, budget analysis, and historical comparisons can be viewed in the context of a strategic audit of operations in the host country. Above all else, the top management of a multinational corporation has the responsibility to ensure that the MNC contributes to and reinforces the functioning of the host nation rather than frustrating or undermining its government and culture.

DISCUSSION QUESTIONS

1. What differentiates a multinational corporation from an international corporation?

2. The Common Market in 1982 considered the adoption of the *Vredeling proposal.* This proposal required parent corporations to give workers a semi-annual "clear picture" of the entire corporation's financial situation, development and employment plans, marketing strategies, new products and technologies and "all procedures and plans liable to have a substantial effect on employees' interests."[48] What is your opinion of this proposed legislation?

3. Should MNCs be allowed to own more than half the stock of a subsidiary based in a host country? Why or why not?

4. Should the United States allow unrestricted trade between corporations in the United States and communist countries? Why or why not?

5. In developing an international product portfolio matrix, what specific factors should be included to assess a country's attractiveness?

NOTES

1. B. D. Henderson, *New Strategies for the New Global Competition* (Boston: Boston Consulting Group, 1981), p. 1.

2. A. L. Malabre, Jr., "World Trade Suffers as Economies Slow," *Wall Street Journal* (August 3, 1981), p. 1.

3. J. Fayerweather, *International Business Strategy and Administration* (Cambridge, Mass.: Ballinger Publishing, 1978), p. 1.

4. M. McLuhan, *Understanding Media: The Extensions of Man* (New York: McGraw-Hill Paperbacks, 1965).

5. L. Birger, "Once Threatened by Henry Ford II, European Fords Carrying Detroit," *The* (Albuquerque, N. Mex.) *Tribune* (June 2, 1980), p. C-10.

6. "USAir Orders Engines for Its Boeing Jets," *Wall Street Journal* (August 3, 1981), p. 22.

7. Adapted from W. A. Dymsza, *Multinational Business Strategy* (New York: McGraw-Hill, 1972), pp. 50–51.

8. K. C. Crowe, "The Selling of America," *Next* (May–June, 1981), p. 112.

9. "Mitsubishi: A Japanese Giant's Plans for Growth in the U.S.," *Business Week* (July 20, 1981), pp. 128–131.

   A. Bennett, "A Pioneer from Japan Helps to Clear the Way for Nissan's U.S. Plant," *Wall Street Journal* (August 4, 1981), p. 1.

   B. R. Schlender, "Hitting Home: Foreign Firms Build More Houses in U.S., Upset Some Americans," *Wall Street Journal* (July 9, 1981), p. 1.

   S. Shellenbarger, "Grist for the Mill: Japanese Buy More U.S. Grain Elevators, Making Bigger Inroads into World Trade," *Wall Street Journal* (July 31, 1981), p. 40.

10. "Japanese Tire Concern Still Weighs Purchase of Firestone Facility," *Wall Street Journal* (August 4, 1981), p. 6.

11. Dymsza, p. 5.

12. Dymsza, pp. 5–6.

13. S. J. Kobrin, "Morality, Political Power and Illegal Payments by Multinational Corporations," *Columbia Journal of World Business* (Winter 1976), p. 106.

14. J. D. Daniels, E. W. Ogram, Jr., and L. H. Radebaugh, *International Business: Environments and Operations*, 3rd ed. (Reading, Mass.: Addison-Wesley, 1982), p. 640.

15. Daniels, Ogram, and Radebaugh, 2nd ed. (1979), p. 322.

16. Daniels, Ogram, and Radebaugh, 3rd ed. (1982), p. 513.

17. D. Ricks, M. Y. C. Fu, and J. S. Arpan, *International Business Blunders* (Columbus, Ohio: Grid, Inc., 1974).

18. Daniels, Ogram, and Radebaugh, 3rd ed. (1982), pp. 522–523.

19. "France Plans to Nationalize Key Industries," (Charlottesville, Va.) *Daily Progress* (July 9, 1981), p. 1.

20. A. H. Malcolm, "Canadians are Pursuing Foreign Oil Companies," *New York Times* (June 4, 1981), p. D1.

   A. Pine, "U.S. Resistance to Trade Limits in Canada Grows," *Wall Street Journal* (July 6, 1981), p. 3.

21. B. Paul, "Seagram, a Player in the Conoco Game, Shows Its Skills at Washington Lobbying," *Wall Street Journal* (August 4, 1981), p. 15.

22. J. Seaberry, "Auto Quota Called Boon for Nation," *Washington Post* (May 3, 1981), pp. A1 and A12.

23. Daniels, Ogram, and Radebaugh, 3rd ed. (1982), p. 28.

24. Y. N. Chang and F. Campo-Flores, *Business Policy and Strategy* (Santa Monica, Calif.: Goodyear Publishing, 1980), p. 601.

25. Daniels, Ogram, and Radebaugh, 3rd ed. (1982), p. 301.

26. G. W. Weiss, Jr., "The General Electric-SNECMA Jet Engine Development Program" (Boston: *Intercollegiate Case Clearing House*, no. 9-380-739, 1980).

27. Daniels, Ogram, and Radebaugh, 3rd ed. (1982), pp. 636–638.

28. H. Knudsen, "Explaining the National Propensity to Expropriate: An Ecological Approach," *Journal of International Business Studies* (Spring 1974), pp. 51–69.

29. Chang and Campo-Flores, pp. 602–604.

30. Dymsza, p. 1.

31. Dymsza, pp. 96–102.

32. Daniels, Ogram, and Radebaugh, 3rd ed. (1982), p. 422.

33. Daniels, Ogram, and Radebaugh, 3rd ed. (1982), p. 490.

34. For further discussion of these strategies, refer to a text on international business such as that by Daniels, Ogram, and Radebaugh.

35. G. D. Harrell and R. O. Kiefer, "Multinational Strategic Market Portfolios," *MSU Business Topics* (Winter 1981), p. 5.

36. Harrell and Kiefer, p. 8.

37. R. L. Drake and L. M. Caudill, "Management of the Large Multinational: Trends and Future Challenges," *Business Horizons* (May–June 1981), pp. 84–85.

38. Daniels, Ogram, and Radebaugh, 2nd ed. (1979), p. 359.

39. S. M. Davis, *Managing and Organizing Multinational Corporations* (New York: Pergamon Press, 1979), p. 241.

40. Drake and Caudill, p. 87.

41. G. Hofstede, "Motivation, Leadership, and Organization: Do American Theories Apply Abroad?" *Organizational Dynamics* (Summer 1980), pp. 42–63.

42. W. H. Newman and J. P. Logan, *Strategy, Policy and Central Management*, 8th ed. (Cincinnati, Ohio: South-Western, 1981), pp. 616–617.

43. Daniels, Ogram, and Radebaugh, 3rd ed. (1982), p. 552.

44. Daniels, Ogram, and Radebaugh, 3rd ed. (1982), p. 552.

45. Dymsza, pp. 74–78.

46. Adapted from Fayerweather, p. 124.

47. F. T. Haner, *Business Policy, Planning and Strategy* (Cambridge, Mass.: Winthrop Publishers, 1976), p. 441.

48. T. W. Lippman, "Proposals before EEC Alarm Multinationals," *Washington Post* (March 7, 1982), pp. K1 and K3.

STRATEGIC MANAGEMENT MODEL

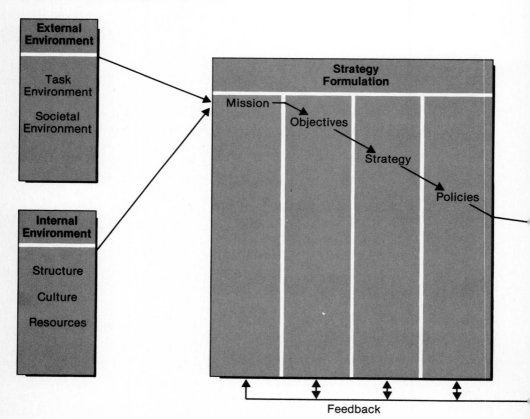

STRATEGIC MANAGEMENT OF NOT-FOR-PROFIT ORGANIZATIONS

CHAPTER 11

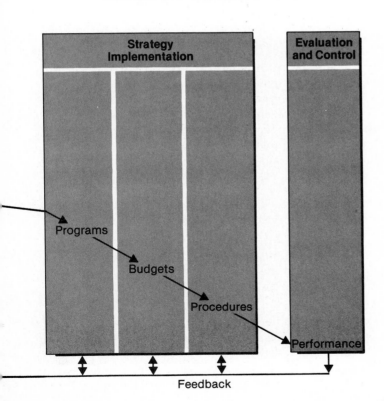

T raditionally, studies in strategic management have dealt with profit-making firms to the exclusion of nonprofit or governmental organizations. The little empirical research that does exist is primarily descriptive or documentary.[1] Wortman, in concluding his comprehensive study of the area, states, "Not-for-profit organizations are just in the initial stage of using the strategic management concept."[2] Nevertheless, a knowledge of not-for-profit organizations is important if for no other reason than the fact that they employ over 20 million people in the United States (compared to approximately 70 million in the profit-making sector).[3] In addition to various federal, state, and local government agencies, there are about 3,500 not-for-profit hospitals, 3,000 colleges and universities, and approximately 300 national church and synagogue bodies, plus hundreds of thousands of local churches and synagogues.[4] These are only a few of the many different kinds of not-for-profit organizations.

The first ten chapters of this book dealt primarily with the strategic management of profit-making corporations. The purpose of this chapter, however, is to highlight briefly the major differences between the profit-making and the not-for-profit organization in order to indicate how their differences might affect the strategic management process.

11.1 CATEGORIES OF ORGANIZATIONS

All profit-making and not-for-profit organizations can be grouped into four basic categories. In some instances, such as Hughes Aircraft, it is difficult to clearly state where one category leaves off and another begins: "The wide and growing involvement of government in all aspects of life has caused a convergence or blurring of the various sectors."[5] Some business corporations, for example, are so dependent on government contracts that they take on certain characteristics of government agencies.[6] Four categories are as follows:

1. *Private for-profit* businesses dependent on the market economy for generating the means of survival (ranging from small businesses to major corporations).

2. *Private nonprofit* organizations operating on public goodwill (donations, contributions, and endowments or government stipends), but constituted outside the authority of governmental agencies or legislative bodies.

3. *Private quasi-public* organizations created by legislative authority and given a limited monopoly to provide particular goods or services to a population subgroup (primarily public utilities).

4. *Public* agencies of government (federal, state, and local) constituted by law and authorized to collect taxes and provide services.[7]

Typically, the term not-for-profit includes private nonprofit corporations such as hospitals, institutes, and organized charities, as well as public governmental units or agencies. Regulated public utilities are in a grey area somewhere between profit and not-for-profit. They are profit making and have stockholders, but take on many of the characteristics of the not-for-profit organization, such as a greater dependence on rate-setting government commissions than on customers.

11.2 WHY NOT-FOR-PROFIT?

The not-for-profit sector of the American economy is becoming increasingly important for a number of reasons. *First*, society desires certain goods and services that profit-making firms cannot or will not provide. These are referred to as "public" or "collective" goods because people who may not have paid for the goods also receive benefits from them. Paved roads, police protection, museums, and schools are examples of public goods. A person cannot use a private good unless she or he pays for it. Generally once a public good is provided, however, anyone can partake of its benefits. The key question thus revolves around who pays for the goods.[8] As a result, many not-for-profit organizations are more concerned with the needs and desires of their funding sponsors or agency than with those of the public that receives the services. The U.S. Post Office, for example, has been criticized by some as being more concerned with lobbying Congress for higher rates than with providing better service. Nevertheless, valuable services, which might not otherwise exist, are provided for society.

Second, a private nonprofit firm tends to receive benefits from society that a private profit-making firm cannot obtain. Preferred tax status to nonstock corporations is given in section 501(c)(3) of the Internal Revenue Code in the form of exemptions from corporate income taxes.[9] Private non-profit firms also enjoy exemptions from various other state, local, and federal taxes. Under certain conditions they also benefit from the tax deductibility of donor contributions and membership dues. In addition, they qualify for special third-class mailing privileges.[10]

11.3 IMPORTANCE OF REVENUE SOURCE

The feature that best differentiates not-for-profit organizations from each other as well as from profit-making corporations is their source of income.[11] The profit-making firm depends upon revenues obtained from the sale of its goods and services to customers. Its source of income is the customer who buys and uses the product, and who, typically, pays for the product when it is received. Profits result when revenues are greater than the costs of making and distributing the product, and are thus a measure of the corporation's effectiveness (a product is valued because customers purchase it for use) and efficiency (costs are kept below selling price).

The not-for-profit organization, in contrast, depends heavily on dues, assessments, or donations from its membership or on funding from a sponsoring agency such as the United Way or the federal government. Revenue, therefore, comes from a variety of sources, *not* just from sales to customers/clients. It may come from people who do not even receive the services they are buying. Such charitable organizations as the American Cancer Society and CARE are examples. In another type of not-for-profit organization—such as unions and voluntary medical plans—revenue comes mostly from the people, the members, who receive the service. Nevertheless, the members typically pay dues *in advance* and must accept later whatever service is provided whether they want it or not, whether it is what they expected or not. The service is often received long after the dues are paid. As a result, some members who have paid into a fund for many years may leave the organization or die without receiving services, whereas newcomers may receive many services even though they have paid into it only a small amount.

Therefore, in profit-making corporations, there is typically a simple and direct connection between the customer or client and the organization. The organization tends to be totally dependent on sales of its products or services to the customer for revenue and is therefore extremely interested in pleasing the customer. As shown in Fig. 11.1, the profit-making organization (organization A) tries to influence the customer to continue to buy and use its services. The customer, in turn, directly influences the organization's decision making process by either buying or not buying the item offered.

In the case of the typical not-for-profit organization, however, there is likely to be a very different sort of relationship between the organization providing and the person receiving the service. Since the recipient of the service typically does not pay the entire cost of the service, outside sponsors are required. In most instances, the sponsors receive none of the service but may provide from partial to total funding of needed revenues. As indicated earlier, these sponsors may be the U.S. Congress (using taxpayers' money) or charitable organizations, such as the United Way (using voluntary donations). As shown in Fig. 11.1, the not-for-profit (NFP) organization may be partially dependent on sponsors for funding (organizations B and C) or totally dependent on the sponsors (organization D).

The pattern of influence on the organization's strategic decision making derives from its sources of revenue. As shown in Fig. 11.1, a private university (organization B) is heavily dependent on student tuition for

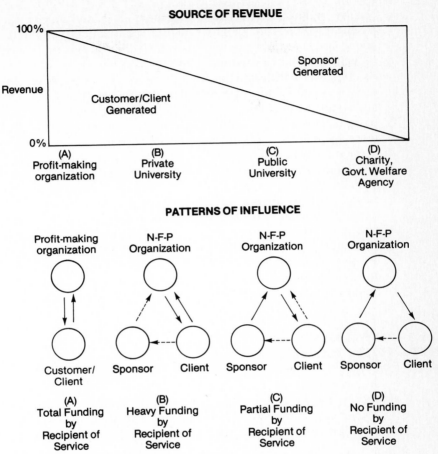

SOURCE: T. L. Wheelen and J. D. Hunger. Copyright © 1982 by Wheelen and Hunger Associates. Reprinted by permission.

Figure 11.1 *The effect of sources of revenue on patterns of client-organization influence.*

revenue. As a result, student desires are likely to have more influence (as shown by an unbroken line) on the university's decision making than are the desires of the various sponsors, such as alumni and private foundations. The relatively marginal influence on the organization by the sponsors is reflected by a broken line. In contrast, a public university (depicted in Fig. 11.1 as organization C) is more heavily dependent on outside sponsors, such as a state legislature, for revenue funding. Student tuition forms a smaller percentage of total revenue. As a result, decision making is heavily influenced by the sponsors (unbroken line) and only marginally influenced directly by the students (broken line). In the case of organization D in Fig. 11.1, however, the client has no direct influence on the organization because the client pays nothing for the services received. In this type of situation, the organization tends to measure its effectiveness in terms of sponsor satisfaction. It has no real measure of its efficiency other than its ability to carry out its mission and achieve its objectives within the dollar contribution it has received from its sponsors. In contrast to other organizations where the client contributes a significant proportion of the needed revenue, this type of not-for-profit organization (D) may actually be able to increase the amount of its revenue by heavily lobbying its sponsors while reducing the level of its service to its clients!

Regardless of the percentage of total funding generated by the client, the client may attempt to indirectly influence the not-for-profit organization through the sponsors. This is depicted by the broken lines connecting the client and the sponsor in organizations B, C, and D in the figure. Welfare clients or prison inmates, for example, may be able to indirectly improve the services they receive by putting pressure on government officials by writing letters to legislators or, even, by rioting. And students at public universities may lobby state officials for student representation on governing boards.

11.4 CONSTRAINTS ON STRATEGIC MANAGEMENT

Because not-for-profit organizations are truly different from profit-making organizations, there are a number of characteristics peculiar to the former that constrain its behavior and affect its strategic management. Newman and Wallender list the following five constraining characteristics:

1. Service is often intangible and hard to measure. This difficulty is typically compounded by the existence of multiple service objectives developed in order to satisfy multiple sponsors.

2. Client influence may be weak. Often the organization has a local monopoly, and payments by customers may be a very small source of funds.

3. Strong employee commitment to professions or to a cause may undermine their allegiance to the organization employing them.

4. Resource contributors—notably fund contributors and government—may intrude upon the organization's internal management.

5. Restraints on the use of rewards and punishments may result from characteristics 1, 3, and 4.[12]

It is true that a number of these characteristics may be found in profit-making as well as in not-for-profit organizations. Nevertheless, as Newman and Wallendar state, the "... frequency of strong impact is much higher in not-for-profit enterprises...."[13] As a result, the strategic management process for any given situation will be different in a not-for-profit organization than in the typical profit-making corporations discussed in earlier chapters.

Impact on Strategy Formulation

Long-range planning and decision making are affected by the listed constraining characteristics and serve to add at least four *complications* to strategy formulation.

Goal conflicts interfere with rational planning. Since the not-for-profit organization typically does not have a single clear-cut performance criterion (such as profits), divergent goals and objectives are likely to exist. This is espeically true if there are multiple sponsors. Differences in the concern of various important sponsors may prevent top management from stating the organization's mission in anything but very broad terms, fearing a sponsor may disagree with a particular narrow definition of mission and choose to cancel funding. In such organizations it is the reduced influence of the clients that *permits* this diversity of values and goals to occur without a clear market check.

An integrated planning focus tends to shift from results to resources. Since not-for-profit organizations tend to provide services that are hard to measure, there is rarely a net "bottom line." Planning, therefore, becomes more concerned with resource inputs, which can easily be measured, than with service, which cannot. Goal displacement, therefore, becomes even more likely than in business organizations.

Ambiguous operating objectives create opportunities for internal politics and goal displacement. The combination of vague objectives and a heavy concern with resources allows managers considerable leeway in their activities. Such leeway makes possible political maneuvering for personal ends. In addition, since the effectiveness of the not-for-profit organization hinges on the satisfaction of the sponsoring group, there is a tendency to ignore the needs of the client while focusing on the desires of the powerful sponsor.

Professionalization simplifies detailed planning but adds rigidity. In those not-for-profit organizations where professionals hold important roles (as in hospitals or colleges), professional values and traditions may prevent the organization from changing conventional behavior patterns to fit new service missions to changing social needs. This, of course, can occur in any organization hiring professionals. The strong service orientation of most not-for-profit organizations, however, tends to encourage the development of static professional norms and attitudes.

Impact on Strategy Implementation

The five constraining characteristics affect how a not-for-profit organization is organized in both its structure and job design. Three *complications*, in particular, can be highlighted.

Decentralization is complicated. The difficulty of setting objectives for an intangible, hard-to-measure service mission makes difficult the delegation of decision making authority. Important matters are therefore centralized and lower-level managers are forced to wait until top management makes a decision. With the heavy dependence on sponsors for revenue support, the top management of a not-for-profit organization must always be alert to how the sponsors may view an organizational activity. This leads to "defensive centralization" in which top management retains all decision making authority to avoid any actions to which the sponsors may object.

Linking pins for external-internal integration become important. Given the heavy dependence on outside sponsors, a special need arises for people in "buffer" roles who can relate to both inside and outside groups. This is especially necessary when the sponsors are diverse (revenue comes from donations, membership fees, and federal funds) and the service is intangible (for instance, a "good" education) with a broad mission and multiple shifting objectives. The job of a "Dean for External Affairs," for example, consists primarily of working with school alumni and fund raising.

Job enlargement and executive development may be restrained by professionalism. In those organizations that employ a large number of professionals, managers must design jobs to appeal to prevailing professional norms. Professions have rather clear ideas about which activities are, and which are not, within their province. Enriching a nurse's job by expanding his or her decision making authority regarding drug dosage, for example, may cause conflict with medical doctors who feel such authority is theirs alone. In addition, promoting a professional into a managerial job may be viewed as a punishment rather than as a reward.

Impact on Evaluation and Control

Special *complications* arising from the constraining characteristics also effect how behavior is motivated and performance is controlled. Two problems, in particular, are often noticed.

Rewards and penalties have little or no relation to perfor-mance. When desired results are vague and the judgment of success is subjective, predictable and impersonal feedback cannot be established. Performance is either judged intuitively ("You don't seem to be taking your job seriously") or on the basis of those small aspects of a job that can be measured ("You were late to work twice last month").

Inputs rather than outputs are heavily controlled. Since inputs can be measured much more easily than outputs, the not-for-profit organization tends to focus more on the resources going into performance than on the performance itself. The emphasis is thus on setting maximum limits for costs and expenses. Because there is little to no reward for meeting these standards, the response of people to the controls is usually negative.

11.5 TYPICAL RESPONSES TO CONSTRAINTS

Not-for-profit organizations tend to deal with the complications resulting from constraining characteristics in a number of ways. Although these responses may occur in profit-making organizations as well, they are more typical of not-for-profit organizations.

Select a Dynamic and Forceful Leader

One approach, which is also used in profit-making firms at times, is to appoint a strong leader to the top management position: "The leader has personal convictions about the values to be used in decision-making and either has enough power to make important choices, or is so influential that her or his values are accepted by others who make decisions."[14] This manager can thus force a change in the planning of the organizational mission and objectives without antagonizing the sponsors, as well as in the organizing and controlling of activities. The danger with this approach, however, is that change can only occur from the top-down. Rather than accepting the normal risks inherent in making an important decision, lower-level managers "play it safe" and either wait for guidance from above to see which way "the wind is blowing" or pass the decision upward in the hierarchy.

Develop a Mystique

The organization can be integrated toward successful goal accomplishment by developing a "mystique" that dominates the enterprise and attracts likely sponsors. A strong conviction shared by all employees, as well as the sponsors, about the importance of a particular mission or service objective can also serve to motivate unusually high performance and client satisfaction. This sense of mission typically focuses on providing a unique service to a highly visible client group, such as mentally retarded children. Once established, the mystique sets the character and values decision makers and others are expected to follow.[15] It is, thus, similar to the earlier-discussed corporate culture. One danger of the use of mystique to focus activities and to motivate performance is that the mission can move far afield from that desired by the sponsoring groups.

Generate Rules and Regulations

Since the constraints may force people in not-for-profit organizations to be more concerned with pleasing the sponsors than with achieving a mission of satisfying the client, top management may respond by generating rules and regulations regarding activities with the client. Minimum standards may be developed regarding the number of contact hours spent with each client, the number of reports completed, and/or the "proper" method of working. The danger inherent in this approach is that it tends to emphasize form over substance and to confuse looking good and keeping busy with actual performance. More goal displacement develops and feeds upon itself. "Burn out" develops among dedicated employees who may feel they are being forced to spend too much energy fighting the system rather than helping the client.

Appoint a Strong Board

The presence of a board of directors or trustees can help ensure vigilence in setting and monitoring the objectives of the organization. To the extent that the board actively represents the sponsors and special interest groups that determine the organization's revenues, it has a great deal of power: "The potential for control by some not-for-profit boards far exceeds that of the boards of a corporation which represents only the owners."[16] The board can perform a watchdog role over the organization by demanding clear-cut, measurable objectives and a mission of client satisfaction. The danger with this approach, however, is that the board may get too involved in operational activities. In organizations with a large number of professionals employed, the senior administrator may be viewed as a "hybrid" professional—part professional and part manager (for instance, a physician serving as a hospital administrator). The board thus tends to involve itself not only with strategic matters, but also with operational matters such as hiring, directing, and developing the budget.[17] Nevertheless, like the boards discussed in Chapter 3, not-for-profit boards can range in their degree of involvement in strategic management from the passive phantom or figurehead boards to the active catalyst type.

Establish Performance-Based Budgets

A fifth approach to dealing with complications in a not-for-profit organization is to institute an information system that ties measurable objectives to budgeted line items. One such system is the *planning, programming, budgeting system* (PPBS) developed by the U.S. Department of Defense. It assists not-for-profit administrators in choosing among alternative programs in terms of resource use. It is composed of five steps:

1. Specify objectives as clearly as possible in quantitative, measurable terms.
2. Analyze the actual output of the not-for-profit organization in terms of the stated objectives.
3. Measure the cost of the particular program.
4. Analyze alternatives and search for those that have the greatest effectiveness in achieving the objectives.
5. Establish the process in a systematic way so that it continues to occur over time.[18]

Another system is *zero base budgeting* (ZBB). It is a planning process that requires each manager to justify budget requests in detail each year a budget is constructed. This procedure serves to avoid developing annual budgets based upon last year's budget plus a certain percentage increase. ZBB forces a manager to justify the use of money for old established programs as well as for new ones. The system requires three steps:

1. Each activity is identified with a program in order to relate input to output.
2. Each activity is evaluated by systematic analysis.
3. All programs are ranked in order of performance.[19]

Zero base budgeting has been used by the United States Department of Agriculture since 1971 and has become extremely popular in many local, state, and federal agencies. Its main value is to tie inputs with outputs, and to force managers to set priorities on service programs. It is also a very useful adjunct to MBO, which is being increasingly adopted by many not-for-profit organizations.

The danger with emphasizing performance-based budgets is that members of an organization become so concerned with justifying the existence of pet programs that they tend to forget about the effect of these programs on achieving the mission. The process can just be another variant of trying to please the sponsors and to look good on paper.

11.6 SUMMARY AND CONCLUSION

Strategic management in not-for-profit organizations is in its initial stages of development. Approaches and techniques, such as MBO, which work reasonably well in profit-making corporations, are being tried in a number of not-for-profit organizations. Nevertheless, private nonprofit and public organizations differ in terms of their sources of revenue and thus must be treated differently. The relationship between the organization and the client is also more complicated. Moreover, not-for-profit organizations have certain constraining characteristics that affect their strategic management process. These characteristics cause variations in the way managers in not-for-profit organizations formulate and implement strategic decisions. Not-for-profit organizations are therefore more likely than profit-making corporations to look for dynamic and forceful leaders who can pull together various constituencies, develop a mystique about their activities, generate many rules and regulations regarding the client, appoint a strong board of directors/trustees to represent sponsoring agencies and special interest groups, and to develop performance-based budgets.

Not-for-profit organizations form an important part of American society. It is therefore important to understand their reason for existence and what makes them different from profit-making corporations. The lack of a profit motive does often result in vague statements of mission and unmeasurable objectives. This coupled with a concern for funding from sponsors may cause a lack of consideration for the very client the organization was designed to serve. Programs may develop that have little or no connection with the organization's mission. Nevertheless, it is important to remember that not-for-profit organizations are usually established to provide goods and services judged valuable by society that profit-making firms cannot or will not provide. It is dangerous to judge their performance on the basis of simple economic considerations because they are designed to deal with conditions under which profit-making corporations could not easily survive.

DISCUSSION QUESTIONS

1. Are not-for-profit organizations less efficient than profit-making organizations? Why or why not?

2. Is client influence always weak in the not-for-profit organization? Why or why not?

3. Why does the employment of a large number of people who consider themselves to be professionals complicate the strategic management process? How may this also occur in profit-making firms?

4. Why do many not-for-profit organizations tend to be centrally controlled?

5. How does the lack of a clear-cut performance measure, such as profits, affect the strategic management of a not-for-profit organization?

NOTES

1. M. S. Wortman, "Strategic Management: Not-for-Profit Organizations," *Strategic Management*, eds. D. E. Schendel and C. W. Hofer (Boston: Little, Brown & Co., 1979), pp. 353–381.

2. Wortman, p. 372.

3. B. P. Keating and M. O. Keating, *Not-For-Profit* (Glen Ridge, N.J.: Thomas Horton & Daughters, 1980), p. 18.

4. W. F. Glueck, *Business Policy and Strategic Management*, 3rd ed. (New York: McGraw-Hill, 1980), pp. 22–24.

5. M. D. Fottler, "Is Management Really Generic?" *Academy of Management Review* (January 1981), p. 2.

6. M. L. Weidenbaum, *The Modern Public Sector: New Ways of Doing the Government's Business* (New York: Basic Books, 1969).

7. Fottler, p. 2.

8. Keating and Keating, pp. 21 and 62.

9. Keating and Keating, pp. 23–24.

10. Keating and Keating, p. 24.

11. Keating and Keating, p. 21.

12. W. H. Newman and H. W. Wallender, III, "Managing Not-For-Profit Enterprises," *Academy of Management Review* (January 1978), p. 26.

13. Newman and Wallender, p. 27. The following discussion of the effects of these constraining characteristics is taken from Newman and Wallender, pp. 27–31.

14. Newman and Wallender, p. 27.

15. Newman and Wallender, p. 28.

16. Keating and Keating, p. 130.

17. E. H. Fram, "Changing Expectations for Third Sector Executives," *Human Resource Management* (Fall 1980), p. 9.

18. Keating and Keating, pp. 140–141.

19. Keating and Keating, pp. 143–144.

APPENDIX
CURRENT ISSUES IN
STRATEGIC MANAGEMENT

In industry after industry, U.S. firms are losing their competitive advantage to foreign firms. This loss is the underlying cause for the country's present, serious, economic distress and the many social problems closely related to it. Unemployment, adverse balance of payments, decline in the growth of the gross national product, low rate of productivity gain, and the high level of interest rates and inflation are but symptoms of a seriously weakened position industry by industry, firm by firm. Even a significant upswing in the entire economy would provide only temporary and partial relief from this general weakened condition.[1]

The above quote from Lawrence and Dyer's *Renewing American Industry* epitomizes much of the influential writing being published today in both the business and popular presses. The common theme is concern over the slower economic growth facing not only the United States and Canada, but also European industrialized nations. Current issues and research in strategic management center on finding possible reasons for this decline in productivity and suggesting likely strategies and programs to reverse this trend. An overview of the issues being debated include the changing nature of American business, the increasing importance of the external environment, finding strategies to retain growth, and an increasing concern for the implementation of strategy.

A.1   CHANGING NATURE
OF AMERICAN BUSINESS

Productivity growth in the United States moved in a generally rising trajectory for nearly two hundred years before turning downward in the late 1960s. From 1948 to 1965, the annual average rate in the private business sector increased 3.2%. It declined to a 2.4% increase between 1965 and 1973 and to a 0.8% annual average increase between 1973 and 1979. During the period from 1978 through 1980, the labor productivity growth rate became negative.[2] A number of authorities have suggested that the United States is becoming a "postindustrial society" with an emphasis on service and information rather than on heavy manufacturing. During 1980, the information handling sector employed approximately 47% of the U.S. labor force, the service sector employed 25%, the industrial sector 26%, and the agricultural sector 3%. The combined service-information sector increased from 49% in 1950 to 72% in 1980![3] These trends toward lower labor productivity and increased dominance by the service-information sector have serious implications for strategic managers in government as well as in business corporations.

Decline of
Traditional Industries

Many reasons have been given for the lack of competitiveness of America's steel, textile, automobile, consumer electronics, rubber, and petrochemical industries. Labor has been criticized for demanding high wages. Management has been criticized for losing its commitment to innovation in both product and process technology, and for its emphasis on short-run performance measures. Support can be found for both of these arguments. Many large American companies, such as General Electric, General Motors, and Westinghouse, considerably reduced their investment in research during the period 1965–1975, resulting in a so-called "creativity falloff."[4] Focusing upon high-volume standardized production, major American firms have found to their chagrin that the developing countries of the world have copied their technology. The production costs of the firms in these countries are low because of lower wages, often better access to raw materials, and greater market demand for standardized products in developing countries.[5] A recent study of the textile and clothing industry concludes that this trend is likely to continue for the following reasons:

1. The technology is easily available.
2. Wage differentials are so large they are unlikely to be counterbalanced by any technological lead.

3. The area least amenable to automation is garment assembly, a task mastered in developing countries.

4. Past attempts to revitalize the textile and clothing industry have generally failed.

5. Overall demand for these products is not projected to increase dramatically.[6]

Arguing against this implicit life cycle theory of industrial development, Abernathy, Clark, and Kantrow propose that much of U.S. industry is particularly vulnerable to competition from Japanese firms because U.S. firms have failed to properly integrate people into the manufacturing process. People's skills and abilities need to become and remain a point of competitive leverage. By relying on a standardized mass production core technology, U.S. firms are failing to reach the next stage of manufacturing development.[7]

In response to this problem of maturity and decline of U.S. heavy industry, numerous articles have recently been written suggesting strategies and programs a firm should consider when it is faced with a probable future of declining sales.[8] Some have found that businesses in slow-growth industries with low market share can be very profitable.[9] This is good news to those firms who have to live with a "dog" business (see Fig. 6.2, page 132) because of barriers preventing exit from that business. Some of these barriers are:

☐ Interdependence among business units

☐ Legal/political constraints

☐ Societal expectations

☐ Lack of ability to internally shift resources to a "star" or "question mark" business

☐ Corporate cultures that value mature products[10]

Growth of Service-
Information Industries

The service-information sector includes the communications, transportation, wholesale and retail trade, finance, insurance, real estate, health care, advertising, entertainment, government, and educational services industries.[11] Referring to the decade of the 1980s as "the end of the Industrial Revolution for developed nations," Collier, an authority on the service sector, predicts that the service sector will provide four out of every five jobs in the United States by the year 2000.[12] This continues the trend noted by other authorities that economic development has been characterized by a steady evolution from an agricultural to an industrial to a service-dominated economy.[13] The implications of this transformation to a postindustrial society where the strategic resource may be information over capital are very important to today's strategic managers.[14] United States business corporations are already considering moves out of their traditional businesses into telecommunications and financial services, among other industries.

Role of the National Government

A major issue surrounding the changing nature of business in the industrialized nations of the world is the role of the national government. The state has emerged in many nations as an active influencer of industrial policy, as well as a major supplier of capital.[15] Arguments are being made in the United States for a better connection between national economic policies and business development.[16] Nations with a clear industrial policy seem to be more competitive.[17] Reich, in his influential book *The Next American Frontier,* points out that the broad array of tariffs, quotas, voluntary export agreements, and bailouts for declining businesses indicates how deeply the U.S. government is already involved in business activities. He states that American society should accept the fact that the economic effects of public policies and corporate decisions are completely intertwined. Therefore he proposes that the nation develop a better system to help move U.S. industry more quickly out of high-volume standardized production into more flexible, quality-oriented systems of production using skilled labor.[18] Nevertheless, recent data suggest that national industrial policy has not been as successful as claimed in other countries. Korea, for example, is phasing out its policy of extending preferential access to credit and treatment in taxation to strategic industries because of a resulting structural imbalance in its economy.[19]

In their book, *Industrial Renaissance*, Abernathy, Clark, and Kantrow contend that it is the responsibility of business management to reverse the decline of firms in manufacturing industries. They disagree with Reich and others that there is an irreversible tendency of products to become standardized over time. Arguing that manufacturing corporations can indeed arrest and perhaps even reverse the life cycle process toward maturity and decline, they propose the possibility of industrial "dematurity." They claim that an increased emphasis on technological innovation and workforce management can bring about an "industrial renaissance."[20]

In a similar vein, Lawrence and Dyer propose a readaptive framework for business corporations as a way to help them maintain competitive vitality in their maturity. Arguing that the readaptation process requires that people in organizations be stimulated to constantly learn (in order to be innovative) and to constantly strive (in order to be efficient), they propose strategic roles in this process for both government and business management.[21] Their model states that a certain amount of *information complexity* in a corporation's environment is healthy because it promotes creative thinking. For example, too few competitors and a single type of customer tend to induce passivity in a firm; whereas, many competitors, a large number of customer types, and many government regulations tend to overload a firm's ability to deal with the situation. The model also includes a second key variable—*resource scarcity.* For similar reasons, the model states that either too much or too little resource scarcity can slow down the striving for efficiency in a corporation. When resources are plentiful (as in the United States during the 1950s and 1960s), there is little motivation to increase efficiency. Too much scarcity, however, means that resources needed to achieve efficiency and innovation are lacking. In applying their model, Lawrence and Dyer suggest approaches business management and government leaders can take to alter the mix of information complexity and resource scarcity within an industry. This is done in order to provide the conditions necessary to encourage both innovation and efficiency.

A.2   INCREASING IMPORTANCE OF EXTERNAL ENVIRONMENT

Recent surveys of large U.S. industrial corporations reveal an increasing concern with environmental scanning and analysis.[22] Seventy-three percent of the responding companies reported that they perform organized environmental analysis. An identical percentage stated that their environmental analysis activity was either important or crucial in terms of usefulness. Its future usefulness was believed to be even greater. The following seven major "payoffs" were reported to result from environmental analysis activity:

1. Increased general awareness by management of environmental changes
2. Better strategic planning and decision making
3. Greater effectiveness in government matters
4. Better industry and market analysis
5. Better results in foreign business
6. Sound diversification and resource allocation decisions
7. Better energy planning[23]

Stakeholder Analysis

Following Schendel and Hofer, and Hofer et al.,[24] a number of writers in strategic management have proposed a fourth level of strategy called *enterprise strategy* that identifies the relationship of a business corporation with society. It addresses the role the corporation assumes in society and the processes by which that role is defined.[25] As proposed, the enterprise or "societal" strategy forms the top of the hierarchy of strategy (as discussed previously on page 5). Beneath it lay the *corporate strategy* (concerned with selecting the specific portfolio of businesses for the firm), the *business strategy* (concerned with how the firm can compete in a particular industry), and the *functional strategy* (concerned with maximizing resource productivity in an operational part of the corporation, e.g., manufacturing or marketing). Even though recent research has failed to find any significant relationship between a business corporation's social responsibility and its profitability,[26] there appears to be a developing consensus that a firm must be very concerned with its relationship to other institutions and groups in society and must seek to manage these relationships.[27]

An increasingly popular approach to highlight and clarify a business corporation's many relationships with key groups in its task environment is through stakeholder analysis. A stakeholder is typically defined as "any group or individual who can affect or is affected by the achievement of the firm's objectives."[28] An increased emphasis on the task environment is suggested in order to better understand the degree of competition in an industry and to provide focus for environmental scanning. To the extent that a stakeholder seriously affects or is affected by the actions of the corporation, environmental scanning can be directed toward those issues of mutual concern.[29] This can serve to increase the efficiency of the scanning activities. Freeman, an authority on stakeholder analysis, proposes a "stakeholder audit" to "create and certify a roadmap of the external environment of the firm."[30] This information can then be added to Porter's model of five competitive focuses determining the level of competitive intensity in an industry (Fig. 4.3 on page 81). This sixth force, entitled "relative power of other stakeholders," serves to fill an important gap in Porter's conceptualization of the forces that shape competitive strategy.[31]

External Orientation of Strategic Managers

A series of interviews in 1980 with forty-seven chief executive officers (CEOs) of large American corporations found that these executives were spending more time than their predecessors dealing with social and political issues. They reported spending on the average from 25 to 50

percent of their time on these kinds of activities. In addition to the traditional qualities of leadership, technical, and administrative capacity
required from their predecessors, CEOs reported needing:

- ☐ Sensitivity to social and political pressures
- ☐ The ability to balance the interests of different interest groups
- ☐ Skills in communication to act as spokesperson
- ☐ Understanding of and involvement in government
- ☐ A global perspective and a generalist background
- ☐ The poise to handle political and social pressures[32]

The boards of directors of most large U.S. corporations are finding
themselves to be a key part of the strategic management of the firm. As
such, they are increasingly expected to be concerned with the external as
well as the internal affairs of the corporation. In addition to the responsibilities mentioned on page 47, should be added "consideration of
stakeholder interest." This means that boards are going to be expected to:

- ☐ Monitor product quality
- ☐ Facilitate employee quality of work life
- ☐ Review labor practices and policies
- ☐ Keep community relations at a high level
- ☐ Use influence to improve governmental, professional, and educa-
  tional contacts
- ☐ Maintain a good public image[33]

The current trend of increasing the percentage of outside directors
on a board of directors in order to make the board more objective and to
better reflect key environmental concerns is receiving some criticism.
Stanley Vance, after many years of research with boards of directors,
concludes that "directors close to the scene, competent, and dedicated,
are far more effective than part-time directors of questionable interest,
availability, or competency."[34] He argues that the most profitable firms are
those with primarily insiders (officers or owners) as board members. This
is supported by a recent study that found the level of concern for the
external environment among the members of the board to be better
related to corporate profitability than was that of a large number of
outside directors.[35] This suggests that it is more important for a corporation's board of directors to have a developed concern for environmental
matters, than it is for a board to have a large percentage of outside

directors. A recent study of codetermination in West Germany concluded that legislation requiring firms to put employee representatives on boards lowered dividend payments, led to a more conservative investment policy, and reduced firm values.[36] Results like these may cause top management to think twice in the future about adding union, government, or other interest group representatives to a business corporation's board of directors.

A.3   STRATEGIES TO RETAIN GROWTH

Sparked by the hope of economic recovery and rising corporate profits, merger and acquisition activity in the United States reached a nine-year high in 1983. W. T. Grimm and Company, a Chicago-based merger consulting firm, reported 2,533 merger and acquisition announcements in 1983, up 8 percent from 1982.[37] Attempting to reverse a trend of declining sales and profits, a number of business corporations are choosing growth strategies of horizontal integration, vertical integration, and joint ventures with other firms, especially foreign corporations. Given that most business and academic types agree that no one strategy is always best for all firms, the key issue appears to be determining which strategies work best in particular business situations.

Horizontal Integration— Concentric Versus Conglomerate

As pointed out on page 147, concentric diversification is the addition to a corporation of *related* products or divisions so that the corporation's lines of business still possess a common thread. Conglomerate diversification, in contrast, is the addition of *unrelated* products or divisions so that there is little commonality among the corporation's lines of business. Beginning with a classic study by Rumelt, researchers in the area have consistently concluded that diversification into other industries (unrelated or conglomerate) does *not* increase the profitability of a business corporation.[38] As a whole, studies in the United States have generally found that "mergers do not benefit the acquiring firm with a greater return than it would receive from other investment-production activities with similar levels of risk."[39] Like results have been found in Britain.[40] Peters and Waterman in their recent book, *In Search of Excellence*, support the developing chorus in favor of concentric over conglomerate diversification.

> Our principal finding is clear and simple. Organizations that do branch out (whether by acquisition or internal diversification) but stick very close to their knitting outperform the others. The most successful of all are those

diversified around a single skill—the coating and bonding technology at 3M, for example.

The second group, in descending order, comprises those companies that branch out into related fields—the leap from electric power generation turbines to jet engines (another turbine) from GE, for example.

Least successful, as a general rule, are those companies that diversify into a wide variety of fields. Acquisitions especially, among this group, tend to wither on the vine.[41]

Despite research concluding that mergers and acquisitions (especially into unrelated industries) typically do not result in substantial increases in corporate profitability, conglomerate diversification continues at a rapid pace. Conglomerate mergers, for example, accounted for 83 percent of all mergers between 1966 and 1970 and continued at a high level into the 1980s.[42] Characterized as "paper entrepreneurialism," Reich strongly criticizes conglomerate diversification as an attempt by managers to maintain or increase their firms' earnings without new productive investment.[43] Supporting his argument that paper entrepreneurialism, if left unchecked, will drive corporations into decline, is the increase in spinoffs of formerly acquired units. In the past few years ITT, RCA, Gulf & Western, Beatrice Foods, Quaker Oats, and General Electric have sold off major holdings.[44]

Vertical Integration— A Contingency Approach

A study of 1,649 manufacturing companies found that vertical integration can increase profits in some instances and decrease them in others.[45] A recent analysis of the petrochemical industry concluded that cost savings from vertical integration are normally overestimated. The study also warned of greater risks in forward over backward integration because of a likely "domino effect" of other competitors following suit. The resulting increase in competitive conditions causes corporations to accept lower margins, leading to an overall lowering of profitability in the industry.[46]

A closer look at vertical integration reveals a continuum of four generic substrategies:

1. *Full integration.* These firms buy or sell all of their requirements for a particular material or service internally.

2. *Taper integration.* These firms rely on outsiders for a portion of their requirements.

3. *Quasi-integration.* These firms do not own 100 percent of the adjacent business units, but they effectively control much of the relationship through joint venture agreements, loan guarantees, or minority equity investments.

4. *Contracts.* Long-term contracts provide some guarantee of a relationship without the risk of high investment in assets.[47]

In her in-depth study of vertically integrated corporations, Harrigan proposes a type of life cycle theory of vertical integration.[48] Assuming that an industry goes through distinct phases of economic development, she recommends that for each phase a particular strategy will have a higher probability of success than will others. She proposes an inverted U-shape curve to signify the relationship between the degree of vertical integration and the degree of maturity in a particular industry. For example, *embryonic* industries do not enjoy the sales volume or assets necessary for any substrategies other than contractual or quasi-integration. Firms in *emerging* industries, however, can successfully take advantage of taper and even full integration. Sales are rising, capital is easy to get, and the cost savings give them a real advantage over nonintegrated competitors. Corporations in *established* industries need to be fully integrated in order to keep costs as low as possible when sales growth stabilizes. Nevertheless, strategic managers need to decide how they are going to face the decline phase. They need to begin to sell off some of their assets and move toward taper integration to free capital for better use in growing businesses. Firms in *declining* or "endgame" industries should be disintegrating unless they face serious exit barriers or intend to be the last survivor to harvest whatever sales remain after decline. The suggested substrategy in this situation is a quasi-integration move toward contracts.

A.4   INCREASING CONCERN FOR STRATEGY IMPLEMENTATION

Over the past few years, the primary emphasis in strategic management research and business practice has been the formulation of strategy—including mission, objectives, and policies. Recently, however, the emphasis has been slowly shifting to the implementation of strategy. A number of strategic managers feel that the big challenge in management is in making a strategy work.[49] In a study of ninety-three company presidents or division heads, the following ten implementation problems were experienced by over 50 percent of the managers:

1. Implementation took more time than originally allocated.
2. Major problems surfaced during implementation that had not been identified beforehand.
3. Coordination of implementation activities was not effective.

4. Competing activities and crises distracted attention from implementing the strategic move.
5. Capabilities of employees involved were not sufficient.
6. Uncontrollable external environmental factors had an adverse impact on implementation.
7. Leadership and direction provided by departmental managers were not adequate.
8. Training and instruction given to lower-level employees were not adequate.
9. Key implementation tasks and activities were not defined in enough detail.
10. Information systems used to monitor implementation were not adequate.[50]

Although a number of people contend that many of the problems occur because of the tendency to separate implementation from formulation,[51] research and discussion continues on specific strategy implementation issues. In many instances, the process of evaluation and control (presented as a third element of strategic management in this book) is discussed as a part of strategy implementation.

Relationship Between Strategy and Structure

Thanks to the pioneering work by Chandler in the early 1960s detailing the development of business corporations like DuPont and General Motors, it is well accepted that changes in strategy tend to be followed by changes in structure. The recent decision by General Motors to restructure its automotive divisions is another example of how strategic decisions are often reflected in structural changes in implementation. It is also becoming accepted that strategy can follow structure.[52] Hall and Saias propose that structure partly determines strategy in three ways.

1. *Structure determines the introduction and subsequent development of strategic planning.* Bureaucratic structures, for example, create very formal planning systems which can choke creativity.
2. *Structure conditions strategic perceptions.* Bureaucratic structures, again for example, can delay the flow of incoming information about the environment so that certain strategic options are ignored.
3. *Structure influences decision making.* A rigid, centralized structure tends to be less open to new information because it is so focused on only one objective.[53]

Corporate Culture: One Best Way?

The concept of corporate culture is a very "hot topic" in management literature. Whole issues of scholarly journals are being devoted to its study.[54] A clear, well-accepted definition of the term is still being sought, but most strategic managers and academics seem to agree that the concept is worth developing further. Peters and Waterman, in their best-selling book *In Search of Excellence*, argue persuasively that the dominance and coherence of culture is an essential ingredient of the excellent companies they studied.

> The top performers create a broad, shared culture, a coherent framework within which charged-up people search for appropriate adaptations. Their ability to extract extraordinary contributions from very large numbers of people turns on the ability to create a sense of highly valued purpose. Such purpose invariably emanates from love of product, providing top-quality services, and honoring innovation and contribution from all.[55]

Peters and Waterman also state that poorer performing companies tend to have cultures which focus on internal politics instead of the customer, and on "the numbers" instead of the product or the people who make it. A recent study of America's large corporations supports this contention of Peters and Waterman. It concludes that "corporations with first-class reputations are seen to put quality, integrity, and respect for the customer alongside profits on the bottom line."[56]

Other studies of culture question the existence of a universal one-best-kind of culture as proposed by Peters and Waterman.[57] Agreeing that a strong culture is essential to high performance, one study proposes the existence of four types of corporate culture: "Tough-Guy/Macho," "Bet-Your-Company," "Process," and "Work Hard/Play Hard."[58] It is suggested that, depending upon the situation, any one of these cultures may be related to high performance. Clearly, there is plenty of room for further research and debate concerning whether a "universalistic" or a "contingency" view of corporate culture is best.

Organization Types and Strategic Groups

One method of integrating the wealth of information on the interactions between strategy, structure, and culture is through the development and study of patterns of corporate behavior. From their research and interpretation of strategic management activities, Miles and Snow propose the existence of four organization types.[59] They contend that strategic managers consciously develop and articulate an internal organizational image to support the firm's product–market image. The combination of these images tends to place the corporation in one of the following categories:

☐ *Defenders* are corporations with a limited product line who focus on improving the efficiency of their existing operations. Their focus makes them less likely to innovate in new areas.

☐ *Prospectors* are corporations with fairly broad product lines who focus on product innovation and market opportunities. They tend to emphasize creativity over efficiency.

☐ *Analyzers* are corporations who operate in two different product–market areas, one stable and one changing. In the stable area, efficiency is emphasized. In the changing area, innovation is emphasized.

☐ *Reactors* are corporations who lack a consistent strategy–structure–culture relationship. They tend to respond (often ineffectively) to environmental pressures with piecemeal strategic changes.[60]

A study of the relationship between organization type finds that defenders outperform prospectors in terms of current profitability and cash flow.[61] Prospectors outperform defenders in terms of market share in innovative industries. The costs and risks of product innovation thus appear to be very significant in the short run for prospectors.

Miles and Snow's category of organization types can be related to Porter's three business level strategies (discussed on page 158). Defenders tend to emphasize a strategy of overall cost leadership; whereas, prospectors emphasize differentiation or focus. Given the ability of analyzers to work in two different product–market situations, they appear to use combinations of all three business strategies. The introduction of Miles and Snow's typology and Porter's business competitive strategies is stimulating research into "strategic groups," groups of corporations within one industry who follow similar strategies. Studies so far have concluded that commitment to at least one of the three business strategies will result in higher performance than a firm who fails to develop a strategy and thus becomes a "reactor."[62]

Matching Managers
With Strategy

The effectiveness of strategy implementation appears to depend upon organization structure, corporate culture, and the characteristics of the general manager responsible for overall corporate or divisional performance. The current executive staffing process in many corporations typically contains fundamental weaknesses leading to either selection of the wrong person or failure to best utilize the existing person.[63] Job descriptions at this level are often vague and inadequate. Given the lack of clear job specifications, there is usually no attempt to collect all of the relevant background data on a likely candidate. The biggest problem is that a large number of people continue to believe in the existence of a "universal manager." It is often assumed by those who select strategic managers that a good manager is a good manager in any situation.[64]

Recent research is concluding that corporations should match key attributes of the strategic manager to the requirements of a particular strategy.[65] One study of business executives found that strategic business units (SBUs) with a "build" strategy as compared to SBUs with a "harvest" strategy tend to be headed by managers with a greater willingness to take risks and a higher tolerance for ambiguity.[66] Another study also found that managers with a certain mix of behaviors, skills, and personality factors tend to be more successful in implementing a specific strategy than others with a different mix. For example, SBUs with a stability strategy tend to do better if headed by a manager with a conservative style, a production or engineering background, and experience with controlling budgets, capital expenditures, inventories, and standardization procedures.[67] Consequently, there is increasing support for matching executive "stereotypes" or "archetypes" with the dominant strategic direction of a business unit.[68] Unfortunately, little work has been done to ascertain the type of manager most needed when a corporation or SBU does not have a specific strategy in place.

A.5 SUMMARY AND CONCLUSION

The study of strategic management is moving quickly from practical armchair philosophizing to a related series of concepts and techniques based upon research in actual corporations. Strategic management is increasing in importance as a field of study in response to a critical need for guidance by modern industrialized societies and their business corporations. Facing the development of an increasingly interdependent global economy and the likelihood of slower economic growth, strategic managers are looking for new and better methods to promote efficiency and effectiveness. Their major concerns are with (1) the changing nature of American (and worldwide) business, (2) the increasing importance of the external environment to business success, (3) finding strategies to retain or generate growth in sales and profits, and (4) improving methods to implement strategic decisions. These concerns are being addressed by current research activities. Regardless of whether the world is entering into an industrial renaissance, the consideration of these strategic issues may provide the information needed to generate a new understanding of successful business management.

NOTES

1. P. L. Lawrence and D. Dyer, *Renewing American Industry* (New York: The Free Press, 1983), p. 1.

2. K. Hughes, *Corporate Response to Declining Rates of Growth* (Lexington, Mass.: Lexington Books, 1982), p. 14.

3. Hughes, p. 12.

4. G. Petroni, "The Strategic Management of R & D, Part II—Organizing for Integration," *Long Range Planning* (April 1983), p. 51.

5. R. B. Reich, *The Next American Frontier* (New York: Times Books, 1983).

6. J. Fitzpatrick, "Why Textile and Clothing Industries Are Shifting to the Third World," *Long Range Planning* (December 1983), pp. 44–45.

7. W. J. Abernathy, K. B. Clark, A. M. Kantrow, *Industrial Renaissance* (New York: Basic Books, 1983), p. 83.

8. K. R. Harrigan, *Strategies for Declining Businesses* (Lexington, Mass.: Lexington Books, 1980).

   R. F. Zammuto and K. S. Cameron, "Environmental Decline and Organizational Response," *Proceedings, Academy of Management* (August 1982), pp. 250–254.

   D. C. Hambrick and S. M. Schecter, "Turnaround Strategies for Mature Industrial-Product Business Units," *Academy of Management Journal* (June 1983), pp. 231–248.

   W. C. Napper, "Tools for Managing in Mature Operations," *The Journal of Business Strategy* (Summer 1983), pp. 91–96.

   T. C. Settle and B. McIntosh, "Coalition Formation Within Industries: A Strategy for Dealing with Niche Decline and Interorganizational Dependence," *Proceedings, Southern Management Association* (November 1983), pp. 190–192.

   K. R. Harrigan, "Managing Declining Businesses," *The Journal of Business Strategy* (Winter 1984), pp. 74–78.

9. C. Y. Woo and A. C. Cooper, "The Surprising Case for Low Market Share," *Harvard Business Review* (November–December 1982), pp. 106–113.

   D. C. Hambrick and I. C. MacMillan, "The Product Portfolio and Man's Best Friend," *California Management Review* (Fall 1982), pp. 84–95.

10. H. K. Christensen, A. C. Cooper, and C. A. DeKluyver, "The Dog Business: A Reexamination," *Business Horizons* (November–December 1982), pp. 12–18.

11. Hughes, p. 12.

12. D. A. Collier, "The Service Sector Revolution: The Automation of Services," *Long Range Planning* (December 1983), pp. 10, 19.

13. Hughes, p. 11.

   R. Bolling and L. C. Krauthoff II, "National Policy-Making in a Global Economy: The Case for U.S. Economic Planning," *Long Range Planning* (December 1983), p. 26.

14. J. Naisbitt, *Megatrends* (New York: Warner Books, 1982), p. 15.

15. R. A. Bettis and C. K. Prahalad, "The Visible and the Invisible Hand: Resource Allocation in the Industrial Sector," *Strategic Management Journal* (January–March 1983), pp. 27–43.

16. J. F. Welch, Jr. "World Competitiveness: The Practical Test of U.S. Economic Policy," *The Journal of Business Strategy* (Fall 1983), pp. 63–65.

17. Bolling and Krauthoff II, p. 33.

18. Reich.

19. K. Kihwan, "A Case Study in the Perils of Industrial Policy," *The Wall Street Journal* (June 27, 1983), p. 23.

   A. Pine, "Industrial Policy? It's No Panacea in Japan," *The Wall Street Journal* (September 19, 1983), p. 1.

20. Abernathy, Clark, and Kantrow.

21. Lawrence and Dyer.

22. J. Diffenbach, "Corporate Environmental Analysis in Large U.S. Corporations," *Long Range Planning* (June 1983), pp. 107–116.

   R. E. Linneman and H. E. Klein, "The Use of Multiple Scenarios by U.S. Industrial Companies: A Comparison Study, 1977–1981," *Long Range Planning* (December 1983), pp. 94–101.

23. Diffenbach, p. 109.

24. D. Schendel and C. Hofer, eds., *Strategic Management: A New View of Business Policy and Planning* (Boston: Little, Brown, and Co., 1979).

   C. Hofer, E. Murray, R. Charan, and R. Pitts, *Strategic Management: A Casebook in Business Policy and Planning* (St. Paul: West Publishing Co., 1980).

25. A. B. Carroll and F. Hay, "Integrating Corporate Social Policy into Strategic Management," *The Journal of Business Strategy* (Winter 1984), p. 49.

26. K. E. Aupperle and A. B. Carroll, "Profitability and Corporate Social Responsibility," *Proceedings, Southern Management Association* (November 1983), pp. 362–364.

27. D. Windsor and G. Greanias, "Long Range Planning in a Politicized Environment," *Long Range Planning.* (June 1983), pp. 82–91.

   C. Fombrun and W. G. Astley, "Beyond Corporate Strategy," *The Journal of Business Strategy* (Spring 1983), pp. 47–54.

28. R. E. Freeman, *Strategic Management: A Stakeholder Approach* (Boston: Pittman Publishing Co., 1984), p. 25.

29. A. L. Mendelow, "Setting Corporate Goals and Measuring Organizational Effectiveness—A Practical Approach," *Long Range Planning* (February 1983), p. 73.

30. R. E. Freeman, p. 111.

31. R. E. Freeman, p. 141.

32. B. Taylor, "Key Social Issues for European Business," *Long Range Planning* (February 1983), pp. 61–62.

33. S. C. Vance, *Corporate Leadership: Boards, Directors, and Strategy* (New York: McGraw-Hill Book Co., 1983), pp. 15–16.

34. Vance, p. 274.

35. J. A. Pearce II, "The Relationship of Internal versus External Orientations to Financial Measures of Strategic Performance," *Strategic Management Journal* (October–December 1983), p. 305.

36. L. H. Clark, Jr., "What Economics Says About Business—and Baboons," *The Wall Street Journal* (June 7, 1983), p. 33.

37. D. Graham, "Mergers, Acquisitions Hit Nine-Year High in 1983," *Des Moines Register* (January 14, 1984), p. 65.

38. R. P. Rumelt, *Strategy, Structure, and Economic Performance* (Boston: Harvard University Press, 1974).

    R. W. Hearn, "Fighting Industrial Senility: A System for Growth in Mature Industries," *The Journal of Business Strategy* (Fall 1982), pp. 3–20.

    R. P. Nielsen, "Should a Country Move toward International Strategic Market Planning?" *California Management Review* (January 1983), pp. 34–44.

39. M. Lubatkin, "Mergers and the Performance of the Acquiring Firm," *Academy of Management Review* (April 1983), p. 218.

40. B. Taylor, "Social Issues for European Business," *Long Range Planning* (February 1983), p. 46.

41. T. J. Peters and R. H. Waterman, Jr., *In Search of Excellence* (New York: Harper and Row, 1982), pp. 293–294.

42. S. A. Rhoades, *Power, Empire Building, and Mergers* (Lexington, Mass.: Lexington Books, 1983), pp. 81, 103.

43. Reich.

44. "The Big Sell-Off," *Time* (August 29, 1983), p. 45.

45. R. D. Buzzell, "Is Vertical Integration Profitable?" *Harvard Business Review* (January–February 1983), pp. 92–102.

46. A. R. Burgess, "Vertical Integration in Petrochemicals-2. Strategies and Problems," *Long Range Planning* (December 1983), pp. 33–34.

47. K. R. Harrigan, "A Framework for Looking at Vertical Integration," *The Journal of Business Strategy* (Winter 1983), pp. 30–37.

48. K. R. Harrigan, *Strategies for Vertical Integration* (Lexington, Mass.: Lexington Books, 1983), pp. 22–27.

49. W. Kiechel III, "Corporate Strategists Under Fire," *Fortune* (December 27, 1982), pp. 34–39.

    J. M. Stengrevics, "Corporate Planning Needn't Be an Executive Straitjacket," *The Wall Street Journal* (September 26, 1983), p. 22.

50. L. D. Alexander, "Towards an Understanding of Strategy Implementation Problems," *Proceedings, Southern Management Association* (November 1982), pp. 146–148.

51. Y. Datta, "Toward a Holistic Theory of Strategic Management," *Proceedings, Southern Management Association* (November 1983), pp. 25–27.

    L. T. Hosmer, "The Importance of Strategic Leadership," *The Journal of Business Strategy* (Fall 1982), pp. 47–57.

    R. Lamb, "Is the Attack on Strategy Valid?" *The Journal of Business Strategy* (Spring 1983), pp. 68–69.

52. D. J. Hall and M. A. Saias, "Strategy Follows Structure," *Strategic Management Journal* (April–June 1980), pp. 149–163.

    A. C. Hax and N. S. Majluf, "Organization Design: A Case Study on Matching Strategy and Structure," *The Journal of Business Strategy* (Fall 1983), p. 73.

    L. G. Hrebiniak and W. F. Joyce, *Implementing Strategy* (New York: Macmillan, 1984), p. 87.

53. Hall and Saias, pp. 153–160.

54. *Administrative Science Quarterly* (September 1983).

    Organizational Dynamics (Autumn 1983).

55. Peters and Waterman, p. 51.

56. N. J. Perry, "America's Most Admired Corporations," *Fortune* (January 9, 1984), p. 56.

57. A. K. Gupta and J. M. Stengrevics, "Strategy, Culture, and Climate: A Conceptual Reevaluation" (Paper presented at the Forty-Third Annual Meeting of the *Academy of Management*, Dallas, Texas, August 1983), pp. 4–6.

58. T. L. Deal and A. A. Kennedy, *Corporate Cultures: The Rites and Rituals of Corporate Life* (Reading, Mass.: Addison-Wesley, 1982), pp. 108–113.

59. R. E. Miles and C. C. Snow, *Organizational Strategy, Structure, and Process* (New York: McGraw-Hill, 1978).

60. Miles and Snow, p. 29.

61. D. C. Hambrick, "Some Tests of the Effectiveness and Functional Attributes of Miles and Snow's Strategic Types," *Academy of Management Journal* (March 1983), p. 24.

62. G. C. Dess and P. S. Davis, "Porter's Generic Strategies as Determinants of Strategic Group Membership and Organizational Performance," A Working Paper (Columbia, South Carolina: College of Business Administration, University of South Carolina, 1983), p. 26.

63. M. Gerstein and H. Reisman, "Strategic Selection: Matching Executives to Business Conditions," *Sloan Management Review* (Winter 1983), pp. 33–49.

64. H. Deresky and T. T. Herbert, "The Strategy Implementation Imperative: Strategy-Contingent Implementation Actions and Skills," Working Paper (Montreal, Canada: Management Department, Concordia University, 1984), p. 1.

65. M. Leontiades, "Choosing the Right Manager to Fit the Strategy," *The Journal of Business Strategy* (Fall 1982), pp. 58–69.

L. J. Stybel, "Linking Strategic Planning and Management Manpower Planning," *California Management Review* (Fall 1982), pp. 48–56.

66. A. K. Gupta and V. Govindarajan, "Business Unit Strategy, Managerial Characteristics, and Performance," *Proceedings, Academy of Management* (August 1982), p. 35.

67. Deresky and Herbert, p. 9.

68. J. G. Wissema, H. W. Van Der Pol, and H. M. Messer, "Strategic Management Archetypes," *Strategic Management Journal* (January–March 1980), pp. 37–47.

R. A. Bettis and W. K. Hall, "The Business Portfolio Approach—Where It Falls Down in Practice," *Long Range Planning* (April 1983), pp. 95–104.

AUTHOR INDEX*

*For authors referred to in Chapters 1–11 only. Case contributors are listed on pp. xxi–xxiv.

SUBJECT INDEX*

*For Chapters 1–11 only.